D... Due

THEORY OF HARMONY

Harmonielehre

THEORY OF HARMONY

Harmonielehre

by

Arnold Schoenberg

TRANSLATED BY ROBERT D. W. ADAMS

PHILOSOPHICAL LIBRARY
NEW YORK

PHILOSOPHICAL LIBRARY, INC.
15 EAST 40TH STREET, NEW YORK 16, N. Y.

PRINTED IN THE UNITED STATES OF AMERICA

To the Memory of

GUSTAV MAHLER

FOREWORD

THIS book I have learned from my pupils.

In teaching I have never sought to "tell what I know" to the student. Rather what he did not know. Even this was not the main thing, though it did make it necessary for me to discover something new for each student. Mainly it was my care to show to him the heart of the matter, from the ground up. Hence there have never been for me those stiff rules that so carefully entwine their tentacles about the student's brain. Everything was resolved into directions, which were no more binding upon the student than upon the teacher. If the student does better without the directions, then let him do without. The teacher must also have the courage to be in the wrong. He must not pose as infallible, all-knowing and never erring, but as the tireless one who always seeks and sometimes finds. Why must he be a demigod? Why not rather fully human?

I have never tried to persuade my pupils that I was infallible; I have often had to risk saying what I might later retract, to give directions that proved faulty when applied and had therefore to be revised. My mistakes may not have been of use to the student, but they can scarcely have harmed him much. That I often acknowledged them may have given him food for thought. For me, however, who gave out these unproved cogitations, each new error pointed to the need for more proving and better formulating.

In this way, this book has come into being. From the mistakes made by my pupils in following inadequate or wrong directions I have learned how to give the right directions. Successful solutions justify my attempt, without misleading me into the fallacious belief that I have really solved the problem myself. I believe we both have not come through badly. Had I only told what I knew, then they would know that and no more. Perhaps they know even less now. But they do know that all depends on one thing: on seeking!

I hope that my pupils will be seekers! For they will learn that we seek, only to seek further; that finding, which to be sure is the goal, may easily put an end to striving.

The world today seeks many things. Before all else it has found one thing: *comfort*. This ideal, with all its implications, has forced itself even into the world of ideas and makes us more complacent than we have ever dared to be. Today more than ever before, man knows how to make life pleasant. Problems are solved to eliminate something disagreeable. But—how are they solved? And do we altogether believe that they have been solved? Herein is seen the essential weakness of the philosophy of comfortableness: its superficiality. It is easy to have a "world outlook" ("*Weltanschauung*") if one looks only at that which is pleasant, counting the rest not worth looking at. Actually the rest is much more important. Hence we can understand that these world outlooks fit their wearers as if made to measure; also that the motives from which they arise come mainly from an attempt to escape all blame. It is almost ludicrous: the men of our time, who establish new moral laws (or rather overthrow the old), *cannot live with guilt*.

But comfort gives no thought to self-control; guilt is either denied or made into a virtue. The thinker, who still seeks, does the opposite. He recognizes that there are problems and that they are unsolved. As Strindberg, that "Life makes everything ugly." Or as Maeterlinck, that "Three fourths of our brothers are condemned to misery." Or as Weininger and all others that have thought earnestly.

Comfort as a life philosophy (*Weltanschauung*)! The least possible activity, no commotion. Those who so love comfort will never seek except where there is definitely something to find.

There is a mechanical puzzle which consists of three small metal tubes of different diameters enclosed in a glass covered box; the object is to manipulate the box so that the tubes are placed one within another. One can work it out methodically; then it generally takes a long time. One can also do it otherwise: shake at random till the tubes are in place. Is that pure accident? So it appears, but I do not think so. There is a thought hidden here, namely that activity can succeed where deliberation fails. Is it not thus with learning? What does the teacher accomplish with a method? At best, activity. When things go well! But things can also go badly, and then he accomplishes stagnation. Stagnation produces nothing. Only activity is productive. Then why not begin at once with activity? But comfort!? Comfort avoids activity; hence will not start seeking.

Whether activity brings seeking, or seeking brings activity, is unimportant: only activity accomplishes what can really be called culture (*Bildung*). Namely: education, training (*Ausbildung*, *Durchbildung*). The lukewarm teacher who just tells "what he knows," also exerts his pupils too little. The activity must proceed from him; his restlessness must infect the students. Then they will seek, as he does. He will not spread culture, and it is well. For culture, today, means: to know a little of everything without understanding anything. The real sense of this fine word is something different; but since it has today fallen into disrepute it must be replaced by education, training.

It should be clear, then, that the teacher's first assignment is to shake up the students thoroughly. When the uproar has died down, everything should be in its proper place.

Or it never will be!

The activity that proceeds thus from the teacher comes back to him again. Also in this sense I have learned this book from my pupils, and I must take this opportunity to thank them.

There are some that I should thank in another sense, those who have helped me in the work, by proof reading, etc., by agreeing, which was always a joy, and by criticism, which gave me energy and also called my attention to many a defect: Alban Berg (who made the index), Dr. Karl Horwitz, Dr. Heinrich Jalowetz, Karl Linke, Dr. Robert Neumann, Josef Polnauer, Erwin Stein and Dr. Anton von Webern. Some of these will soon be heard from.

And so perhaps this activity returns to me.

ARNOLD SCHOENBERG

Vienna, July, 1911.

TRANSLATOR'S PREFACE

This translation of Schoenberg's monumental work into English is intended as a student edition, for practical use, and is considerably abridged from the original. Much philosophical, polemic material has been omitted, but the essentials,—explanations, directions, examples,—have been included. The portions of the text used are those indicated in Erwin Stein, *Praktischer Leitfaden zu Schönbergs Harmonielehre*.

Some American readers may be surprised, perhaps a bit disappointed, to find here a treatise on traditional harmony, handled from a conservative, even strict point of view, when they may have expected a dissertation on the twelve-tone system or a survey of "ultra-modern" harmony. It is important to realize that the most striking, the most difficult of the ideas found in the works of Schoenberg's later period are actually based, by clear laws of historical succession, upon the musical development of the past. The most "strange" ideas of Schoenberg have grown as logically out of the harmony of Brahms and Wagner, as the "immoral" ideas (as they were once called) of the *Eroica* from the structure of Haydn, or the harmonies of Monteverdi or Gesualdo from Des Pres and Palestrina. Hence it is not surprising that Schoenberg insists that his pupils have a thorough grounding in the harmony that man has spent a thousand years in building.

On the other hand teachers of harmony will find here much that is unusual, especially in the manner of presentation,—in the kind of student exercise. A glance through the book will disclose numerous illustrations or models, but no "exercises." Figured bass, given melodies to harmonize,—none of these appear. The student makes his own exercises from the start, under careful directions, creating his harmony as he learns it.

The text used here is from the III. VERMEHRTE UND VERBESSERTE AUFLAGE, Vienna, 1921.

ARNOLD SCHOENBERG

Arnold Schoenberg was born in Vienna, September 13, 1874. As a young man he played violin and cello in amateur chamber music groups. He showed some manuscripts to Zemlinsky (a friend of Brahms), who was much impressed and accepted him as a pupil in counterpoint. The study under Zemlinsky was the only formal instruction Schoenberg had in musical theory; he was largely self-taught.

The works of Schoenberg's first period were in the romantic spirit of Wagner and Brahms, and while some of the songs aroused opposition there was little of a revolutionary nature. *Verklärte Nacht*, for string sextet, appeared in 1899. It aroused opposition, controversy and fist fights; one critic called it "a calf with six (!) feet." The *Gurre-Lieder* were begun in 1900 but the work was constantly interrupted by the scoring of operettas by other composers. It was on the strength of the first part of the *Gurre-Lieder* that Richard Strauss obtained for him a teaching position at the Stern Conservatory in Berlin. The score was finally completed in 1911.

Meanwhile, in 1902-3 he completed the symphonic poem *Pelleas and Melisande*, after the dramatic poem by Maeterlinck.

Schoenberg's first important change of style came about 1905, in the orchestral songs Op. 8 and the String Quartet Op. 7. Here there is a wealth of very active and complicated counterpoint, but the work remains tonal. In 1906 the *Chamber Symphony* was performed amid protests.

The Second Quartet Op. 10 and the Piano Pieces Op. 11 bring in the second change of style (1907-11), and atonality appears. In 1910 and 1911 he spent most of his time painting, exhibiting an "expressionistic" style akin to that in his music. His pictures were exhibited in Vienna in 1910. In 1912 he wrote the chamber music melodrama *Pierrot Lunaire*. Soon after appeared the music dramas, *Erwartung* and *Die Glückliche Hand*.

By 1924 the genius of Schoenberg was so far recognized that his fiftieth birthday was publicly celebrated in Vienna, with the assistance of the State Opera Chorus and an address by the mayor of the city. He then moved to Berlin again to teach in the Prussian Academy of Arts.

In 1933 he came to the United States and has made his home in Southern California, where he has been active as a teacher, first at the University of Southern California, and thereafter, until 1944, at the University of California at Los Angeles.

In 1923 occurred the final development of style, with the rigid adherence to the twelve-tone principle. Tonality has entirely disappeared, with its tonic-dominant relationship; the twelve tones of the chromatic scale are of equal value. The elaborate contrapuntal technique of the preceding period is now carried out with a melodic theme in which each of the twelve tones appears once only and any resemblance to a folksong type of melody is studiously avoided. The tones of the theme may appear vertically (harmonically) as well as horizontally; iiberal use is made of the fifteenth century devices of lnversion and cancrizans. Following his theory of the emancipation of the dissonance, the harmonic combinations now avoid consonances more carefully than the classical writers of the past avoided dissonances.

Yet Schoenberg feels that his most advanced ideas are the logical outgrowth of musical theory and practice of the past. Hence he guides his own pupils first through a thorough discipline in the traditional harmony, as presented in this book.

TABLE OF CONTENTS

THEORY OF HARMONY

Harmonielehre

THE DIATONIC TRIADS OF THE MAJOR SCALE

In *C* major the following triads are built from the diatonic scale:

The tones of the scale, each of which is the root or lowest tone of a triad, are called degrees. Thus *c* in the triad *c-e-g* is the first degree, *d* in the triad *d-f-a* is the second, *e* in *e-g-b* is the third, etc. The triads vary in structure. Reckoned from the bottom up, some have a major third with a superimposed minor third to form a perfect fifth; in some this order is reversed, a minor third with a major third on top, still forming a perfect fifth; in one a diminished fifth is formed from two minor thirds. Triads of the first sort, major triads, are found on degrees I, IV and V; the second, minor triads, on degrees II, III, and VI; the third, the diminished triad, only on VII. At this point an important distinction should be made. The triad on the first degree is of course a major triad, for it is from this triad that the major mode or key takes its name. The two other similar triads, on IV and V, are also commonly called major triads, and are sometimes referred to as the *F* major or *G* major triad,—an incorrect and confusing practice. In *C* major there is only one triad which should be called a major triad, the one on the first degree. Those on the fourth and fifth should never be called *F* major or *G* major, as thus a false impression may be given that a key or tonality is meant, the key of *F* or *G* major. Likewise it is incorrect to speak of the triads on II, III and VI as *D* minor, *E* minor, or *A* minor triads. The best usage is to identify the triads as "on the first, second or third degrees" (or "I, II, III," etc.), or "triad on *G* (or *A*) with major (or minor) third." It has already been indicated which have major or minor thirds, which are major or minor in structure. One may also use the terms Tonic for I, Dominant for V, Under- or Sub-Dominant for IV, Mediant for III, Sub-Mediant for VI, Diminished Triad for VII. The second degree is given a name at certain times; this will be discovered when the need arises.

Placing the Chords

Our presentation of chord succession through moving voice parts is based on the fact that the majority of harmonic situations use four voices, a combination of the four main types of the human voice: soprano, alto, tenor and bass, giving the so-called four part harmony.

As far as concerns us here, the individual ranges of the human voices (and likewise of nearly all instruments) are those shown in Example 3. There is one range (or register) in which every normal, healthy voice sings easily and without strain: the middle range; also two ranges which require more effort and cause tiring: the high and the low. The middle range is less expressive and penetrating than the high or low extremes. Since, however, in presenting harmonic structure we are concerned less with such considerations than with pure harmony, the following suggestions are given for the treatment of voice parts (as a foundation principle which to a degree may even develop a style of writing): In general each voice should sing in its middle range; only when special conditions require it (difficulty of voice leading, avoiding monotony, etc.) will the higher or lower ranges be used. The practical range of the voices, then, is indicated approximately by the half notes:

The quarter notes in parentheses indicate the extreme high and low tones that can be used when necessary. The middle or preferred range is found a fourth or a fifth from the highest or lowest note, namely:

Obviously the student cannot work exclusively in the middle range and will find it sometimes necessary to use higher or lower tones,—mainly the adjoining ones, of course, but occasionally even the highest or lowest, if there is no other way out. In general, however, the compass of an octave should seldom be exceeded; one who wishes to write suitably for voices will avoid the practice of letting a voice sing long in an extreme range.

The two outer ranges should therefore be entered by the student only briefly.

Chords may be placed in close or in open position. Open position usually sounds less intense, close position more intense. The student is not faced with the problem of evaluating these two positions, in the theoretical study of harmonic relations. Hence we may be satisfied with the statement of this distinction, and use both positions without considering cause or effect. In close position the upper three voices lie so close together that no other chord tones could be inserted among them. How far removed the bass is from the tenor is of no consideration, if the distance is not *too* great. If one or more chord tones can be inserted among the tones of the upper three voices, the chord is then in open position.

5 close position open position

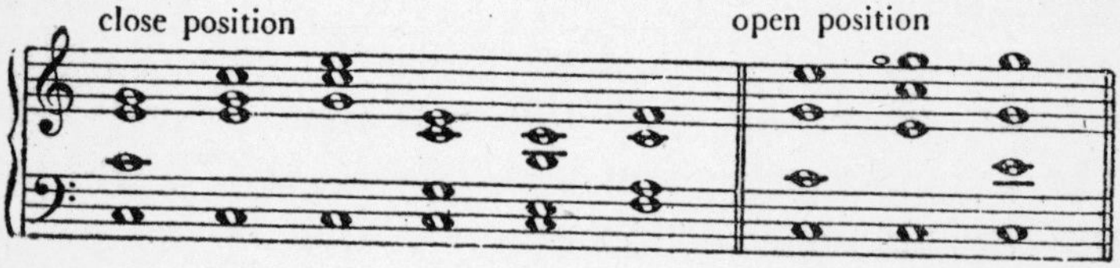

Experience teaches that a uniformly smooth harmonic effect can best be had when any two of the upper three voices (*i.e.*, soprano and alto, or alto and tenor) are never more than an octave apart, though the bass can be more than an octave from the tenor.

In dividing the three chord tones among four voices it is necessary to double one of the tones. First choice for doubling is the root, also called the fundamental, second the fifth, and only as a last resort the third. Since at first the doubling of the fifth or the third is unnecessary, we shall double only the root.

In example 6 the triad on I in *C* major is written in various close and open positions. As a first exercise, the student should likewise write, with due regard for the vocal ranges already given, the chords on II, III, IV, V and VI (the seventh degree triad will be dealt with later), and should also repeat this exercise in

close position — open position

6 — etc.

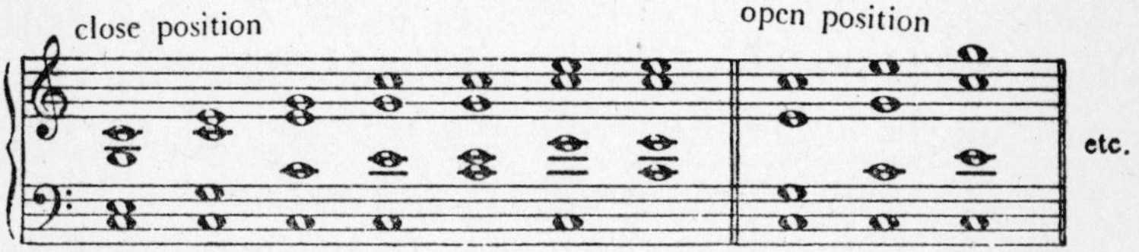

several other keys. The exercises will be notated on two staves with treble and bass (G and F) clefs. The student will do well to place soprano and alto on the upper staff (with treble clef), tenor and bass on the lower (with bass clef). Sometimes the tenor is written on the upper staff, with the bass alone on the lower. The examples are given here mostly in *C* major, but the student must always practice what he has learned in other keys; otherwise they will always be foreign to him.

To be learned now is the method of the so-called Thoroughbass, or Figured Bass, a kind of musical shorthand, which was once used to indicate to the accompanist the harmonic structure of a composition, which he then realized in his improvisation by filling in the indicated chords. For this purpose figures were placed under the bass, indicating the intervals of the chord tones from the lowest tone, *i.e.*, from the bass, without considering, however, whether the interval lay in the same or a higher octave. For example:

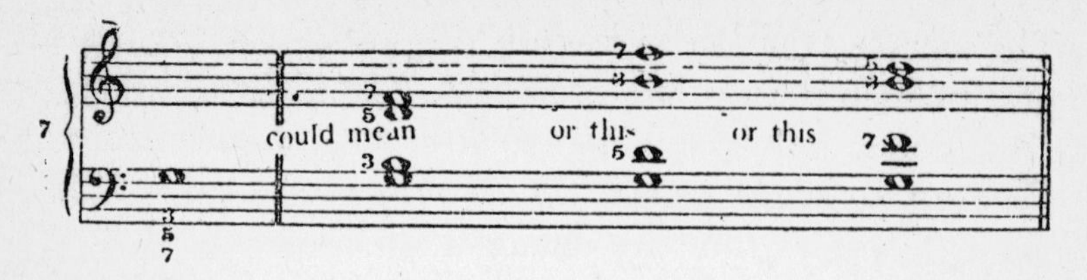

In itself, 3, 5, 7 indicated the orderly arrangement of the chord members in the smallest space; but to the 3, 5 or 7 one or more octaves could be added. 3 meant that there was a third above the bass in some higher octave, 5 meant likewise a fifth, 7 a seventh, 9 a ninth, 6 a sixth, etc. The arrangement of the tones, in the order 3, 5, 7 or 5, 3, 7 or 7, 3, 5 or any other way, was left to the judgment of the accompanist, and was decided by considerations of voice leading. In the absence of an accidental (♯, ♭ or ♮) beside the figure, the chord was built from the tones of the scale indicated by the key signature. A triad in root position, of which the indication would have been $\substack{5\\3}$, was left unmarked. If the figure 8, 5 or 3 appeared under a bass note, it meant that the highest voice (the soprano) took the 8, 5 or 3, respectively. This was called then the octave position, the fifth position or the third position of the chord.

Connection of the Primary and Secondary Triads of the Scale

The good solution of the problem of *joining chords together* is tied up with the fulfillment of certain conditions. These conditions will be given (as has been intimated and will be repeated at many opportunities), not in the form of laws or rules, but as directions or advice. Laws or rules must apply always and unvaryingly.

The saying that the exception proves the rule, is true only of such rules as are proved only by the exceptions. Directions, however, supply directly the means for reaching a certain goal. Hence they are not eternally valid, like laws, but are changed whenever the goal is changed. Although the following directions correspond in part with composition practice, they do not arise from aesthetic considerations, but have a limited goal: namely, to guard the student against faults which can only later be clearly described as such. The first of these directions, applying to voice leading, is *to do only what is absolutely necessary for the connection of the chords.* In other words, each voice will move only when it must, then stepwise or by the smallest possible skip, and in such manner as to enable the other voices to move as little as possible. The voices then follow the "law of the nearest way" (as I once heard Bruckner call it). It follows that, when two chords to be connected have a tone in common, this tone will be taken by the same voice in the second chord as in the first; hence that voice "remains stationary." To simplify the problem still further, we shall choose for our first connections only chords that have one or more common tones (two triads cannot have more than two common tones) and let the common tone or tones serve as a *harmonic bond.* The following table shows the chords to be connected, having common tones:

The Roman numerals indicate the degrees of the scale.

It will be seen that a triad on any degree has a common tone with every other triad except those on the next higher or lower degrees. The second degree triad (II) is *d-f-a.* The roots of triads on neighboring degrees

I	.	III	IV	V	VI	.
.	**II**	.	IV	V	VI	VII
I	.	**III**	.	V	VI	VII
I	II	.	**IV**	.	VI	VII
I	II	III	.	**V**	.	VII
I	II	III	IV	.	**VI**	.
.	II	III	IV	V	.	**VII**

Triad on	has common tones with			
I	III	IV	V	VI
II	IV	V	VI	(VII)
III	I	V	VI	(VII)
IV	I	II	VI	(VII)
V	I	II	III	(VII)
VI	I	II	III	IV
VII	II	III	IV	V

(*c* and *d*) are one degree apart; it follows that the thirds (*e* and *f*) and the fifths (*g* and *a*) are likewise one degree apart. Hence there is no common tone. There is always one common tone between chords whose roots are a fifth or a fourth apart, two common tones when the roots are a third or a sixth apart.

According to the table, the first degree triad (I), under the condition of the common tone, can be joined with III, IV, V or VI.

In these first exercises the root is to be used always as the lowest tone of the chord, hence in the bass. The bass

F							*F*
E						*E*	
D					*D*		*D*
C				*C*		*C*	
B			*B*		*B*		*B*
A		*A*		*A*		*A*	
G	*G*		*G*		*G*		
F		*F*		*F*			
E	*E*		*E*				
D		*D*					
C	*C*						

voice should always be the lowest, the tenor the next higher, then the alto, with the soprano as the highest. Crossing of voices, *i. e.*, a lower going above a higher (as the tenor going above the alto or soprano), should be avoided by the student. The student will write first, under the lower staff, the degree numerals of the chords to be connected, then the bass note of the first chord, placing above it the first chord in the other voices. Whether in close or open position, third, fifth or octave position, he must choose for himself, *before he begins to work out the exercise. To this extent he sets the problem for himself;* we shall follow this practice during the entire course of study. In writing the chords the student will most easily avoid errors if he will answer the following series of questions:

I. Which tone is placed in the bass? (The scale degree, root or fundamental.)

II. Which tone in the soprano? (The octave, fifth or third of the triad, depending on his choice of 8, 5 or 3 position, which he should indicate by placing the corresponding figure beside the chord numeral).

III. What is missing? (The remaining tones are so placed that the chosen close or open position results.)

In proceeding to chord connection the student will do well to ask himself the following questions:

1. Which tone is the root? (Note carefully: place in bass!)
2. Which is the common tone? (Remains stationary!)
3. What tones are missing?

To postpone again consideration of faults to be avoided, we shall double in the first lessons always the root. Hence the chords will not appear with doubled third or fifth.

The connection of I and III may be presented as follows (Example 8*a*):

1. Bass (third degree): *e*.
2. Common tones: *e* and *g* (soprano and alto remain stationary).
3. What tone is missing: *b* (the tenor moves from *c* to *b*).

Here it must be pointed out that the student should always think of chord connection as the result of voice movement. He should not say, "Place *b* in the tenor," but "The tenor moves from *c* to *b*;" nor "Place *e* in the soprano, *g* in the alto," but "*E* remains stationary in the soprano, *g* in the alto."

The student must distinguish between the *root* (*i.e.*, the tone on which the triad is built, as *d* for II, *e* for III, etc.) and the *bass* (*i.e.*, the tone that is placed in the bass or lowest part). In our first exercises, until directed otherwise, we shall invariably place the root in the bass. Later, however, other chord members may be placed in the bass; hence the student must guard against confusing the two ideas.

The preliminary examples are worked out in whole notes without division into measures.

8

a) b) c) d)

I III I IV I V I VI

Example 8*a* shows the progression I—III, in which there are two common tones (*e* and *g*); in 8*b* and 8*c* (I—IV and I—V) there is in each progression only one common tone, in I—VI again two common tones. The student should indicate with a tie the common tone remaining in the same voice.

In like manner the connection of the triads on the other degrees of the scale should be practiced, connecting each with those indicated in the table as having common tones; hence II with IV, then with V and with VI (the seventh degree triad will be omitted at first, as it demands special treatment); III with I, V and VI; IV with I, II and VI, etc., through VI (VII also omitted here).

Connection of Primary and Secondary Triads of the Scale into Short Phrases

The next assignment for the student is to construct short phrases with the six chords which are at his disposal. These phrases, as far as the means at hand permit, should have considerable variety, and should be as interesting as possible. We should also, even though in elementary fashion, aim at a certain effect which we shall later with more adequate material strive for more energetically: namely, to establish to some extent the tonality or key. The phrases will evidently have to be short, since there are only six chords to be used, and since their connection is limited by certain conditions (the common tone). Repetitions, unless given a differently colored sense by the surroundings, or used for a special purpose, can easily be monotonous, needlessly monotonous; or, since repetition usually gives emphasis, the repeated chord is given a towering significance among the other chords. Repetition is therefore, on the whole, to be avoided, unless one intends to give great emphasis to a chord. This intention we can have at first only with one chord, the Tonic or first degree triad (I), by which the key is expressed. Through repetition, in a short phrase, this chord is given special significance; hence the key is somewhat, though not conclusively, established. The most effective arrangement for this repetition is to place this chord at the beginning and at the end. First and last impressions are strongest, and one achieves some variety if the repetition of the chord is postponed as long as possible, so that some contrast may appear in between. The first condition, then, that we set for ourselves, is this: *The phrase begins and ends with the triad on the first degree.* It will then be seen that, to have a common tone, the chord just before the last must be one that can be connected with I as in our table; hence III, IV, V or VI. In order to guard against faults that might be unavoidable with too great length, we shall be satisfied at first with the connection of four to six chords. The first and last will be I; between these will appear at most two to four other triads.

It may be pertinent here to make two further suggestions regarding voice leading. Two successive similar skips of a fourth or a fifth in the same direction should be avoided, because the extreme tones form a dissonance; or, put in general terms: two skips in the same direction which add up to a dissonant interval are unmelodic. As for example:

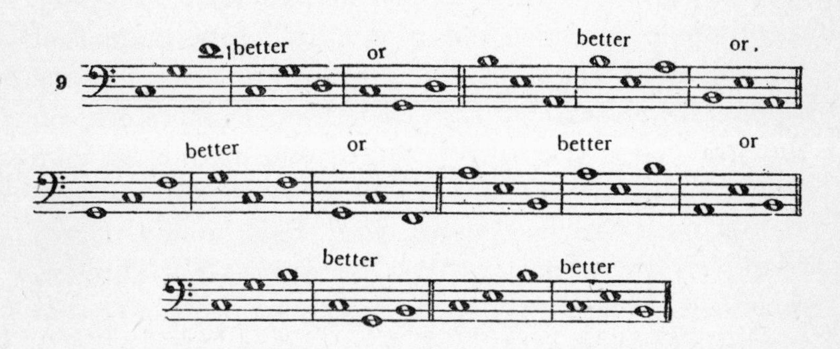

Also, no voice should make a greater leap than a fifth (the leap of an octave, which has nearly the same effect as repetition of the same tone, is naturally allowed).

The student can now, with the help of the table, work out the problem for himself, beginning with I and following it with a triad that has one or more tones in common with it; for example, III. Then he will look in the table for a triad that can follow III. I, V and VI appear as possibilities. Since I has already been used, its repetition now would bring the exercise to a close; hence we choose V or VI. Supposing we choose V, we have so far, I, III and V. After V, as the table shows, I, II or III can be used. Since I and III have already appeared, II naturally follows, except that the exercise would then be extended to at least six chords. To keep the first exercises as short as possible, we now take I to close. The exercise then runs: I—III—V—I. The working out of these progressions takes place now, as already indicated for chord connection, by answering the three questions (see Example 11*a*).

In constructing other phrases, the student will do well to begin again with I—III, with a different continuation. As, for example, I—III—VI; after VI can come I again, or, another time, IV followed by I. When all possibilities beginning with I—III have been used, he may then begin with I—IV, then with I—V, and lastly with I—VI, using various continuations.

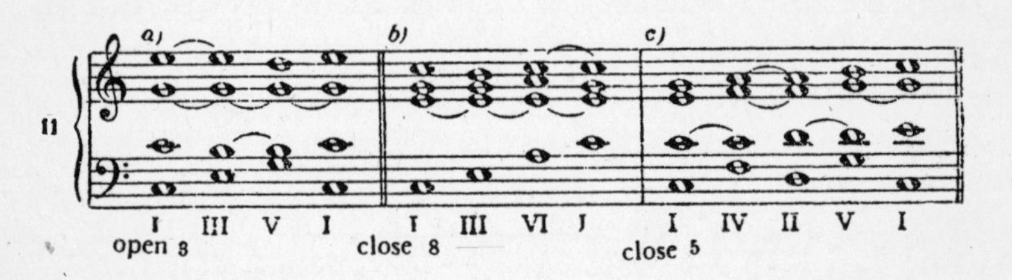

The student can also work out these same examples in different positions—close or open, or beginning with third, fifth or octave in the soprano. It is especially necessary to work out each example in various keys,—not by a simple transposition, but by carrying out the whole process in each key.

The Triad on the Seventh Degree

Special treatment is required for the seventh degree triad because of its dissonant diminished fifth. The first and simplest form of approach to this chord is by *preparation*. By preparation is meant that the tone that creates the dissonance has been sung as a consonance in the preceding chord by the same voice. The object of this preparation is obviously to sound the tone first where as a consonant part of a major or minor triad it causes the singer no difficulty, then to sustain it while the other voices move in such a manner that it becomes dissonant.

When we progress from a dissonance, some kind of *resolution* is required. As the first form of resolution we shall choose a method the effectiveness of which can easily be perceived psychologically. If the introduction of the dissonance may be thought to interpose an obstacle to the smooth flow of the harmony, somewhat comparable to a weir in a brook, then this holding back may be said to cause an accumulation of strength by which the obstruction may be pushed aside. By a strong move, it seems, we force our way through. The progression from V to I may be considered such a strong move, or, in general, any progression to a chord whose root is a fourth higher.

If for the resolution of the dissonant fifth in the diminished triad we let the root leap a fourth upwards (or a fifth down), the chord of resolution of VII is III.

The resolution of the dissonant tone itself is accomplished here in its stepwise downward movement, from *f* to *e*. There are various ways by which a dissonance can move into the chord of resolution. It can descend,

ascend or remain stationary, or even move by a skip. In this instance we choose to let it descend, *i.e.*, move stepwise one degree downward.

Here frequently the common tone must be given up, if we wish to keep a complete chord. If we kept the common tone, the *b*, stationary (example 12*b*, *c*, *d*), then the voice that has the *d* would be obliged to leap up or down to *g*, very likely causing difficulties, as for example in 12*b*, where the alto by this leap crosses below the tenor, or, if the upward leap is chosen, would cross above the soprano. *Crossing of voices*, however, as has already been said (Page 9), should be avoided. Good and useful is the solution in example 12*c*; only it is necessary here, since the highest voice makes a leap, to give some attention to its melodic line, which should be the next consideration. On the other hand there arises in example 12*d*, whether the alto leaps up or down, too wide an interval between neighboring voices; in one case alto and tenor are a tenth apart, in the other alto and soprano. Such a position we shall where possible avoid, since it is one of those that experience has shown to give an unsymmetrical impression. (When an example occurs in music such an effect may have been deliberately intended, or it may have arisen from its subordination to other purposes.) Here therefore the solution at 12*e* (without stationary common tone) is to be preferred. The student may safely, according to the needs of each situation, sometimes keep the common tone, sometimes give it up. These considerations will be explained later in the discussion of the melodic requirements of the voices. For the present it is recommended to stay in the same position (close or open) in which the phrase begins, or if it is necessary to change to another, to seek the first opportunity to return to it.

As to which tone in the seventh degree triad is best to double, this may be said: Preferable of course is the root, for the same reason as in the other triads. It is otherwise, however, with the third and fifth. The third here receives more consideration for doubling, because VII is neither major nor minor, but a diminished triad. The third here does not determine the nature of the triad, is hence less striking. The fifth on the other hand is, as a dissonance, the most striking tone of VII, and should therefore not be doubled. Besides it has, as a dissonance, which requires resolution, a strong tendency downward. If it is doubled, then also the other voice in which it appears should descend (12*f*). Thus arises a form of voice leading about which more will be said later. For the present only this: two voices make the same melodic progression. That is superfluous, since one would suffice. Hence the diminished fifth is not to be doubled.

Now for the preparation. The dissonant tone should appear as a consonance in the preceding chord and then remain in the same voice while it becomes a dissonance. Each tone of the scale appears in three triads,—once as a root, again as a third and again as a fifth. Our dissonant fifth, the *f*, is also the root of IV, the third of II. Hence IV or II may precede VII. To the three questions that we have indicated for the connection of consonant chords another is now added. The questions now stand:

1. Which tone is in the bass?
2. Which tone is dissonant? (If there is one, then prepare and resolve.)
3. Common tone? (Remains stationary where possible, but not invariably.)
4. What tone or tones are missing?

Example 13 illustrates preparation and resolution in several situations; in 13*a*, *b*, *c*, the preparation occurs in IV (since here the preparing tone is the root of the preparing chord, we have the term, *preparation by the root*); in 13*d* and *e* the preparing chord is II (*preparation by the third*).

The student should now practice the preparation and resolution of VII in as many examples as possible (also in other keys!). The chord succession will be: IV—VII—III or II—VII—III. After VII will appear, for the present, only III; before VII only IV or II. When the student has become sure enough in the treatment of the seventh degree triad, he may try using it in short phrases. Obviously here also VII must be followed by III and preceded by IV or II. For the rest, the student can be guided entirely by the table, remembering that it does not show the restrictions applying to the seventh degree triad.

Inversions of Triads

In the lessons worked out thus far, the arrangement of the chord members among the upper three voices was immaterial, as long as the one condition was satisfied, that the root was always in the bass. There are various situations, however, which require—and permit—the appearance of other chord tones than the root in the bass. They require it and they permit it; a necessity and an advantage.

There is no doubt that the sounding in the bass of another tone than the root gives a different effect, probably a weaker effect, because of the greater resemblance of the chord in root position to its ultimate prototype, the fundamental and upper partials of the overtone series. Thereby arises the possibility of sounding a chord once with stronger, then with weaker effect, or with stronger or weaker significance,—a distinct artistic advantage! If in the course of a longer phrase, which is to have, say, ten chords, it is necessary to repeat a chord (since only seven chords are available), then this chord, as has already been indicated, is given a special emphasis over the others. If this emphasis is desired, well and good; otherwise it is well to consider how the effect of this repetition can be weakened so that the repeated chord is not made too conspicuous. If for this purpose one allows a chord in its strongest form to be followed by one of its weaker forms, the weaker form will not so easily injure the effect of the preceding one, and will likewise prepare the possibility of a later repetition in the stronger form.

Placing some tone other than the root in the bass has not only the advantage of varying the effect of a chord, in a seeking for variety; it answers also to the needs of the bass in two ways. On the one hand, the use of a chord of the sixth often makes possible in the bass a better and more interesting melodic line; on the other hand requirements of the vocal range may make it advisable.

Inversion of an interval or of a chord means that the lowest tone is raised an octave, or the highest tone is lowered an octave, without affecting the other tones. In the *inversion of a triad* the lowest tone of its original form (root) is inverted, or raised an octave. Thus the *c* (14*a*) is placed above the *g*. The third of the triad is then the lowest tone, and we have the *first inversion*. This should strictly be called a 6-3 chord, but, since

it is the first in a series of sixth chords, it is known as the *chord of the sixth*. Now if the lowest tone of the chord of the sixth is inverted, the fifth becomes the lowest tone, and we have the *second inversion* (14*b*), the *six-four chord*. In other words, when the third of a triad is in the bass the triad is in the 6 position; when the fifth is in the bass it is in the $^6_4$ position. The essential value of a chord is the same whether it is in root position (root in bass) or in an inversion.

The Chord of the Sixth

In comparing the positions of triads the decisive element, since the chord tones are the same, must be the tone in the bass. The especial importance of the bass voice is not that it is the foundation of the harmony, since in relation to the harmonic roots it has more the character of a lowest inner voice, but that it has been made the foundation of the visible harmonic structure. At one time it was the foundation of the harmony, *i.e.*, when it consisted only of roots. Then the ear became accustomed to give it especial attention. Also it is conspicuous as being the second outer voice, the boundary of the tonal structure. Another weighty factor: the analogy with the overtone structure of a tone, of which the chord is an imitation. In the tone, which is itself a complex structure, its lowest element is recognized as that from which the entire complex is generated, and from which the entire phenomenon receives its name. The weightiest reason, however, for the conspicuousness of the bass, lies in the fact that the bass tone, lying the farthest from the upper limits of human hearing, has clearer and more intense overtones than do the upper voices,—though of course the overtones of the bass are weaker than the tones actually present above it, which have also their own overtones. But unconsciously the ear receives the impression of the overtones. If now the chord built by the actual voices coincides with the overtones of the bass, then the result is similar to the perception of a single tone: the entire complex is named from the lowest tone, the bass, and is recognized as fulfilling the needs of the bass. Through this strengthening by the upper voices the bass becomes the predominant factor. If however the upper tones do not coincide with the overtones of the bass, then there are clashes between the elements above the bass. These clashes can be looked upon as an obstacle, to which the bass, since it has the most audible overtones, is the one to offer the most resistance. Thus the bass is still the most conspicuous.

There is hence some justification for regarding the bass as fundamental, since it is the voice most affected by these tonal combinations. Now when we compare the 6th and $^6_4$ chords with the root position, we see that the overtones of the bass (*e* or *g*) are contradicted by the upper tones. Hence the 6th chord and the $^6_4$ chord are less consonant than a triad in root position. It is for this reason that the 6th chord is recognized in musical practice as less suited for establishing tonality. But there must be also some distinction between these two chords, for the $^6_4$ chord is regarded as a mild dissonance. Since the chord members are the same, the difference must be sought again in the overtones. If we now compare the overtones of the various chord members, we discover the following: the bass tone of the $^6_4$ chord finds in the overtones of the other chord tones earlier, hence stronger support than does that of the 6th chord. The second overtone of *c* is *g* (supporting the bass); likewise the second of *e* is *b* (an overtone of the bass). In the 6th chord, on the other hand, the earliest overtone support for the bass is the fourth of the *g*, namely *b* (the second of *e*); likewise the *e* appears first as fourth overtone of the *c*.

e			*e*		*b*		*e*	*g*♯	*b*			Sixth
	g			*g*		*d*	*g*		[*b*]	*d*		Chord
		c			*c*		*g*			*c*	[*e*]	
g			*g*		*d*		*g*	*b*	*d*			Six-
	c			*c*			[*g*]		*c*	*e*	*g*	Four
		e			*e*			[*b*]		*e*	*g*♯	Chord

In the $^{6}_{4}$ chord the overtone structure of the chord members resembles that of the bass *more* than in the 6th chord. The bass tone of the $^{6}_{4}$ meets *less resistance* in the chord tones, or (as one might also look at it) its chord tones are *more inclined to yield to the supremacy of the bass tone*. If we conceive the bass tone as striving to establish in the chord a sound as like to its own as possible,—to make its own overtones as effective as possible,—then the bass of the $^{6}_{4}$ chord has more chance to do so than has the bass of the 6th chord. There are problems in both chords. Both are really dissonances. But the problem of the $^{6}_{4}$ chord has a better prospect of a solution; it is hence *more intensive, more striking*. A problem is also evident in the 6th chord; but it is farther from its solution. The disturbance is not great enough to force its way through; it *can be overlooked*. But it has not been entirely ignored, for it has been noticed how it is less suited for establishing a tonality than the root position. These problems are of course very small —as if expressed in the last decimal places. But still they have been clearly recognized; otherwise no distinction would ever have been made between the two inversions of a triad. Since the ear has shown itself so sharp in this problem pertaining to the overtones, one may well hope that in the further development of music it also will not fail,—even if that development should follow a course which aestheticians will condemn as sure to bring the art of music to an untimely end.

Since the chord of the sixth has melodic rather than harmonic significance, it is suited to bring variety in the leading of the bass and also in the other voices. It may be freely used, with due consideration for the requirements of the third of the chord, which is in the bass. We have already indicated that the third is only third choice for doubling. Since it is the last tone of the chord to appear in the overtone series, and since it is the most conspicuous sounding member of the chord, as the determinant between major and minor, its doubling serves to emphasize an already striking sound. Hence it is clear that in general, if a well-balanced sound is desired, it will be superfluous, that is, *in poor taste, to double the third,*—especially *in the chord of the sixth,* where the third is already conspicuous because of its position in the bass. Obviously this restriction applies only as long as it is not necessary (exceptions will be noted later) to use the third also in an upper voice. Whatever is necessary may be done; what is superfluous should be avoided.

Example 15 shows the first inversion of the triad on the first degree in various positions: at *a* with the root doubled, at *b* with the fifth doubled. The student should practice these, and do the same with the other triads.

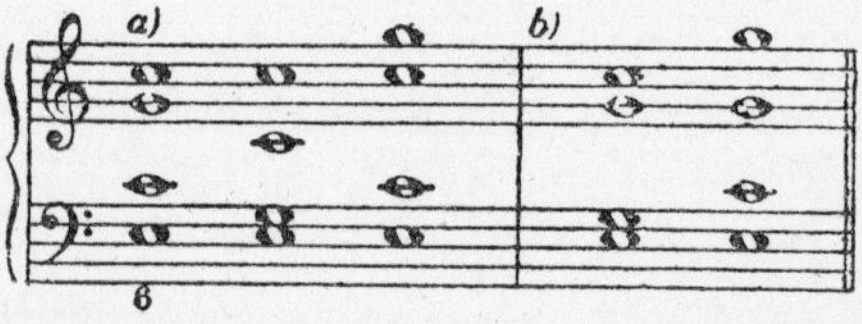

The doubling of the fifth makes necessary a new observation for connecting the chord of the sixth.

Consecutive Octaves and Fifths

In chord connection there are three possible relationships between the movements of two voices:

1. While one voice moves, the other is stationary (*oblique motion*), 16*a*.
2. While one voice descends, the other ascends (*contrary motion*), 16*b*.
3. Both voices move in the same direction, up or down, at the same time (*similar motion*), 16*c*.

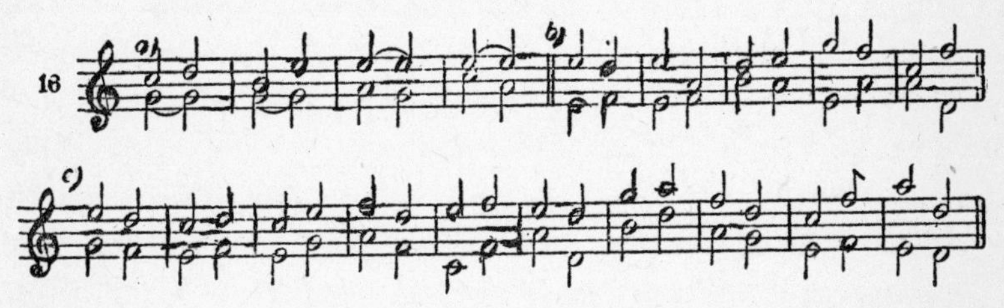

In almost every four-voiced harmonic progression, two or often three of these kinds of motion appear. Thus in example 17 oblique motion occurs between soprano and alto, also between tenor and alto, also bass and alto; similar motion between soprano and tenor; contrary motion between soprano and bass, and between tenor and bass.

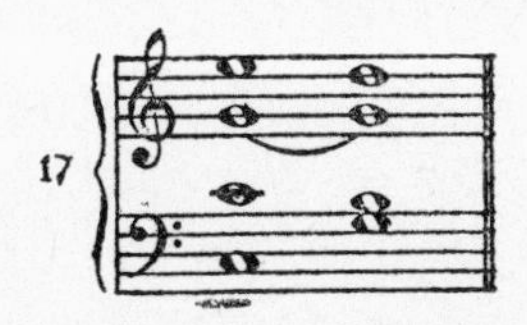

While the older theory permitted oblique and contrary motion freely, it often forbade similar motion, in some instances conditionally, sometimes absolutely. The latter instances are known as consecutive octaves and consecutive fifths.

Example 18*a* shows consecutive octaves, 18*b* consecutive fifths.

This law defined the forbidden situation as follows: When two voices move in similar motion from an octave

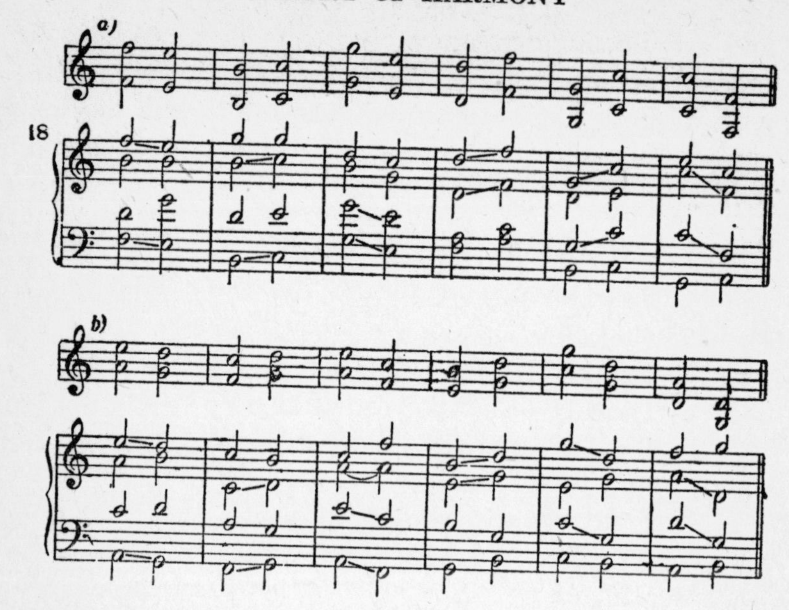

interval to another octave interval, or from a fifth to another fifth, there arise *consecutive octaves*, or *consecutive fifths*.

The stricter form of the rule forbade similar motion of two voices into a perfect consonance (octave or fifth). This form of the rule forbade what are called *covered* (or "hidden") *octaves* and *covered fifths*, and could be stated also as follows: When two voices proceed from any interval (fifth, octave or other) in similar motion into an octave or fifth, there arise consecutive or covered octaves or fifths.

The student will avoid entirely consecutive octaves and fifths as long as he needs to be guided by teaching. He may employ them later as soon as inclination, taste and artistic understanding place him in a position to proceed on his own. Covered octaves he may write with discretion in a few situations, which will be discussed when the time comes. Covered fifths may be used at any time.

Triad Connection Using Chords of the Sixth

The connections indicated in the three tables (A, B, C) should now be studied and worked out.

A. Triad I with 6th chord of I, III, IV, V, VI
Triad II with 6th chord of II, IV, V, VI, VII
Triad III with 6th chord of III, V, VI, I
etc., to
Triad VII with 6th chord of III.

B. 6th chord of I with root position of I, III, IV, V, VI
6th chord of II with root position of II, IV, V, VI, VII
etc., to
6th chord of VII with root position of III.

C. 6th chord of I with 6th chord of III, IV, V, VI
6th chord of II with 6th chord of IV, V, VI, VII
etc., to
6th chord of VII with 6th chord of III.

The student will do well to work out these entire tables (if possible in several keys). Here for the first time we have difficulties in voice leading, which it will be best to overcome at once; it is well to gain the necessary practice now, so that one may not later go astray with more important matters because one is not successful in voice leading.

Here I only is worked out. The student should join likewise the other triads (don't forget: other keys!).

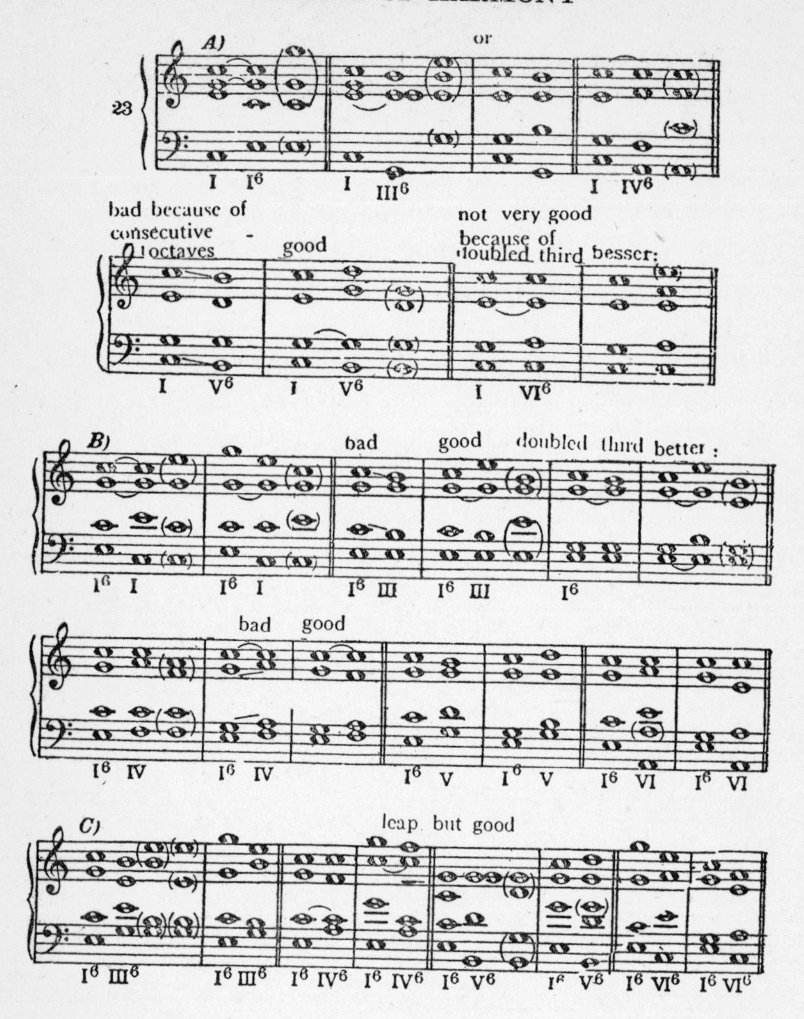

In some progressions the student must watch for, and avoid, consecutive octaves and fifths. In others the stationary common tone must be given up, as otherwise the third is needlessly doubled.

The connection of a triad with one of its inversions ($I—I_6$ or $II_6—II$ or $IV—IV^6_4$ or $V_6—V^6_4$) is called a *change of position*. There is no real change of harmony (hence change of position has only melodic significance); two or more voices (here one is the bass) exchange places.

The student will do well to work out each example twice (at least twice!), once doubling the root in the 6th chord, and again doubling the fifth. Thus arise various solutions, and often new difficulties. All of these the student should investigate, finding if possible more than two solutions. Nearly every one will suggest another. It is especially important to try this situation: doubling the fifth in the first chord.

VII demands special care.

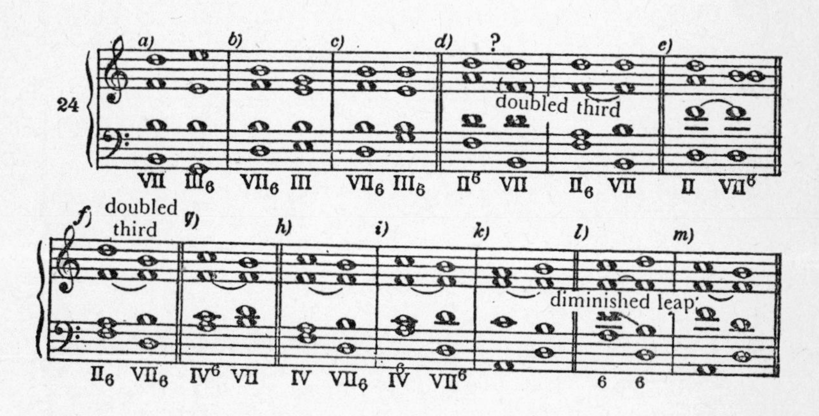

In example 24*d* we meet a new situation. As II is in the 6 position, the *f*, which should prepare the diminished fifth, is in the bass, which will proceed to *b* in the next chord. Hence the diminished fifth cannot be prepared unless the *f* is also in an upper voice. Therefore the third, the *f*, should in this instance be doubled. Here we have a noteworthy example of how any instruction may be modified when necessary. Another is in

24*i* and *l*. In *i* the *c* of the tenor cannot go to *b* because of consecutive octaves with the soprano, nor to *f*, which as a dissonance should not be doubled. The only possibility is for the tenor to go to *d*, even though it doubles the third in the 6th chord of VII. Another solution of the same problem, at *k*, doubles the third in the first chord. In 24*l* the tenor is obliged, for the same reasons as at *i*, to make a leap of a diminished fifth. A leap of this interval was avoided under the old rules because it is unmelodic, or, perhaps more truthfully, because it is difficult to sing in tune. On the whole we shall also avoid this leap, so as not to destroy the smoothness of style. But when we find it necessary to make such a skip (which is sometimes unavoidable in the bass), then we shall try as it were to resolve the dissonance (= difficulty of intonation) implied in the diminished or augmented interval. Hence we lead *b*, the "rising leading tone," upward to *c*, and *f*, the "falling leading tone," downward to *e*. But since this procedure is not always possible, example 25 shows also several other possibilities. (Measures 5-10.)

The careful watching of such details may make possible a formal finish which seems to me well suited for the development of a feeling for form. Naturally the examples will not sound especially "moving;" but they should no longer be as stiff as the first ones.

The student may now employ the chord of the sixth in building phrases, with the following suggestions: In general, a chord of the sixth can be used anywhere except at beginning and end, where I in root position will always appear. When it is necessary to repeat a chord, it is well to use a 6th chord. It is not good to use too many 6th chords. The phrases can now extend to eight or twelve chords; more would be inadvisable, necessitating too many repetitions. Example 26 shows several phrases.

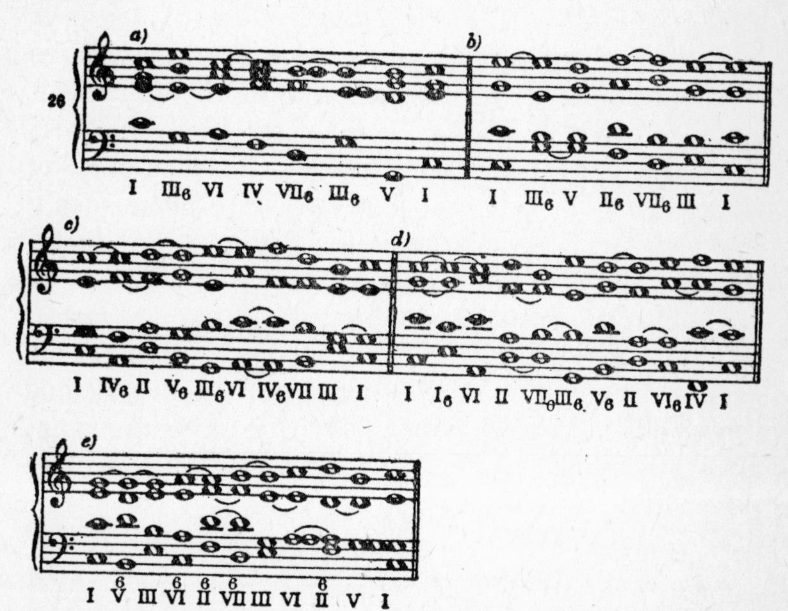

In deciding whether to use a chord in root or 6 position, naturally the melodic line of the bass must be considered. In general the bass should not be allowed to remain stationary. This can often be avoided, as in example 26*a*, by leaping an octave, often by choosing a 6th chord instead of root position, or the reverse. Repetition of the same bass note, even when one or two other tones intervene, can give a lame effect. If, for example, in 26*a* the VI had been taken in 6 position instead of root position, it would not have helped much even to take the leap to the lower octave (*c*). Such repetitions should as far as possible be avoided by the student and corrected by the teacher, for where the repetition is not justified by a motive the effect is bad. The situation is different in 26*e*, where the repetition of the *c* and the *e* can do no harm; not so much because in one instance two, in the other three chords are in between, as because the bass proceeds both times in the opposite direction after the repeated note. In judging whether a bass part is good, then, the first melodic consideration is the question of variety. When tone repetitions are unavoidable, at least two other tones should intervene, or the melodic direction should change. The student should also give special attention to the highest tone of a melodic line. This should always be treated as the high point, *i.e.*, it should appear only once, for its repetition has usually a worse effect than that of less conspicuous tones.

The Six-Four Chord

Under the old rules the $^6_4$ chord was to be either prepared and resolved, or treated as a passing $^6_4$; in any event it was to be approached and left without skips in the bass. Hence the bass remained stationary or moved only stepwise in approaching and leaving the $^6_4$ chord.

The preparation of the $^6_4$ chord differs from that of a dissonance in that two tones are to be considered for preparation. Either the fifth (in the bass) or the root may be prepared; *i.e.*, one of these tones should be a member of the preceding chord, and should appear in the same voice in the $^6_4$ chord. In resolution either the bass remains stationary while the upper voices move to form another chord, or the bass moves one degree up or down and becomes root or third of the next chord. *A $^6_4$ chord should neither precede nor follow another $^6_4$ chord.* It is too much like following an unsolved problem immediately with another unsolved problem, a construction clearly opposed by a feeling for form. Also this progression seems to recall consecutive fifths, which mostly arise in the melodic progression from the fifth of one triad to the fifth of another. The treatment of the passing $^6_4$ chord concerns only the bass, which, like a passing tone, is approached and left stepwise in one direction. We are concerned here not with harmonic, but with melodic considerations, for the effect of this progression lies in its calling attention to a melodic movement. Such a melodic movement is every scale passage of three notes of which the middle note carries a $^6_4$ chord. The scale can be considered as a melody, though the simplest, most primitive melody,—primitive in its slight organization and variety: it has just one principle of tone succession (step by step) and just one direction (up or down). A more complicated, more interesting melody is more varied in its organization; the direction and size of the intervals change more often, even continually; and repetitions, in which one recognizes system, show, if not more principles, at least variations. But the scale is still a melody. It has system and structure; a primitive melody, a relatively artless construction, but yet a melody, already an art form. I make these observations on the nature of the scale because there will be many opportunities when certain seeming harmonic problems can be shown to be melodic.

Example 27*a* shows several preparations, 27*b* some resolutions: in 28 each $\frac{6}{4}$ with its preparation and resolution.[1]

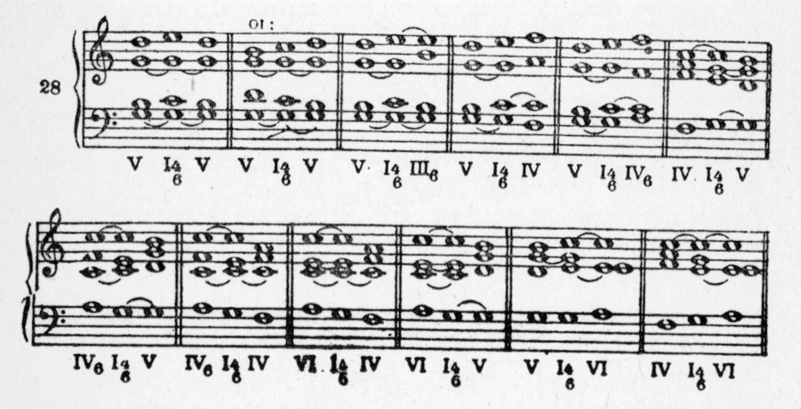

The student should practice the preparation and resolution of the $\frac{6}{4}$ chord of other triads besides I. While not available for constant use, the $\frac{6}{4}$ chord is frequently met with.

[1]The figure $\frac{6}{4}$ and other composite figures ($\frac{6}{5}$, $\frac{4}{3}$, etc.) will appear inverted n Schoenberg's illustrations, which follow the German practice of placing the smaller digit above. The translated text follows English and American usage, with the smaller digit below. There is no musical significance in the order of the digits.—Translator's note.

VII$^6_4$ should be treated with especial care, since the fifth is already a dissonance. Obviously here again only IV (root position) or II (6) can be used for preparation, and only III (root position) for resolution; hence the succession with VII$^6_4$ will be IV—VII$^6_4$—III or II$_6$—VII$^6_4$—III.

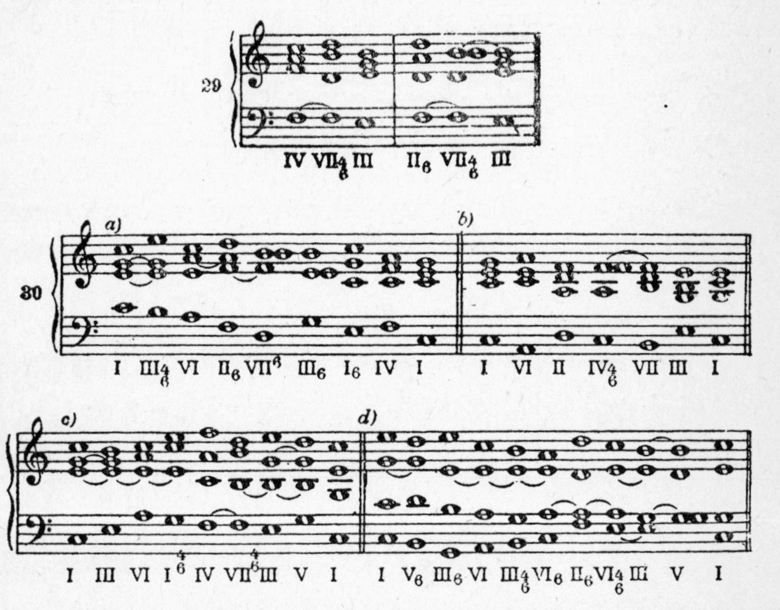

Example 30 shows several phrases. In 30*d* III and VI appear each three times. Without wishing to recommend these repetitions, I give them here in order that the student may see how they can be improved by a good melodic bass with change of position.

Seventh Chords

A seventh chord consists of three superimposed thirds, hence has a root, a third, a fifth and a seventh. As the seventh creates a dissonance it requires preparation and resolution. At first we shall use the simplest method of treating the dissonance, taking for the resolution the same fundamental progression that we chose for the resolution of the seventh degree triad, with the *root leaping up a fourth*. The descending dissonance here becomes the third of the next chord, whereas in VII it became the root of the chord of resolution.

The *preparation* of the seventh chord is accomplished in the same manner as with VII. The tone to be prepared (the seventh) should be a consonance in the preceding chord. If we wish to prepare the seventh chord on the first degree (I_7), the seventh, the *b*, can be in the preceding chord the root of VII, the fifth of III or the third of V. There are then three types of preparation possible, which we shall consider in turn. We choose first preparation by the third, because the root makes the upward leap of a fourth. Here nothing new needs be said concerning preparation and resolution, in addition to what has been said concerning VII.

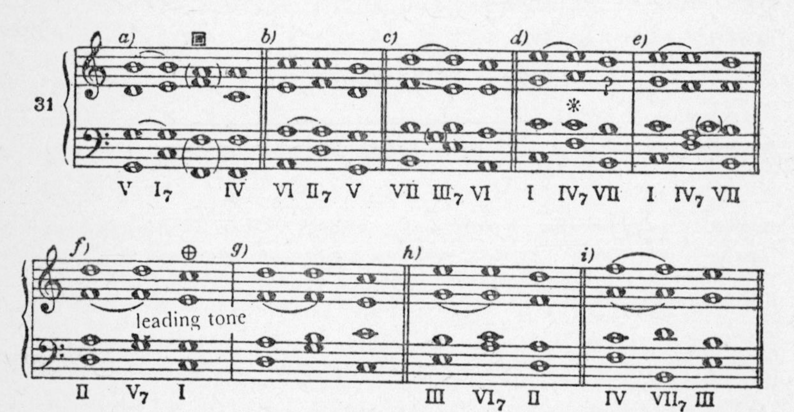

The preparation and resolution of the seventh chords are handled here with root position chords (inversions will be used later). In the resolution it is necessary, if we wish to have a complete chord, to lead the third of the 7th chord (in 31*a*, the *e*), not to the root of the chord of resolution, which would be the nearest move, but a third downward to the fifth. This, however, is evident from Question 4: "What is missing?"

Especially must every appearance of VII be watched, since it contains a dissonance. So in 31*c* the *f* must descend to *e*, so that it will be impossible to have III_7 as a complete chord. The seventh and the root naturally cannot be omitted, since they form the characteristic interval. On the other hand the third or the fifth could be left out, since neither is here especially characteristic. If one of the two were characteristic, the other could more suitably be omitted; as, for example, if the fifth were diminished, or the third major (as in *A* minor). In 31*d*, IV_7 cannot be a complete chord, because VII, the chord of resolution, requires preparation for the *f*; hence the *f* in IV must be doubled, and the third or fifth omitted (31*e*). In 31*i*, where VII_7 is treated, both fifth and seventh of VII_7 must be prepared and resolved, since both are dissonances. In 31*f*, the *b* of the tenor, for reasons already given, should go to *g*. There is one opposing rule which would require the *b* to go to *c*. *B*, the seventh tone of the scale, is called the *Leading Tone*, or, more exactly, ascending leading tone; to lead it upward into the eighth, corresponds to the model of the ascending major scale. However, it is only when it is part of a real melodic movement that it is necessary to follow this melodic tendency, the leading tone tendency, and also when it is the third of V and the following chord is I. The seventh tone has this leading-tone character only in the ascending major scale. In the descending scale the *b* goes easily to *a*, otherwise the resolution of I_7 would be impossible. The melodic necessity of leading the *b* to *c* need for the present apply only to the highest voice. Even there it can often be ignored (especially when other important grounds oppose it); but, particularly in a close, when it is in the highest voice, we shall lead it into the *c* rather than downward.

The student should practice preparation and resolution of seventh chords on all degrees of the scale, at first in the necessary three-chord phrases (in various keys), then in phrases of from eight to twelve chords, including one seventh chord in each. The plan of the fundamental progression should be the same as before, always according to the Table. Supposing for example we intend in the first phrase to use the seventh chord on the first degree. Since I is first and last chord, and in root position both times, it will here be difficult to avoid monotony. One should never bring in the I_7 too soon after the beginning, but allow at least three or four chords between. So perhaps: I—VI—II—V; now I_7, then for the resolution IV, and for a close II—V—I. This example is of course rather bad because of the repetition of II—V—I.

Note how in example 32, through the use of the 6 position of II, the phrase changes from close position to open. Here again variety should be considered.

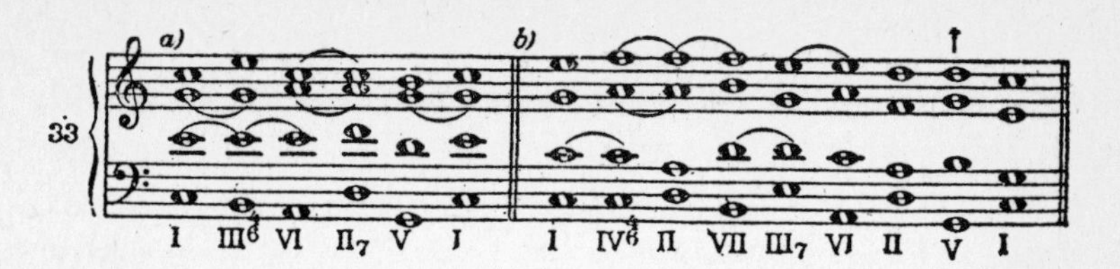

Example 33*a* illustrates the handling of II_7; *b*, III_7.

The student may now, as soon as he is sufficiently practiced in avoiding forbidden consecutives, on occasion lead the voices otherwise than by the nearest way, if by so doing he can obtain a better melody (as in 33*b* at †). Obviously the highest voice is here considered the melody part, and all that can be done to improve it is to avoid too much monotony, as from too frequent repetitions of the same note. It is to be noted that it is not a tone remaining stationary that causes monotony, for it is not being sounded anew, produces no movement. Easily monotonous, however, is the repetition of a certain succession of tones or the repetition of a tone with two or three other tones between, without a satisfying change in the melodic direction. The student need not be over-anxious in considering such melodic questions. For the present the results consistent with smoothness will be very limited. As our materials increase, so will our pretensions.

Preparation by the fifth follows the same supposition as by the third.

34

III I_7 IV II_7 V III_7 VI IV_7 VI IV_7 VII VII V_7 I VI_7 II VII_7

In these examples there are always three common tones, which can remain stationary as a harmonic bond. In IV_7 the root must again be doubled, to provide preparation for the *f* in VII. VII is not suitable for the preparation of V_7, since it does not meet the conditions for a chord of preparation. The preparing tone must be a consonance in the preceding chord; the *f*, however, is the diminished fifth in VII, a dissonance. One might disregard this, since the *f* would have been already prepared for the VII, then continued in the same voice for the V_7. But the progression has something weak about it, because the striking effect of the *f* as a dissonance in V_7 is killed by its being already dissonant with the *b*. The appearance of the *g* in the bass hardly increases this effect, but rather gives the impression that the *g* has simply been omitted until now. Therefore this progression should not be used.

The preparation of the seventh chord by the root will be omitted for the present. We shall return to it later. To be considered now are the preparation and resolution of seventh chords by 6 and $^6_4$ chords.

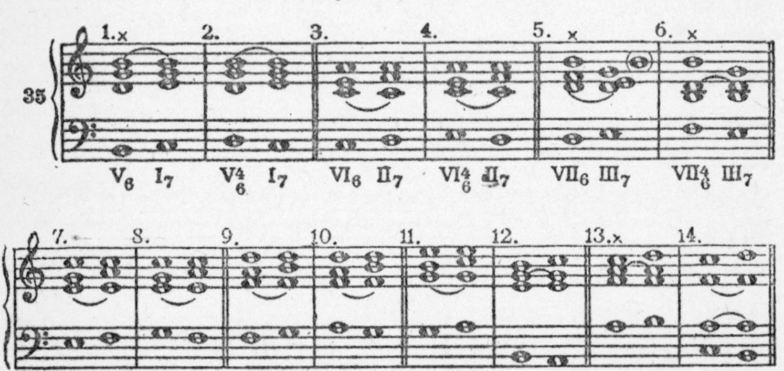

In the preparation of the 7th chord by the third, with the preparing chord in 6 position, the third must be doubled (35[1, 3, 5, 7, 9, 11, 13]). Preparation by a $\substack{6\\4}$ chord causes no difficulty.

This necessary doubling of the third in the chord of the sixth shows how undesirable it would have been to state as a rule: "in the chord of the sixth the third must not be doubled." For it can be seen that it must sometimes be doubled. Our direction was valid, as long as it really implied: "it is superfluous to double the third;" here, however, it is necessary, hence no longer superfluous. Even if I had given a rule, I should not have done so without adding that every rule may be superseded by a stronger necessity. I might almost say: that is the only rule that one ought to give.

If VII_6 is used to prepare III_7, the III_7 cannot be complete; the third or the fifth will be missing, because the resolution of the diminished fifth, *f*, compels the doubling of the root, *e*. Here there are two things to watch. 1. Obviously the preparing chord (VII) must itself be prepared. 2. Question 2 becomes "What dissonances?" for there are two: the diminished fifth of the preparing chord, which must descend, and the seventh of the III_7, which must be prepared (by stationary voice). In preparation by the fifth it is advisable in a preparing chord of the sixth to double the fifth rather than the root; but it is also possible to double the root, if no account is taken of the covered fifths. One could also double the third here, if it is felt to be important to have all voices remain stationary. This, however, is not necessary (36[1, 1a, 1b]).

I cannot recommend resolving a 7th chord into a chord of the sixth. We shall see later (ex. 244) that this progression, which we must avoid for the present, can be entirely satisfactory under certain conditions

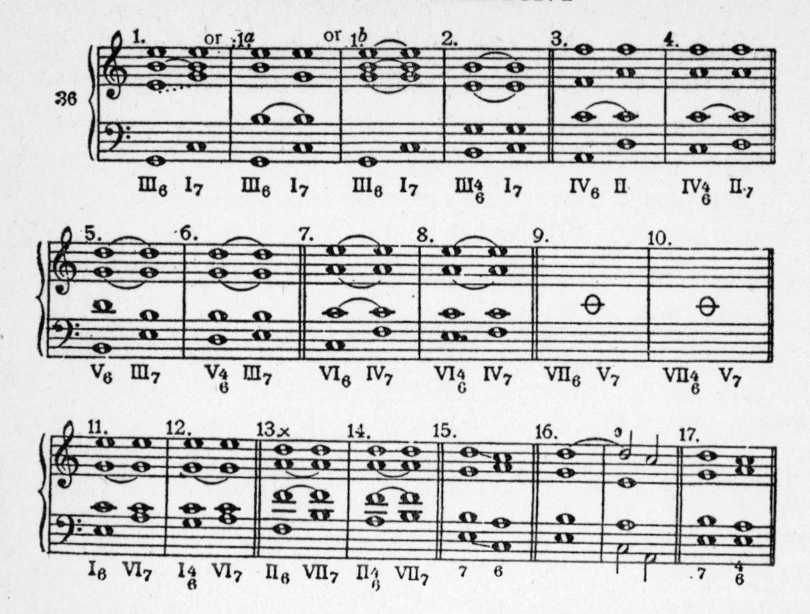

(36[16]); but for the present we must decide to do without it. The covered octaves which would now result (36[15]) from the resolution of the seventh into the same tone as that approached in similar motion by the bass (root), are the only covered octaves that I find really bad in harmonic structure.

On the other hand the resolution to a $^{6}_{4}$ chord causes no difficulty (36[17]).

Here again the student should practice these progressions, at first singly, then systematically in phrases.

The planning of the bass voice is now less simple than before. With the possibility of a choice comes the obligation to make a good choice. At all events such inversions should be used as will permit a more melodic bass. There are also other considerations. If, for example, it is desired to prepare a seventh chord by a $^{6}_{4}$ chord (the student should always think of the problem in this way), then the $^6_4$ chord must also be prepared; it is best to start in the midst of things with the progression under consideration, then work from there both ways toward beginning and end.

Suppose for example I decide to place the following in a phrase: III_7 prepared by V^6_4, VII_7 prepared by IV_6. I write first the bass notes of these progressions, with the triad numerals and figures:

37

V^4_6 III_7 VI IV_6 VII_7 III

The *d* in the bass of the V^6_4 can be preceded only by *d, e* or *c*. *E* could be the bass note of III, I_6 or VI^6_4; the $^6_4$ chord on *e* is of course unsatisfactory, as resulting in two successive $^6_4$ chords; III would be a poor choice, since another III would be the second chord following. I_6 is certainly possible, but the repetition of the tone *e* should be avoided if possible. Hence the preceding bass note should be *d* or *c*. *D* can only be II or VII. VII will not do, as it must resolve to III; II remains, and would be quite satisfactory if it did not make the bass stationary—a slight fault, to be sure. If *c* precedes the *d* of the V^6_4, then only I is possible (at least for now), for IV and VI have no common tone with V. So the best solution is to place the V^6_4 which prepares the 7th chord just after the opening I.

Example 38 shows how the opening might have been constructed otherwise. Example 39 shows the entire phrase worked out.

38

6 $^4_6$ III_7 or I IV II $^4_6$ III_7

Here appears another difficulty. The resolution of the III_7 closes with *a* in the bass, and the preparation of VII_7 by IV_6 begins with *a*; here at least three or four chords should have been placed between the two *a*'s, and it is doubtful whether a good bass would then have resulted. It is the least tasteless to join the two progressions by the stationary *a*, unless one makes the still better choice not to use these two problems in the same short exercise, but replace one of them with some other.

Inversions of Seventh Chords

Like triads, seventh chords can be inverted; *i.e.*, a chord member other than the root may be in the bass. When the third is in the bass the chord is called a $\substack{6\\5}$ chord (more exactly, $\substack{6\\5\\3}$ chord); when the fifth is in the bass, a $\substack{4\\3}$ chord (more exactly, $\substack{6\\4\\3}$ chord); when the seventh is in the bass, a 2 chord (more exactly, $\substack{6\\4\\2}$ chord).

Inversions of seventh chords may now be used, following the same principles as with inversions of triads, namely with a view to variety in the bass voice and to the avoidance of undesirable repetitions. No new directions are needed.

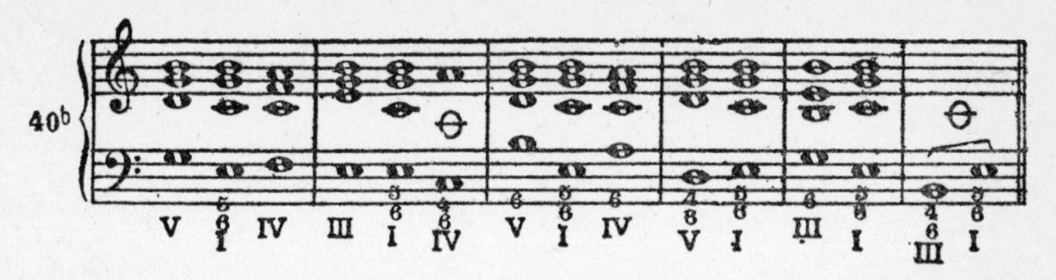

In 40*b*, I^6_5 is prepared and resolved. For preparation by the third (V) root position is suitable, as also 6 and $^6_4$ position; by the fifth (III), root position and 6 position, but not $^6_4$ (because of the skip in the bass, *b*—*e*). Resolution of the $^6_5$ chord (always to a chord with root a fourth higher) may be to a root position or a 6 chord, but not to a $^6_4$ chord. In the resolution of the $^6_5$ chord to a 6 chord one might give preference in the bass to contrary motion to the descending seventh, but this is not absolutely necessary. Other $^6_5$ chords may be treated likewise, with due regard to the special conditions of VII.

40*d* shows preparation of the $^4_3$ chord by the third and by the fifth, and resolution in root position and 6 position; a $^6_4$ chord is impossible here because of the leap in the bass (40*d*[3] and [4]).

In the 2 chord the seventh must be prepared in the bass. It is therefore not often possible. The resolution can be only to a 6 chord, since the seventh must descend.

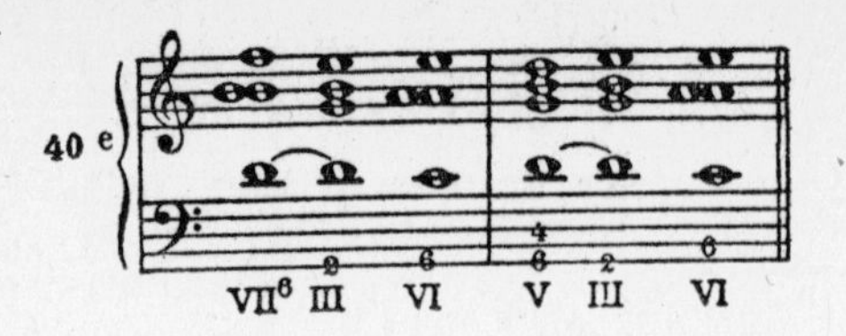

$40f$, g shows inversions of VII_7.

It must be remembered here that not only the seventh but also the diminished fifth must be prepared and resolved. Note especially $40g^1$, where the f, even in the bass, must be prepared. A doubled third will sometimes be necessary, as in the resolution of the $^6_5$ chord to a 6 chord ($40f^2$), or in a preparing 6 chord ($40f^5$) in order to prepare the diminished fifth. Preparation of VII^4_3 by IV_6 will not work, because the diminished fifth must be prepared ($40g^2$; note likewise $40g^4$ and ^{6}). Likewise VII^4_3 cannot be resolved to a 6 chord, because the f should not ascend but descend. VII_2 can be prepared only by IV_6 or by II^6_4.

The student should practice preparation and resolution of inversions of seventh chords in various keys, and then use them in phrases.

Connection of Successive Seventh Chords

If we follow only the most important direction for the resolution of seventh chords, namely that the seventh descends one degree, and are satisfied in the preparation if the tone preparing the seventh is a consonance in the preceding chord (hence is free, has no prescribed path!), then we can join one seventh chord to another. The two conditions must be fulfilled: the preparing tone is a consonance; the resolution is by the descending seventh.

Example 40*k* shows the preparation of a $^{4}_{3}$ chord by a seventh chord (preparation by the third) and the preparation of a $^{6}_{5}$ chord by the same seventh chord.

40*l* shows a succession of such progressions; naturally the position (inversion) of the seventh chords is determined by the bass. Carried so far, such a succession need not interest us. It is cited here because, with older composers, the harmonic framework for the repetition of motives in sequence is often constructed in this manner.

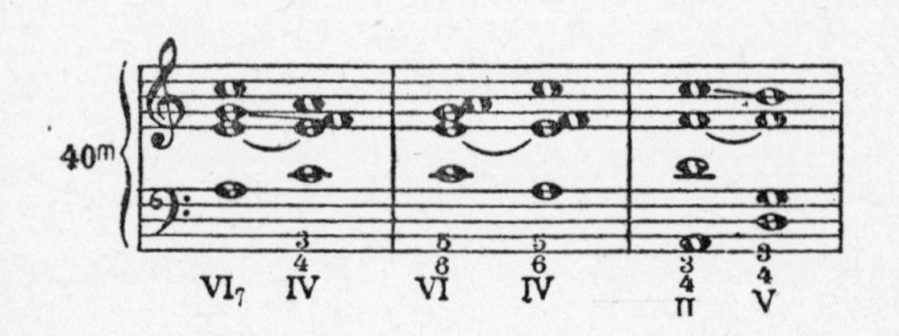

In 40*m* are shown several progressions in which the bass skips, while the seventh resolves and a consonant tone prepares another seventh. At the same time the two other voices exchange positions.

THE MINOR MODE

Our minor scale today is a survival of the old Aeolian: *a*, *b*, *c*, *d*, *e*, *f*, *g*. Sometimes, when the seventh tone proceeded to the eighth, the seventh was changed into a leading tone: *g* was altered to *g*♯. Thus arose the augmented interval *f*—*g*♯, which was to be avoided. Hence the *f* was likewise altered to *f*♯, so that when a leading tone was desired, the scale went *e*, *f*♯, *g*♯, *a*.

As a result we have two forms of the minor scale known as the *melodic minor*, the *ascending* form, which raises the sixth and seventh tones, and the *descending*, which uses the original series of unaltered tones. The two series are not mixed; in ascending the raised tones are to be used, in descending only the unaltered tones. Reducing these statements to rules, we have the *Four Turning Points of the Minor Scale:*

First Turning Point, *g*♯: *g*♯ must go to *a*, for *g*♯ is employed only as a leading tone. In no event can *g* or *f* follow *g*♯; nor can *f*♯ (at least for the present).

Second Turning Point, *f*♯: *f*♯ must go to *g*♯ as it was brought into the scale only as an approach to the *g*♯. In no event can *g* or *f* follow it. Neither (for the present) can *e*, *d*, *a*, etc.

Third Turning Point, *g*: *g* must go to *f*, for it belongs to the descending scale. In no event may *f*♯ or *g*♯ follow it.

Fourth Turning Point, *f*: *f* must go to *e*, for it belongs to the descending scale. In no event may *f*♯ follow.

The following of these directions must be invariable;

otherwise it is nearly impossible to preserve the essential character of the minor mode. Chromatic progressions we must forego for a while, since we have not yet discovered their special conditions. And any other use of the raised sixth and seventh tones can easily have the effect of destroying the feeling of tonality, which for the present we wish to keep entirely clear. When we have more adequate materials and skill, it will be easy enough to avoid too great errors, but just now we are hardly ready. The third and fourth turning points can later be handled more freely, if one intends to suggest the Aeolian mode. This coincides, in the absence of raised tones, with the Ionian, or our relative major. The turning-point rules answer to the character of the modern melodic minor mode, in which there seldom occur passages without raised tones. The absence of these is characteristic of the Aeolian, where the unaltered sixth and seventh tones are freely used. In this sense a freer treatment could even now be permitted. It would then not be out of the question (perhaps in an inconspicuous inner voice) to follow a *g* with an *a*, or an *f* with a *g*. But in the neighborhood of raised tones it can easily produce a rough effect similar to that of the so-called cross relation (about which more will be said). Then the *g* or the *f* must, so to speak, be resolved, the *g* to *f*, the *f* to *e*, near the appearance of raised tones. In any event this restriction will always hold: that *g* and *f* must never go to *f*♯ and *g*♯. But it is more expedient to defer any free treatment till later.

The Diatonic Triads in Minor

Example 41 shows the triads possible in minor keys. Since of course the raised tones are included in chord

building, there are six more than in major, and their placing, character and connection are evidently different. On the first degree is a minor triad; on the second a diminished and a minor; on the third a major triad and another whose form is new. (This is the so-called augmented triad, which will be given special consideration. It consists of two superimposed major thirds adding up to an augmented fifth. The augmented fifth does not appear among the first overtones, hence is a dissonance.) IV is minor or major, as likewise V. VI is major or diminished, as likewise VII. In connecting these chords we shall still at first join only those that have common tones; hence we can use the same Table as before (p. 8). The chords that have no raised tones cause no difficulty in connections *among themselves*. The situations are no different from those in the relative major. Obviously the diminished triads that appear will be handled as before: II (*b-d-f*, identical with VII of the relative major) is prepared by IV (*d-f-a*) or VI (*f-a-c*) and resolved to V (*e-g-b*). It can, however, also resolve to V (*e-g♯-b*), as will be shown later. On the other hand, in the connection of these triads with those that have raised tones, or the latter among themselves, the turning-point rules must be observed. Here naturally there will be some difficulties, and it will not be practicable at first to construct a series of progressions.

The student will again use the Questions (p. 18). Answering to the new conditions imposed by the turning-point rules, the second question will now take the following form:

Question 2: What dissonance (or dissonances) or turning point (tone with prescribed path) is to be observed?

42 shows connections of I with the other unaltered triads, all easily carried out. In like manner the student can work out connections of the other unaltered triads. (At first only in root position.)

43 attempts connection with chords having the raised sixth or seventh tone. The connection of I with the augmented triad (III) may be omitted for the present. On the other hand its connection with the altered IV is satisfactory, but restricted to a certain continuation, since after the altered IV the only possible chord is the altered II. The connection of I with the altered V follows smoothly, but that with the altered VI is not usable, since VI altered (root raised) is a diminished triad, hence must be resolved to a chord with root a fourth higher, an impossible progression because the *f*♯ in the bass must go to *g*♯ (second turning point), hence is not free to leap.

diminished fifth

44 1. 2. 3.

IV II V VI II V II IV II V II VI VII

44 shows the connection of II (diminished) with V, with preparation by IV, then by VI. (Prepare and resolve!)

44^3 shows the altered II progressing to IV, entirely possible but not practical, because, as will be shown, IV can be followed only by II, and the II can be preceded only by IV, as the remaining examples show. The example would then be: IV—II—IV—II, giving a superfluous repetition. II to V, both altered, may be used without hesitation, but II to VI (altered) is useless, since the altered VI cannot be used; likewise II to VII (altered), since also VII, as will be shown, is for the present not usable.

The unaltered III naturally cannot be connected with chords containing *f*♯ or *g*♯. With VI, which we might consider if we were going to ignore the third turning point (as of course we shouldn't), we might manage to avoid *g*—*f*♯ by letting the *g* leap to *c*; but then the *c* (diminished fifth) would not be prepared; also there are the two *f*♯'s, both tending toward *g*♯. Even if the *f*♯ were not doubled, there would still be the *f*♯

in the bass. *The augmented triad on the third degree we shall omit for the present;* it will be considered in a different connection.

In joining the unaltered IV with an altered triad, since III and VII are not practicable, only V is possible; here, however, there is no common tone. It clearly cannot be connected with altered II or VI, for *f* should not go to *f*♯, and if another voice takes the *f*♯ it violates the so-called cross relation rule.

The Cross Relation Rule: The chromatic alteration of a tone must appear in the same voice in which this tone has appeared unaltered. For example, if *f*♯ appears in the second chord, and *f* in the first, the same voice that has the *f* must sing the *f*♯. Hence if the alto has just sung *f*, the tenor should not have *f*♯ in the next chord. I do not wish to make this rule too emphatic, as it is too often contradicted in accepted practice. Our turning-point rules will regulate the handling of these tones, and chromatic progressions will for a time be avoided.

The altered IV can easily be joined with the altered II, but not with the unaltered II, nor with the altered VI (diminished), since the diminished fifth, *c*, must be prepared. Unusable also is the connection with the diminished triad on VII, *g*♯-*b*-*d*, since this triad is not to be used for a while. Later it will be given special consideration. Connection with I is not possible, for *f*♯ must go to *g*♯.

The unaltered V (by similar reasoning as with the unaltered IV) cannot be joined to chords containing *f*♯ or *g*♯. Altered V, however, joins well with I, while its connection with II altered or unaltered, or with VII, is not possible. The II will not work because the *g*♯ must not go to *f*♯ (or *f*); besides, the unaltered II is a diminished triad, of which the *f* should be prepared. III will be omitted for the present.

The unaltered VI cannot be joined to chords containing *f*♯ or (at least for now) *g*♯. The diminished VI, *f*♯-*a*-*c*, cannot now be used at all, since the *f*♯ must go to *g*♯, while the diminished triad demands the upward leap of a fourth by the root.

Now again phrases should be constructed. In general it will be advisable to use the triads with raised tones less often than those without. An example in which several altered and unaltered triads appear, will necessarily be relatively long, because nearly always several chords are necessary in going from the one region to the other. In general it is a good idea to use altered triads near the end, where they properly belong. A succession of altered chords will always discharge into I; repetitions will result from their use in the middle. Also the introduction of the raised tones is possible, for the present, only after I or II. The student should use V next to the last chord, and always with the raised tone (as a dominant chord). The raised tones are indicated in the figures under the bass; beside the figure indicating the raised interval appears the appropriate sharp or natural, as for example 3♯, 5♯, etc. (or in *C* minor 3♮, 5♮).

49^1 has only unaltered chords, with the exception of the closing V. In 49^2, besides the two I's, all the chords are in the altered form. Neither example could well have been longer, unless one had wished to continue beyond the I. 49^1 might have been extended by using an unaltered V following the II; but then one should have used another series of chords to bring a close. Perhaps: II—V—III—VI—II—V—I, which, as can be seen, nearly duplicates the preceding series of chords, hence would hardly be in the best taste. To be sure, it would be permissible to close differently, with IV—I. In no event should the student use III just before the closing chord, for it includes *g*, which cannot go to *a*, and for a good close we use the leading tone *g*♯. Also a IV—I close would be possible, or even VI—I; but these should be used by the student only when an exercise otherwise would turn out to be too long. Generally one should try for a V for next to the last chord. With these materials, not very many examples and no great variety will be possible; therefore the student should practice the little that is possible in as many different keys as possible.

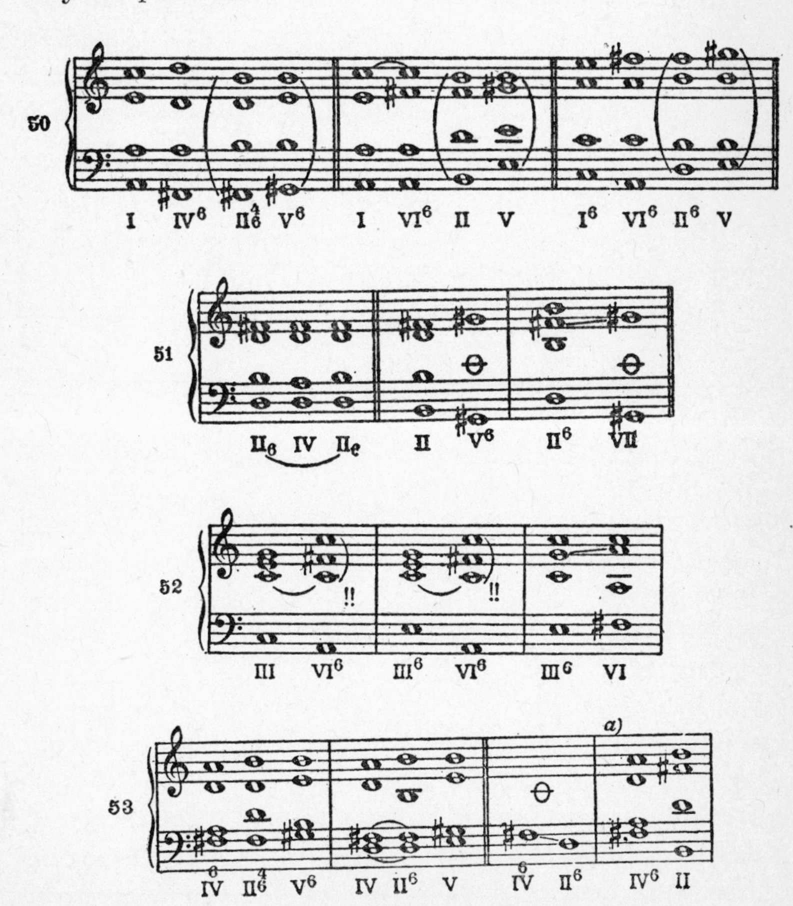

55

VI II6 V6 VI6 II V VI6 II6 VI6 II II6

Inversions of Triads in Minor

By the use of 6 chords and $\frac{6}{4}$ chords some progressions become possible which otherwise could not be used. Nothing new need be said concerning inversions. It still holds, as in major, that the 6th chord may be freely used, and that the bass note of the $\frac{6}{4}$ may not be approached or left by a skip.

In examples 50-55 appear several progressions that were unusable without inversions. The student will be able to find others. Only he must watch carefully the turning points, and must not forget that the diminished fifth (at least for the present) should be prepared and resolved, hence not doubled. Thus for example one cannot leap from the bass note of IV_6 altered, because *f*♯ should go to *g*♯; but yet it would be possible to progress to the altered II, by placing the *f*♯ in a different voice, which will then take over the responsibility of leading the *f*♯ to *g*♯ (53*a*). This procedure would satisfy the harmonic, but not the melodic requisites, from which these directions have arisen.

6th chords and $\frac{6}{4}$ chords can now be used in phrases.

In 56*a*, *b*, several progressions are used which are made possible by the use of inversions. For example: altered IV_6 can progress to altered II^6_4, then to V_6 (altered, as dominant), then to I. The example does not on that account need to close here, for the bass melody may well continue in the same direction, and the melodic force which is developed by this continuation is well suited to cover up the chord repetition which it brings with it. There is no disadvantage in the progression V_6—I—V^6_4—I_6. The melodic line of the bass, *g*♯, *a*, *b*, *c*, improves the effect of the whole in a thoroughly satisfying manner.

In 56*b* altered VI_6 progresses to altered II. Note in this example the tenor going from the *g* in the second chord to *a*. Since a *g*♯ appears soon after, this progression will be felt as faulty. A better solution is at *c*, where the *g* is resolved to *f*, and the *g*♯ comes in with no unpleasant effect. Also inadvisable is the progression of the alto from *f*♯ to *e* in the next to the last chord (56*b*). Later under different conditions we shall find a way to get around this difficulty, as otherwise the V_6 could not be used here.

The augmented triad (III) can now also be used in the examples. About this chord much will be said later, for it has had a great influence on the development of modern harmony. As a diatonic triad in minor its use is fairly simple. Its augmented fifth demands dissonance treatment. Since, however, as first turning point it cannot descend, the resolution takes place, here for the first time, by rising. The preparation, on the other hand, occurs as before. For preparation only V can now be considered, though before long also VII; for resolution, I or VI.

Here a peculiarity of this chord should be mentioned: the interval from *c* to *e* is four half-steps, from *e* to *g*♯ likewise four half-steps, and from *g*♯ to *c* above, the octave of the root, again four half-steps. The tones *e* and *g*♯ therefore divide the octave into three equal parts. Hence the constitution of this triad shows the remarkable fact that the interval of any two tones is always the same, so that the relation of the tones is not altered by inversion; whereby it is essentially different from all other chords so far considered. This peculiarity, about which more will be said later, makes it possible now to permit what soon (next chapter) will be done with all other chords, namely, to connect it with chords with which it has no common tone. More than that, we can dispense with the preparation of the augmented fifth. From this liberty arise many possibilities which will be of value in building phrases. In all this the turning points must be carefully observed. Our free treatment of this chord, with so many restrictions in the use of other chords, is explained by the fact that the application of these restrictions to the augmented triad does not really fit. I would have to re-formulate them, but I would rather not just here, as we are about ready to loosen the other restrictions.

Progressions shown in 57*a* and *b* are possible. Preceding the III: I, II, IV, VI and (see 58) VII; following it: I, IV, VI and V (not II, because *g*♯ must go to *a*).

The diminished triad on the seventh degree (VII) must be prepared (by IV or II) and resolved (to III).

58 a) b) c) d)
IV6 VII III$^{4}_{6}$ VI6 II6 VII6 III IV VII6 III6 II VII$^{4}_{6}$ III

Naturally neither the diminished fifth nor the root can be doubled, for the diminished fifth should descend and the root, being the leading tone (turning point) should ascend. Therefore only the third can be doubled.

SEVENTH CHORDS AND THEIR INVERSIONS IN MINOR

59

Through the use of the raised and unraised tones we can build on each degree of the minor scale two seventh chords; on VII even four. Not all of these are usable, however, if we are to follow the directions so far given. It is evident that there will be no difficulty in connecting seventh chords without raised tones with triads without raised tones. On the other hand several of the seventh chords that have one raised tone can be used only under certain conditions; others (including VII with two raised tones, *g♯-b-d-f♯*) are entirely useless for the present, as long as the foregoing directions are to be followed.

60

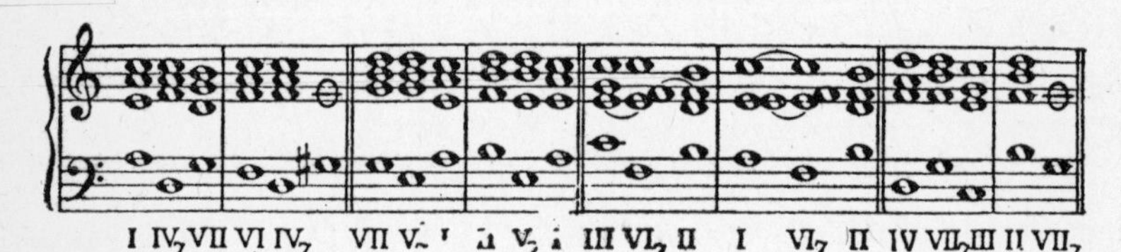

60 shows preparation and resolution of 7th chords without raised tones; preparation by the third and the fifth, resolution by progression to a chord with root a fourth higher. For these progressions no new instruc-

tions are necessary. Connection of these 7th chords with triads having raised tones is possible, under our foregoing instructions, only in one situation: resolution of II_7 to V with raised third. All others are unworkable; for example, the resolution of I_7 to IV (altered) is impossible, because the *g* cannot go to *f*♯.

In 61 the 7th chords with raised tones are examined.

I_7, *a-c-e-g*♯, is not usable for the present, since the seventh, *g*♯, must as leading tone rise, but must as the seventh of the chord descend. In II_7 (*b-d-f*♯*-a*), *f*♯ and *a* should both go to *g*♯: *f*♯ as a turning point, *a* as the seventh. The *g*♯, however, cannot be doubled, because then both *g*♯'s would have to go to *a* (consecutive octaves or unisons). VII (altered) cannot prepare III_7, because the *g*♯ should not leap. For the same reason VI_7 cannot resolve to II (root position). The resolution to II$^6_4$ is of course possible. Likewise VII$_7$, *g*♯-*b*-*d*-*f*, is barred for the present. The other forms of VII$_7$, *g*-*b*-*d*-*f*♯ and *g*♯-*b*-*d*-*f*♯, are unusable, because the seventh, *f*♯, would have to go to *g*♯, also because these forms tend to weaken the sense of tonality. IV$_7$ cannot resolve to unaltered VII because *f*♯ must go to *g*♯, nor to altered VII because of the doubling of the *g*♯. The latter can eventually be avoided by resolving to VII$^6_4$. By use of inversions of these three chords naturally much is possible. The student is by now in a position to examine these chords for himself and to recognize their special conditions; hence I leave the proof to him.

The preparation and resolution of seventh chords should now be worked out in phrases. Example 62 gives some models.

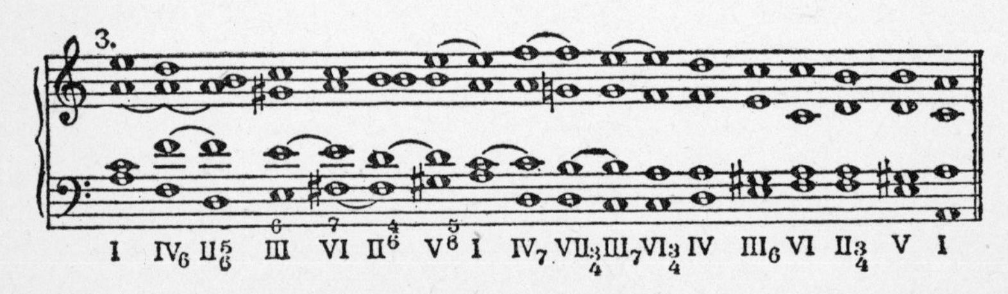

For *inversion* of seventh chords in minor keys no new directions are needed, but only the heeding of those already given. Through their use a few progressions are made possible that so far have had to be avoided. Most of these occur when the raised sixth or seventh tone of the scale is in the bass and the progression permits it to remain stationary. Obviously seventh chords may also be connected with seventh chords. While much of this may be little used, the student will do well to practice all of it. He will increase his understanding and his skill, which also are important. Besides: must one insist on a profit from everything one does?

CONNECTION OF CHORDS THAT HAVE NO COMMON TONES

Here we consider the connection of a chord with those on neighboring degrees of the scale,—the next higher or lower; *e.g.*, II with I or with III. If we moved all voices by the nearest way, consecutive octaves and fifths would result.

Hence it is not possible here to go by the nearest way. To avoid consecutives we must use contrary motion. The student is advised to ascertain clearly in which voices there is danger of consecutives.

64

With the use of 6th chords, fifths and octaves are more easily avoided.

65

a) b)

6 6 6 6 6 6 6 6 6

In the connection of two such 6th chords it is advisable, but not always necessary, to double the third in one of them.

66

6 6 6 6 6 6 6 6 6 6

Before we work these progressions into phrases we shall add to the preparations of seventh chords the preparation by the root.

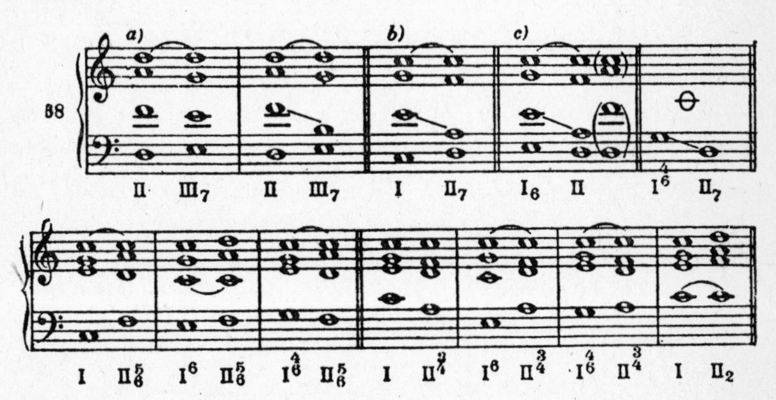

If the student is careful to avoid consecutive fifths and octaves, these examples offer no new difficulties. In the connection of the root positions of both chords (as 68*a*) it is often difficult to have the seventh chord complete; it can be done only by allowing the third of the first chord to leap to the fifth of the second (68*b*). If this leap is a diminished fifth (68*a*), it should properly be avoided as an unmelodic progression; but when advantage or necessity make a complete chord desirable, the student can by now make this leap freely.

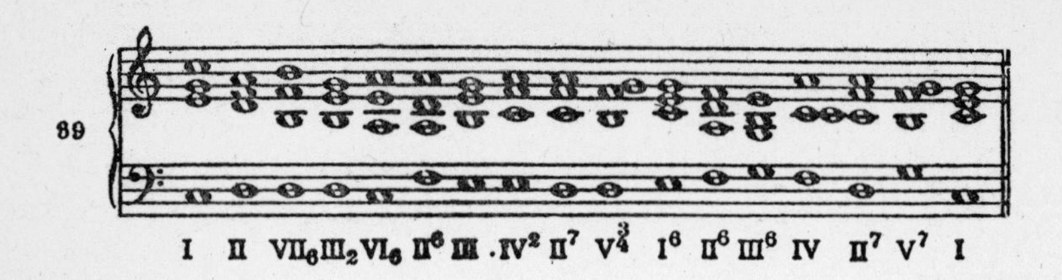

69 illustrates the working into phrases. Obviously the phrases can be more extensive now. (Practice also in minor.)

SOME SUGGESTIONS FOR EFFECTING TASTEFUL PROGRESSIONS; FOR THE MELODIC LEADING OF THE TWO OUTER VOICES; ON CLOSES, CADENCES, DECEPTIVE CADENCES, AND THE SIX-FOUR CHORD IN THE CADENCE

The planning of the bass voice now becomes more difficult. If the many possibilities are to be turned to the best advantage, the assumption of the problems presupposes a certain skill in the construction of the progressions, with the student directing his efforts always toward a certain end. The examples will then approach the point where the pains spent on the design will demand a greater reward than a merely correct solution; we shall have a greater satisfaction in the developing of a feeling for form. In a word, since the means are richer, the phrases should begin to be rounder, smoother. For example, a fault can be seen in example 69 which the student cannot avoid as long as he adheres to the law of the nearest way. The soprano, beginning in the middle range, cannot avoid the continuous dropping into the lower range, at least not with the necessary energy. The resulting monotony is fully justified,—an example of the fact that anything concerning harmonic succession is excusable if it helps to bring about the desired effect. It will be only for such considerations that we shall be concerned with melodic questions. But there is still something wrong. The chord progressions result in too many repeated notes in the other principal voice, the bass. Also the chord successions do not always result in a really good harmonic effect. We shall now therefore have to give attention to the bass melody and to the chord successions.

First the chord successions. We have already discovered that the strongest progression is to a chord whose root is a fourth higher, as it seems to answer to a need or tendency of the root. In this progression one tone changes its function (70): The root or principal

tone of the first chord becomes in the second a subordinate tone, the fifth; the root of the second chord is of a higher category, a higher power, since it embraces the root of the first in its own chord. In the chord on *g*, *g* has a superior significance, but in the chord on *c*, *g* becomes subordinate while *c* is more important. Such a progression, which, so to speak, causes a king to become subject to a prince, can only be a strong one. But the *c* subdues not only the old root, but brings also the other members of the chord to terms, and the new chord includes nothing, outside of the subjugated former root, that recalls the earlier regime. It has otherwise entirely new tones. It is easily understood that any progression that brings about a similar result will be equally or nearly as strong.

Next strongest is the progression to a chord with root a third lower (71). Here the following takes place:

The former root is subdued and becomes only the third. But the former third becomes the fifth, hence advances in importance, and only by one new tone is the new chord different from the first. This is of course the root; but this progression, measured by the victory of the root, cannot be regarded as so strong a progression as that to a chord a fourth higher. It has too much recalling the previous regime, too many tones of the former chord. Yet it is one of the strongest, as can also be seen from the fact that two such progressions in succession give the same result as that to a chord a fourth higher (72).

Somewhat more complicated is the critical estimate of the progression to a chord a second (one degree) higher or lower (II—III or II—I). Many reasons might appear for designating this as the strongest fundamental progression, but its use in music does not corroborate them. When this progression is examined it is apparent that all the tones of the first chord are subdued, since only new tones appear. In this respect it goes even further than the progressions so far estimated. It joins a triad to one of the two triads with which it has nothing in common, to which it is least related. It forces this connection, and here may be why the older theory explains it in a peculiar way: as a combination of two progressions, of which one, the principal, moves to a chord a fourth higher. *E.g.*, V—VI = V—III—VI (73*a*) and V—IV = V—I—IV (73*b*).

Thus the connection (73*a*) of V (*G*) with VI (*A*) would be in reality III (*E*)—VI, with the root of III silent; in V(*G*)—IV(*F*) the silent I(*C*) would play the same role.

I should therefore call this the super-strong progression. Or, since I call the strong progressions *rising* progressions, one might say this is *overleaping*, thereby suggesting the compression of two progressions into one. It is apparent that strong or rising progressions next to weak or falling, will always be permissible as a direct means to normal strength; while for the *superstrong* or *overleaping* a special occasion must appear; also that here as elsewhere rude force must not be confused with the strongest effect.

The two remaining fundamental progressions, to chords with roots a fifth higher and a third higher, I call *falling* progressions. In them the following happens: in that to a chord a fifth higher (75*a*), a tone of relatively subordinate significance becomes the principal tone; the fifth, an upstart, is promoted to become the root,—a decadent situation. One might argue that this advancement shows the power of the up-and-coming one, and that the root is here overthrown. But the power of the ambitious one arises only from the root's releasing of power, an intentional release, out of goodness of heart, so to speak, since the root holds the fifth within itself; the lion forms a friendship with the hare. In still more striking fashion is the weakness shown in the progression to a chord a third higher. Here the third, the weakest chord member, becomes the root, and the new chord differs from the former by only one tone; only the fifth is new (75*b*). This seems therefore to be the weakest progression, as is perhaps indicated also in that two such progressions in succession give the same result as that to a chord a fifth higher (75*c*).

It must now be emphasized, since so sharp a distinction has been drawn between strong and weak progressions, that it is not at all practicable to use strong progressions entirely. Otherwise the use of weak progressions would have to be excluded, for the weak would be bad. For this reason I group the progressions rather, as already said, into *rising* and *falling* progressions, calling those to chords a fourth higher, a second higher or lower, and a third lower, *rising*; to chords a fifth higher and a third lower, *falling*. It should then be indicated what purposes are best served by the one or the other group. That there are such purposes is evident. The construction of a musical phrase demands, as does the spoken phrase, a fall and rise of tone, of inflection. The use of falling progressions is therefore an artistic means, as is the rising. Since we are not now concerned with phrase structure, we shall, in the planning of fundamental progressions, prefer invariably the rising progressions, using the falling progressions for the present in groupings where the total result is still that of a rising progression. For example (76), when a progression to a chord a fifth higher is followed by one a second higher, the end result is to a chord a third lower, hence a rising of the harmony (76*a*); likewise when a third higher progression is followed by a fourth higher (76*b*) or even by a second higher (76*c*).

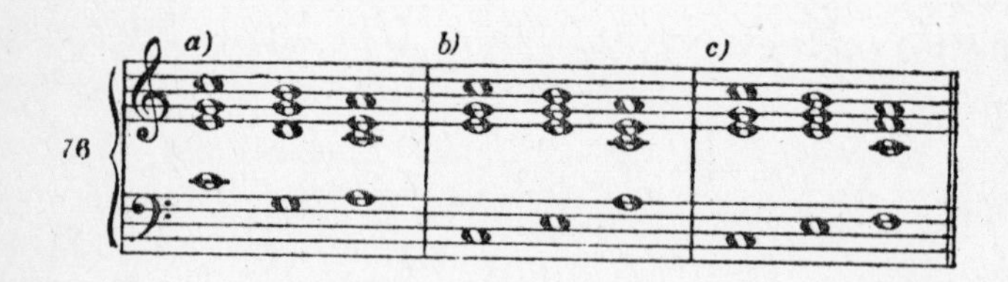

The effect then is as if the intermediate chord were inserted for purely melodic reasons. At any rate the falling progressions should be used in our lessons only in this manner.

To sum up: the fundamental progressions to be used by the student, as long as he is concerned only with harmonic means, and has not yet the ability to develop a characteristic style through melodic, rhythmic or dynamic means, are: to a chord with root a fourth higher, a second higher, a second lower, a third lower, all rising progressions. The falling progressions, to chords a fifth higher or a third higher, are to be used only in those connections illustrated in example 76.

In example 77*a* only rising progressions are used, but yet the phrase is not very good (from a harmonic standpoint of course; a fine melody might lie above it, removing all my objections); for the succession of so many stepwise moves gives a very monotonous, cold effect. The student is advised to allow a little variety. That is, to avoid too many similar progressions, also to mix stepwise progressions with those requiring a skip of the root. For a series of root skips alone would not be very good, as harmony, as it is too mechanical (78*a*, *b*, and *c*).

78 a) etc. b) etc. c)

Thus we are brought to a second demand to be considered in the planning of good phrases: the need for variety. This is difficult to discuss without its opposite, repetition. For if the first brings multiplicity, the second gives to the first coherence, sense, system, and system can rest only upon repetition. We shall find little opportunity to make use of repetition. We must forego for a time the advantage of gaining a certain effect through repetitions, and guard ourselves from the disadvantages that they bring with them. Our bass voice has in any one key a compass of twelve to fourteen tones. If the phrase extends to more than fourteen chords, there is no longer a possibility of avoiding repetition, even by taking the same tone in another octave. It is not so much tone repetition that gives a bad effect, as it is the repetition of tone successions. Even that does not necessarily harm, if over like tones different chords appear; and if between repeated chords there is enough material, they are not necessarily bad. The worst form of repetition occurs when the highest or lowest tone of a melodic line is twice used. To these two points especial attention should be given: the high point and (if I may so call it) the low point. Nearly every melody will present such a tone; the high point especially will hardly ever be repeated.

The repetition of a tone succession is tasteless not only in the highest voice but also in the bass, and often even a change of harmonizing cannot remedy this fault.

To avoid this fault (79*a* in bass, 79*b* in soprano) is usually fairly easy, since it is only necessary in the soprano to change position by a leap, or in the bass to choose a different inversion. But the repetition of tones in a single voice suggests strongly that also chord repetition may appear. Then the fault must be sought out in the first plan and there corrected.

In general the student must not go too far in seeking for variety. Melodic effects are not his problem—because they could not be successful. The thing to do now is to avoid the unmelodic, rather than to try to create melodies.

The following Guide Rules for the use of hitherto learned materials will be repeated and amplified; by observing them the student will be in a position to raise his work to a somewhat higher level. Much—nearly all useless—will be thereby excluded, but the allowed materials will be nearly all usable.

Guide Rules

I. On Fundamental Progressions.

1. The *rising* fundamental progressions: a fourth higher and a third lower are always good, but even here mechanical repetition is to be avoided.
2. The *falling* progressions: a fourth lower and a third higher, only in combinations (as shown on p. 74) which amount to a rising progression.
3. The *overleaping* progressions: a second higher or lower, sparingly; not excluded.

II. Use of the Chords

A. In Major and Minor

1. a) *Triads* can always be used in *root position*.
   b) *Sixth chords* serve the purpose of gaining variety in voice leading, especially in the

outer voices (bass and soprano); also of enabling the preparation of dissonances.

c) *Six-four chords* are in general to be used very sparingly. Best for cadence purposes (as will be shown later). Used as passing six-fours, sparingly, they are of value in the movement of the bass. However, those with stationary bass are to be used with discretion. Sometimes they are necessary for preparation of dissonances.

2. a) *Seventh chords* can be used wherever triads can be used, as long as preparation and resolution are cared for. Yet they will be used for the present where the seventh can serve the purpose of giving the chord a directional tendency, through the feeling for resolution, by which the required progression (V—I and, as will be shown, V—VI and V—IV) will seem to follow from necessity.

   b) *Inversions of seventh chords* under the same conditions as their root positions, to improve the voice leading; the 2 chord is of particular value in introducing a 6th chord.

3. *Diminished triads* (at first only in the progressions already used: II—VII—III and IV—VII—III) are as dissonances well suited to give a semblance of necessity to the appearance of a chord (III). The seventh chord on VII increases this effect. Inversions for the same purpose as with other chords.

B. In Minor.

Here we are subject to the conditions of the turning points and the observance of the two regions: the ascending scale (with raised tones) and the descending (with unraised tones).

1. a) The *Turning Points* must be taken into account in the planning of the chord progressions, so that the tones in question can move in the prescribed manner.

   b) Triads must often be used in inversions, when there is need of preparation or resolution of a dissonance, especially when a turning point lies in the bass.

   c) With seventh chords the same conditions are to be observed as with triads.

   d) The diminished triad or the seventh chord on II (unaltered) is in general better followed by V with major third than with minor third, because this triad, as will be shown later, has a conventional significance in the cadence.

   e) All diminished triads (II, VI and VII), and their seventh chords, are suited to the same purposes as in major: Through the dissonance they receive a definite directional tendency.

   f) With the augmented triad the fact that it can equally well precede or follow the regions of the ascending and descending minor scale, is furthered by its being a dissonance. Hence it is well suited for transition from one region to the other.

2. One cannot remain too long continuously in one of the two regions without endangering the minor mode feeling. This is best kept by suitable alternation and joining of the two regions. The transition from one region to the other cannot take place until all turning point conditions have been satisfied. It takes place:

a) Directly,

i. *From the ascending to the descending*, when the altered III, V or (as will be shown) VII is followed by I or the unaltered IV or VI (chords having the raised sixth tone cannot be followed by an unaltered chord);

ii. *From the descending to the ascending*, when the unaltered II, IV or VI is followed by the altered III, V or (as will be shown) VII. I can be joined to any altered chord; on the other hand chords having the unraised seventh tone cannot be followed by altered chords.

b) Indirectly,

i. *From the ascending to the descending* when chords having the raised sixth tone (II, IV, VI) are first followed by chords permitting the melodic move into the raised seventh;

ii. *From the descending to the ascending*, when chords having the unraised seventh tone (III, V, VII) are first followed by chords permitting the move to the unraised sixth.

III. Voice Leading.

1. Unmelodic moves (dissonant or dissonance suggesting). Such moves should be avoided as long as we are not using chromatically altered chords.
2. Avoid annoying repetitions of tone successions, especially when like harmonies appear on like tones.
3. Where possible preserve a definite, single high point, usually also a low point.
4. Gain as much variety as possible in the use of stepwise melodic progressions and skips, but keep to a certain middle range of the voice.
5. If the voice leaves this middle range by a skip, then if possible lead back to it by another skip or series of tones; even up changes of range in this manner.
6. If the middle range is left through stepwise moves, an octave leap may restore balance.
7. If repetition of tones or tone successions is unavoidable, an immediate change of direction may help.

These directions are of equal value for the soprano and for the bass. If the student could also observe them with the inner voices, the smoothness of the general result would certainly be helped. However, it is not necessary for the present that the student go so far; he will do well if he leads the two outer voices with the greatest possible care.

CLOSES AND CADENCES

Tonality is represented melodically by the scale, harmonically by the diatonic chords. Without special emphasis, however, these elements are not sufficient to establish the tonality. Certain tonalities are so similar, so nearly related that it is not always easy to determine which is implied, unless certain differentiating means are brought into play. It is clear which tonalities are next related: which most resemble each other. In the first place relative keys (*C* major and *A* minor), then like-named keys (*A* minor and *A* major), and then—and here are the most dangerous relatives—those keys whose signatures differ by one sharp or flat (*C* major and *G* major, *C* major and *F* major). If the difference between, say, *A* minor and *A* major is noticeable at practically any moment and disappears only in the V triad (as dominant), the situation is nearly reversed in the last named relationship. Nearly all the tones and a good many of the chords are common to both keys. *C* major differs from *G* major only in having *f* rather than *f*♯, from *F* major only in having *b* rather than *b*♭. It is possible therefore to write passages in *C* major that could be understood as *G* major, or as *F* major.

Is this *C* or *G* major?

Is this *C* or *F* major?

If one avoids the tone *f*, the passage lies as well in *G* as in *C*; if one avoids the *b*, the passage can be understood and employed as of the key of *F*.

If one wishes to indicate *C* major so that there is no doubt about it,—so that no one can be reminded of the key of *F* or *G*,—then he must use *f* and *b*. The surest means, then, to establish the tonality, will be to distinguish it from those that it most resembles,—to fence it off clearly from its nearest neighbors. If one succeeds in preventing any confusion with these, with which confusion could most easily arise, then one has definitely established the tonality.

The often mentioned tendency of a tone to lose itself in a tone a fifth lower, which becomes its root, to which it is the fifth, operates obviously upon the root of the tonic triad (I). For this reason *F* major is the greatest threat to *C* major I. Hence our first care must be to resist the pull to the sub-dominant, the *F* major feeling. This we accomplish melodically by the tone *b* natural. Since *b* belongs to three chords, III, V and VII are indicated as harmonic means to the same end. One could use all three, but V is really entitled to the preference, since its root finds in I the potential root a fifth lower to which it has a strong tendency to become a fifth.

It is clear that a key could be indicated by I alone, especially if it is not contradicted. Certainly any chord joined to I, must as a digression from the keynote weaken the tonality. Only through a certain grouping is it possible to control this weakening and lead things back to the keynote. Hence there is a problem in every harmonic phrase, however short: the straying from and return to the keynote. If the keynote stood alone with nothing to contradict it, the tonality would be established, primitively to be sure, but certainly without ambiguity. The more frequently and the more strongly it is contradicted, the stronger must be the means of reaffirming the tonality. But the more meager the harmonic activity, the simpler will be the work of repair. Thus there are situations in which I—V—I suffices to establish the tonality quite clearly.

The two simplest means for establishing tonality and constructing a close are: using I alone (not usable for us), and using only I and V (also unlikely for us). With this we reach the first, simplest form of cadence.

In a fairly long piece passages will naturally appear which point to the key of the dominant. Hence arises the need to guard against the unintended encroachment of this key. The melodic means is *f* natural; the harmonic, IV, II and VII. Since VII seems suited here as well as for guarding against *F* major, the idea is suggested that it should be completely preferred as a most suitable means for both, and in fact such was the earlier practice. This chord is less effective, however, for this purpose than other means which we shall employ. The charm of tonality is perhaps increased if through a *G* chord the feeling of *G* major is momentarily awakened, and through an *F* chord the feeling of *F* major. Perhaps this satisfaction results from the submission of such triads, each of which could express a tonality, under the will of the potential root a fifth below, as in similar passages yielding their power as confirmation of the strength of the root. It is necessary then, for the overcoming of the *G* major feeling, to use an equally strong chord or fundamental progression as before against the *F* major feeling. II has the advantage of a fourth-higher progression to V. It includes the *f*, but IV is even stronger. Its progression to V is that to a chord a second higher, such as we have construed as a combination of two progressions; here, IV—V = IV—(II)—V; hence II is implied. But IV has another advantage in line with the special charm already mentioned: it is the sharpest contrast to *G* major, and it has a relationship to the fundamental *C* which is the inversion of that of V. Hence the last three chords of our cadences will sound best as IV—V—I or II—V—I. If a phrase is so turned out that one of these patterns of three chords can be used as a cadence, then the harmonic forces have been focussed to a point, and the phrase comes to a satisfying close.

The cadences can be still further defined, and we shall aim at making ever new means serviceable to this end. With the chords already known to us the succession IV—(II)—V—I is the strongest cadence. But even a weaker one may have a kind of charm; hence the qualifications of the other triads should be discussed. First, seeking a substitute for V, we try the possibilities of III. Having two tones in common with I is here a defect. But it has the leading tone, guards therefore against *F* major, and its progression to I is fairly strong (a third lower). Thus it would seem to be suited for the cadence. However, it is not in common use, and we can hardly employ it, but we should notice why not: mainly because it is not customary; *i.e.*, it could be used, its effect would be rather weak, but mainly unaccustomed. I have already indicated that VII was formerly used. It establishes the key, it leads to the closing chord, but today is not in common use, and hence we exclude it. As substitute for IV or II it cannot be considered, for it prates forth noisily the weightiest secret of V, which would follow, the leading tone; it also robs V of the possibility of leading into I with the strength of a seventh chord, because its diminished fifth is identical with the seventh of V (*f* in *C* major). On the other hand it is possible to precede V with VI in place of IV or II. Perhaps the basis of this progression is explained by the hypothesis of the older theory on harmonic progressions of a second: that essentially a silent chord a third or fifth lower (IV or II) makes the connection. This pattern, VI—V—I, is not unusual, hence is available.

The student should first practice cadences in special examples. From now on every phrase is to be closed with a cadence; a few suggestions should be given. It is not customary to use the last chord but one, the V, in an inversion. It is understandable that in this situation one would wish to use the strongest form. It is often used as a seventh chord, but also only in root position. The II can be used in root position or inversions, also as a seventh chord, with suitable inversions (not as a 2 chord). Least usable is the $^6_4$ inversion of II; the $^4_3$ is good. The seventh chord on IV appears seldom, but certainly is not impossible. Of the inversions of IV the 6 is possible, but not the $^6_4$. Inversions of IV_7 are not in good use. VI_7 is not suitable, because of the necessary treatment of the seventh; likewise its inversions are hardly usable. VI^6_4 is useless, VI_6 nearly so

83
1.
2.
IV V I
IV V7 I
3.
4.
IV II V7 I
VI II6 V I
5.
6.
7 II7 V I
VI II V I
7.
8.
II
VI V I
9. minor
10.
IV V I
II6 V I
11.
12.
13.
14.
15.
II V7
VI II V I

because of the weak move of the *c* to the *g* and the following repetition of the *c*; this last can however be used when necessary.

The student will do well (in order to try out many possibilities) to build cadences systematically: much as he did his first exercises following the table. First all the possibilities with IV—V—I; *e.g.*, I—IV—V—I, VI—IV—V—I, III—IV—V—I, etc., with IV both in root position and as a sixth chord. Then all with II—V—I and with VI—V—I. About minor keys nothing special needs be said; it is the same as in major. It is obvious that for the cadence V has the major third; it is for the cadence, for a leading tone, that this major third exists.

Deceptive Cadences

The progression V—I has the name Authentic Cadence; IV—I, Plagal Cadence. These are only names, technical terms, by which we are told nothing of harmonic significance. We have already considered the authentic cadence. There is no need to bother ourselves about the Plagal Cadence, as harmonically it is without any especial importance. It can hardly appear until the conditions of key delimitation have been already fulfilled through the known means, hence does not enrich our cadence in its main purposes. On the other hand the so-called Deceptive Cadences are of constructive harmonic significance. By this term is understood the replacing of the expected V—I progression by V—VI or V—IV. Here is its original form: after the V, I is expected, but instead VI or IV appears. But it is only in the close, in the cadence, that I is expected after V; since it does not come, neither does the end come;—we have not a real cadence but a deceptive cadence. A path is broken for a close, but not used. Naturally this is a very strong effect, for it places one in the position of preparing again for the real close and ending with increased power because of the repetition.

Now we should work the deceptive close into the cadence and turn it to the purpose just named, the delaying of the cadence. One thing must be watched. Since the deceptive cadence uses the *cadencing* V (not just any V), it is important that this V be in root position. The inversions of V are little used for deceptive cadences. There is no objection, however, in other than cadence situations, to the use of an inversion of V in the progressionV—VI or V—IV. On the other hand the seventh chord on V can well be used in the deceptive cadence.

At first we shall treat the seventh as in 91*a*, using only the forms 91*b* (*x* and *y* are of course not to be considered as deceptive cadences) and 91*c* (the same with V_7), excluding the "bad seventh." (The "bad seventh" is a seventh in which the lower tone descends while the seventh remains stationary, or, vice versa, the seventh rises while the lower tone remains stationary, hence resolves into an octave: 92).

When we are not dealing with a deceptive cadence, which we have found of value as a specific means in a close, these same progressions can procede from inversions of the V_7 chord (93); but perhaps those examples

that discharge into a $\frac{6}{4}$ chord should be used with some caution. The $\frac{6}{4}$ chord, as has been said before, has in a certain situation a very weighty function and in this way is used as a sort of cliché; hence it happens that every $\frac{6}{4}$ chord, if it appears in a situation only slightly similar, attracts attention to itself and awakens the expectation of certain things to follow.

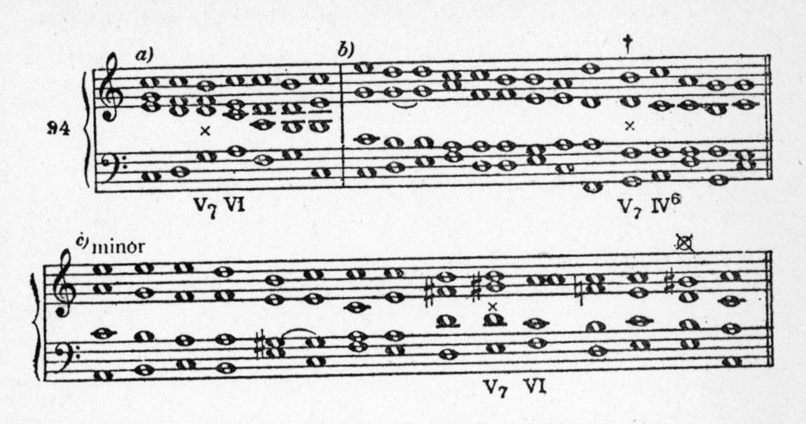

In 94 deceptive cadences with the dominant seventh chord are illustrated at X. At ⊗ and † the dominant seventh is introduced without preparation. I have intimated earlier the eventual free treatment of the seventh. Provisionally the dominant seventh may be given the freedom of appearing without preparation. Especially is the preparation unnecessary when the seventh, as in 94*c* (⊗), is approached and left stepwise in one direction (melodic justification). Other examples of such *passing sevenths* are shown in example 95, including other seventh chords.

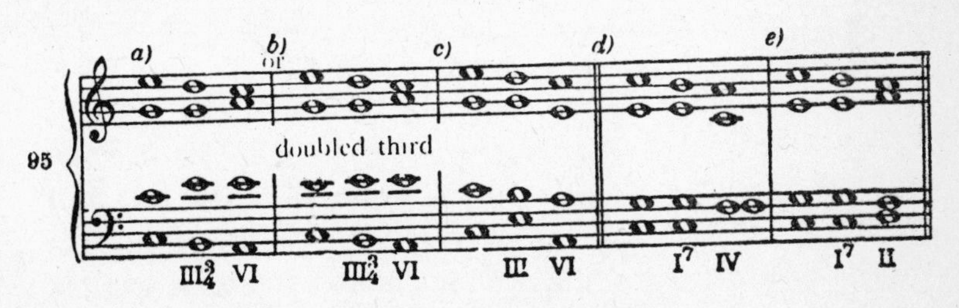

The Six-Four Chord in the Cadence

The cadence can be extended by inserting I before the V (after the IV or II). The original form may have been the I—V—I cadence, which we have noted (p. 84) as the first, simplest cadence.

But it is also explained as IV—V—I:

When V should appear the *c* remains (as a sort of grace note), and the *f* moves through *e* (another grace)

to *d*. The *a* moves normally, to the chord tone *g*. The *e* is hence a *passing tone*; the form in which the *c* delays its move to *b*, making a dissonance, which must be resolved, is called a *suspension*,—of which more later. There is much to be said for this explanation. It seems likely to me however, that although either way could account for the $^{6}_{4}$ chord, the combination of both ideas has led to this cadence formula. In the first way (96) it is sufficient to notice that the two appearances of the *c* in the bass make an undesirable repetition, which can be avoided through an inversion. A 6 chord could be used just as well, and often is. But the $^{6}_{4}$ chord, which is perceived as a sort of dissonance, which must therefore be resolved, and which resolves well into V, is better suited, because it almost compels what the 6 chord only permits. The other explanation is also convincing. The suspension creates tension, which is released by the resolution; the resolution takes place in the desired chord, whose appearance through so careful preparation gains the semblance of necessity and thereby arouses a heightened satisfaction.

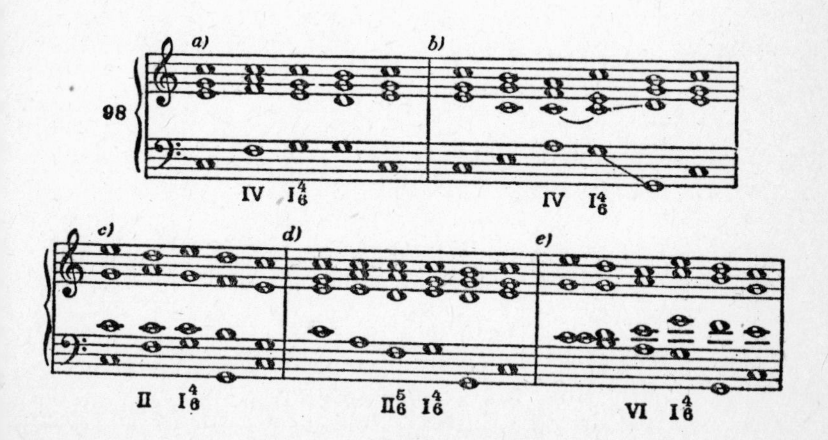

Here are several examples of the use of the $^6_4$ chord, which also show that the one derivation, according to which the $^6_4$ chord results from a passing tone and a suspension, is not a sufficient explanation (98*b*, *c* and *d*). In 98*b* the *c* cannot be considered a suspension, because the necessary resolution is not present (in the tenor). Also the *e* is not a passing tone, as it leaps up to the *g*. In 98*c* the suspension is present, but not the passing tone; likewise in 98*d*. But if the other explanation is considered, the $^6_4$ chord is easily understood. For the critical examination of the fundamental progressions the question of origins is immaterial. If it is to be construed as suspension and passing tone, the following patterns result (since now the $^6_4$ chord is not thought of as a separate chord): IV (I$^6_4$)—V—I or II(I$^6_4$)—V—I or VI (I$^6_4$)—V—I, all strong progressions. But if we look upon the $^6_4$ chord as I, then we have IV—I—V—I, II—I—V—I, VI—I—V—I, thus including a number of weak progressions. These, however, are counteracted by the quasi-dissonant character of the $^6_4$ chord. If we accept the idea that the recognized effect of this form of $^6_4$ chord makes it possible to ignore its origin and use it as a sort of cliché, even if what precedes it is not exactly as it must have been originally, then the freedom shown in 99 is explained, where the $^6_4$ chord is reached from root position II by a leap: a very customary cadence formula.

To avoid the monotony of a stationary *g* (which would not be very bad) it is better to let the bass make the octave leap.

I have mentioned repeatedly that the $^6_4$ chord has its own particular place, and have shown that one must let it be placed there, whether from one's own feeling or from convention. This place, as has just been shown, is in the cadence, as a sort of delaying action, or holding back, before the appearance of the dominant seventh chord. Since this form has become a sort of cliché, which arouses a certain expectation, it is evident why this chord should be handled with caution in situations where that expectation is not to be realized: the feeling of disillusion when the expected continuation does not appear, can easily cause roughness. To be sure, roughnesses can sometimes have a certain charm, but these are effects for which the student is not yet prepared.

FREER TREATMENT OF VII IN MAJOR AND IN MINOR

We learned in handling the triad on the seventh degree in major keys that the simplest treatment of a dissonance is by preparation and resolution. In the seventh chord we have seen that the dissonance can appear without preparation when it is taken in passing (scalewise), and that the resolution can take place otherwise than to a chord a fourth higher. All this can be applied to the diminished triad; the resulting forms are not only available but are more often found in practice than those which we used at first.

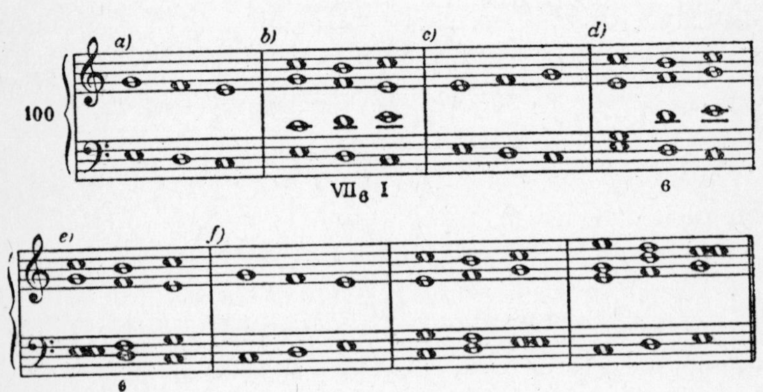

If one plans the movement of two voices as in 100*a*, *c* and *f*, then it is understandable that a VII_6 appearing over the *d* is as well *justified* by this *melodic* movement as it would be by preparation. 100*e* is a striking illustration, which answers to the strict rules of counterpoint and passages in the older music, but is in direct contradiction to what we have been doing. The diminished fifth is not only unprepared and unresolved, but is even doubled!

I shall give several of the most commonly used connections of the triad on the seventh degree, and suggest that in general the root and $^6_4$ positions are of little use; only the 6 position is often found.

In the progression VII—I, VII must be considered as a substitute for V; hence this progression is quite distinct from the already used VII—III. This substitution of VII for V should also be tried in other progressions: VII—VI, VII—IV, VII—II.

101 a) b) c) d)

VI VII_6 I_6 II_6 VII_6 VI II^6 VII_6 IV^4_6 IV^6 VII_6 II_6

Naturally the same treatment is indicated for the diminished triads in minor keys, II, VI, and VII.

The turning point rules must invariably be observed.

Frequent and varied use is made of the seventh chord on the seventh degree in major (identical with II_7 in minor) as will be shown in modulation. Concerning the VII_7 in minor, the so-called diminished seventh chord, the following may be said for the present: In accordance with our first observations we can join it with III (root a fourth higher), as in example 103*a*, *b*, *c*, *d*. In addition we show several other possibilities of this chord of many meanings.

In some connections of the diminished seventh chord covered fifths arise, as at 103*f* and *g*. To eliminate

g) h) i) k) l) m)

VII5/6 I6 VII5/6 I6 VII3/4 I6 VII3/4 I6 VII3/4 I4/6 VII2 I4/6

n) o) p) qu) r) s) t)

VII7 VI6 VII7 IV4/6 VII7 III3/4 VII7 V5/6 VII2 VI VII2 IV6 VII2 V7

these many progressions (103*f*) would have to be avoided, or in others (103*g*) the third would have to be doubled, as in 103*h*. But these covered fifths appear so often in the works of the masters and are so seldom avoided that it seems to me superfluous to demand their avoidance. On the other hand I urge the student, for reasons that will be explained later, to omit the progression from VII to I^6_4 (103*l* and *m*). In the progressions of the diminished seventh chord it is best to let the voices move by the nearest way; but 104 shows several much used progressions involving skips.

Later many reasons will be shown as to why it is possible with the diminished seventh chord more than with others to use skips rather than adhere to the simplest voice leading. For now let the often used reason suffice: the progression is well-known. The voices must not slavishly serve the requirements of the chords, but can follow eventual melodic needs.

MODULATION

The cadence we have seen as a means of strengthening the tonality; modulation aims at leaving it. If it was necessary in the cadence to group together certain chords that closely define the key, then one must do the opposite to accomplish a modulation: avoiding these chords, using instead a succession of chords which do not define the key one is leaving, and then a group that define some other key. If the fetters of tonality are loosened by the omission of those elements which would express the old key, then the new key can be introduced by the same means with which the old key was established, transposed of course to suit the new key. These means of modulation may either be direct, or may lead more or less indirectly to that point where a cadence confirms the new key. Hence the phrases that include modulations will be in three parts:

1. Expression of the old key and the use of such (neutral) chords as allow the turning away from it (not necessarily many chords; I of the old key is often sufficient, as it is often in both keys, hence of neutral tonality).
2. The actual modulation: the modulating chord and any chords necessary to bring it in.
3. The cadence to confirm the new key.

Which chords are suitable, while not going outside the key, to turn the phrase in such a direction that the modulating chord can accomplish the actual change of key, we learn from the same considerations by which we discovered the chords suitable for the cadence. If the problem then was to fence in the key from those nearly related keys into which it might slip too easily because of the leanings of certain triads of the scale, now it is desired to give in to those leanings. The simplest modulations made possible in this way, are: to the *relative minor*, to the keys *a fifth up or down* and *their relative minors*.

Hence from *C* major: its relative, *A* minor; a fifth higher, *G* major (with *E* minor); a fifth lower, *F* major (with *D* minor). Major keys which, as these, differ in signature by only one sharp or flat, and bear this relationship to the old key (a fifth higher or lower) are keys *once removed* on the *Circle of Fifths*. (The relative minor keys are, as we have discovered, only special forms within the major keys. Hence the minor keys, being joined to their relative majors, have a similar relationship of fifths among themselves.)

The term, Circle of Fifths, arises from a diagram in which the names of the keys are placed upon a circle in such manner that the equal distances between neighboring points on the circle correspond to the interval of a fifth between the next related keys. The keys, then, follow in series by the interval of a fifth: *C*, *G*, *D*, *A*, etc., completing the circle as the series of fifths returns to its starting point. Going in one direction, *C*, *G*, *D*, *A*, etc., we have the Circle of Fifths, or, as I prefer to call it, the Upward Circle of Fifths, since it proceeds by upward fifths. Going in the opposite direction we have *C*, *F*, *B*♭, *E*♭, etc., giving what some persons call the Circle of Fourths, a rather meaningless term, since a fifth in one direction is always a fourth in the other; I prefer to call this the Downward Circle of Fifths.

The Circle of Fifths shows, to a certain point, the relationship of any two keys. But not completely. It is clear that two keys that differ in signature by only one sharp or flat can easily be more closely related than those with a difference of five. As that *B*♭ major and *E*♭ major are more closely related than *B*♭ and *A*♭. Likewise *C* major and *D* major should be more nearly related than *C* major and *A* major or *E* major. This, however, is not entirely correct. In determining key relationship the signature is not the only thing to be considered; there are other factors which will be explained later. For example, *C* major and *A* major have a relationship through *A* minor which, as will be shown, is stronger than that of *C* major to *D* major. Hence we shall use the Circle of Fifths not so much to determine the closeness of key relationships, valuable as that might be, as to measure the difference between keys, and to remember the means that have been learned for this purpose.

It can be seen from our Circle of Fifths that *B* major and *A*♭ major are nine fifths apart if one follows the circle upwards from *A*♭ (or downwards from *B*), but only three fifths apart proceeding clockwise from *B* or following the circle downwards from *A*♭. In general the shorter distance will determine the choice for modulatory purposes, but often the seemingly longer way, as will be shown, is really shorter. It is easily demonstrated, if one remembers, that the keys three times removed on the circle are more closely related than those only twice removed. One can deduce from the Circle of Fifths that *F* minor and *F* major are three fifths apart, *F* minor and *D* minor also three fifths, but *F* minor and *D* major are six fifths apart.

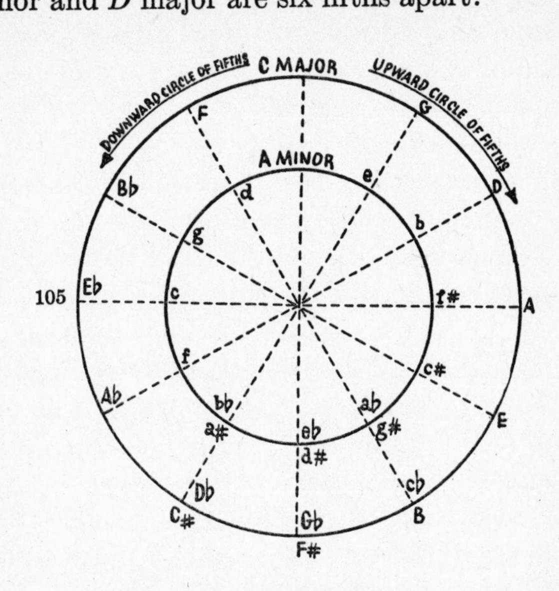

TABLE OF THE CIRCLE OF FIFTHS FOR *C* MAJOR (*A* MINOR)

106

1 fifth removed	*G* maj.	*e* min.	*F* maj.	*d* min.
2 fifths removed	*D* maj.	*b* min.	*B*♭ maj.	*g* min.
3 fifths removed	*A* maj.	*f*♯ min.	*E*♭ maj.	*c* min.
4 fifths removed	*E* maj.	*c*♯ min.	*A*♭ maj.	*f* min.
5 fifths removed	*B* maj.	*g*♯ min.	*D*♭ maj.	*b*♭ min.
6 fifths removed	*F*♯ maj.	*d*♯ min.	*G*♭ maj.	*e*♭ min.
7 fifths removed	*C*♯ maj.	*a*♯ min.	*C*♭ maj.	*a*♭ min.

106 gives a table of the Circle of Fifths for *C* major and *A* minor. The student should determine these relationships for other keys.

The chords that establish firmly the key of *C* major are those that include *f* and *b*; namely, IV, II and VII (for *f*), V, III and VII (for *b*). It is clear that the chords that include *b* will not hinder our purpose of reaching *G* major, but that those in which *f* appears are not suited for this purpose. If then III and V can be considered neutral chords, II, IV and VII must be avoided. But besides V and III there are other neutral triads in relation to *G* major; I and VI. Or, in other words, because of the similarity of scale, *C* major and *G* major have a number of chords common to both keys. If one of these chords is placed by itself, free from context, it cannot be determined to which key it belongs. It can equally well be *C* major or *G* major. In which key it is to be located will depend on preceding and following chords. The triad *c-e-g* can be I in *C* or IV in *G*; the chords which follow it will determine which. If *f-a-c* follows, then it is certainly not *G*; apparently it is *C*, but it could be *A* minor, *F* major or *D* minor. If, however, *c-e-g* is followed by *d-f*♯*-a* (*G* V) or *f*♯*-a-c* (*G* VII), then it is presumably *G* major or *E* minor, or at least is looking in that direction.

In the foregoing we have the first two principal means of modulation. The first: the use of *neutral chords* as intermediary between the old key and the new; the other: the *re-interpreting of chords* that are common to both keys. Usually both work together; the possibility of re-interpreting arises from the use of neutral chords, or at least from the avoidance of chords that would confirm the old key. Vice versa, the neutral chords are forced by the re-interpretation to turn toward the new key. Whether re-interpretation or neutral chords are used, one arrives sooner or later at the point where the turning to the new key must be brought about by some energetic means. What this means can be is clear, if we remember the cadence: for the first choice V, but in general any chord containing the leading-tone of the new key, hence also III and VII. Obviously V will usually be preferred, but the other two are also suited to effect a modulation, especially VII. To make the appearance of the new key clear and definite, a cadence is then added. The length of the cadence depends naturally upon the length and difficulty of the modulation. With a simple modulation a short cadence is sufficient. If more elaborate means of modulation have been used, the cadence can hardly be short. Sometimes it happens, however, that after a long modulation which is very conclusive because of its extent, a short cadence is enough; or sometimes a too briefly constructed modulation demands a stronger establishing of the new key through a longer cadence.

In order to survey the means of modulation, it will be well to proceed systematically, beginning with the shortest and simplest forms.

From *C* major to *G* major:

The key of *C* is understood to have been already established. I in *C* (neutral chord) is IV in *G*. The re-interpreting can well begin here. Hence chords of *G* major can follow, whether neutral or distinctive. To make the first example short, we take at once a distinctive chord, V of *G* major: the modulating chord. This can proceed most simply to I, completing the modulation but for the cadence (107*a*). The cadence can be short, since the modulation is short and clear. If one wishes to avoid the slight fault of the repetition of *G* I, one may follow the *G* V with I_6 or a deceptive cadence (107 *b*, *c*, *d*) or use the V in an inversion ($^6_5$, $^4_3$, or 2), which will vary it sufficiently from the V in the cadence.

Between the first chord and the modulating chord intermediate chords can be placed: the neutral chords, III, V, VI of *C* major (VI, I, II of *G* major).

108*a* uses as a neutral chord I in *G*, taking it as a 6th chord to improve the bass melody and avoid the repetition in the following *G* I; the modulating chord is a V^4_3. In 108*b*, *C* VI (*G* II) is followed by *G* V^6_5. The cadence is made somewhat longer, to cover up the repetition of *G* I. 108*c* (doubled third!) has *C* III (*G* VI) with passing seventh leading into *C* VI (*G* II), which then progresses, likewise with passing seventh (2 position) to V^6_5, then makes a deceptive cadence with the IV^6_4 (passing $^6_4$), leading to another *G* V which resolves to a I_6. Such a repetition of the modulating chord (I call it going through the chord twice) often has a good effect. Here this repetition is hardly needed, but later

we shall find it very useful (since repetition is a strengthening) where a modulation is not sufficiently strong and definite. In 108*d*, *C* VI_7 (*G* II_7) is led to *G* VII^6_5. The latter serves here as modulating chord; the III which follows, since *g* in this example does not appear again until the end, can be regarded as a substitute for I, from which the cadence begins. This example is noteworthy, since it shows that the modulation does not necessarily proceed to a I, but that the cadence can begin with a triad of similar character, as perhaps a

III, a VI or eventually even a IV or a II. Fundamentally this is not much different from 107*c*, where a deceptive cadence appears after the modulating chord, except that the modulating chord in 107*c* is a V and here is a VII. In 108*e* *G* III is used as modulating chord. Here also the I is replaced by a VI. In examples 108*f*, *g*, *h*, likewise VII and III establish the new key. Here too the deceptive cadence is to be recommended, since it veils the purpose without confusing it. Obviously other neutral chords can be interpolated, in other (but good) progressions. The student has here a splendid opportunity to develop skill in such combinations.

Properly one should prefer modulations, such as these, in which the repetition of I and V can be avoided. Since, however, there are sufficient means of neutralizing the harm of such repetitions, and since the repetitions in themselves are not very bad, there is no sense in making an important distinction here. The tonic triad should make an impression; so let it be heard twice.

By similar means and just as simply modulation is accomplished to *A* minor and *E* minor.

A minor (109). Here the first choice for means of modulation is V, but II and VII can also be used. It will be simplest to look upon the first chord (*C* I) as III in *A* minor. Here it is advisable, if the modulation is to be smooth, to consider the Turning Point Rules applying to the sixth and seventh tones. Thus *g* and *f*, as third and fourth turning points, must be satisfied by a downward resolution before tones of the rising scale can appear. Later we shall be less particular and write an *f*♯ following a *g* without a qualm (in the discussion of materials included in the chapter "Secondary Dominants, etc.").

In modulation to minor keys good service is rendered by the II in minor, especially as a 7, $\substack{6\\5}$, $\substack{4\\3}$, or 2 chord. On the one hand it gives an opportunity to lead the sixth tone of the scale (as diminished fifth) to the fifth. On the other hand V follows it easily (II—V); but even in a deceptive progression (II—I or II—III with augmented fifth), it has a characteristic effect.

Much variety is provided by the use of the altered III (augmented triad), VI (triad and seventh chord) and VII (diminished triad and diminished seventh chord). But always the leaving of the seventh (and sixth) tone demands great care.

E minor (110). Neutral chords are *C* I, III, VI, eventually also V. Means of modulation again V, II and VII (of *E* minor). Especially effective, as in *A*

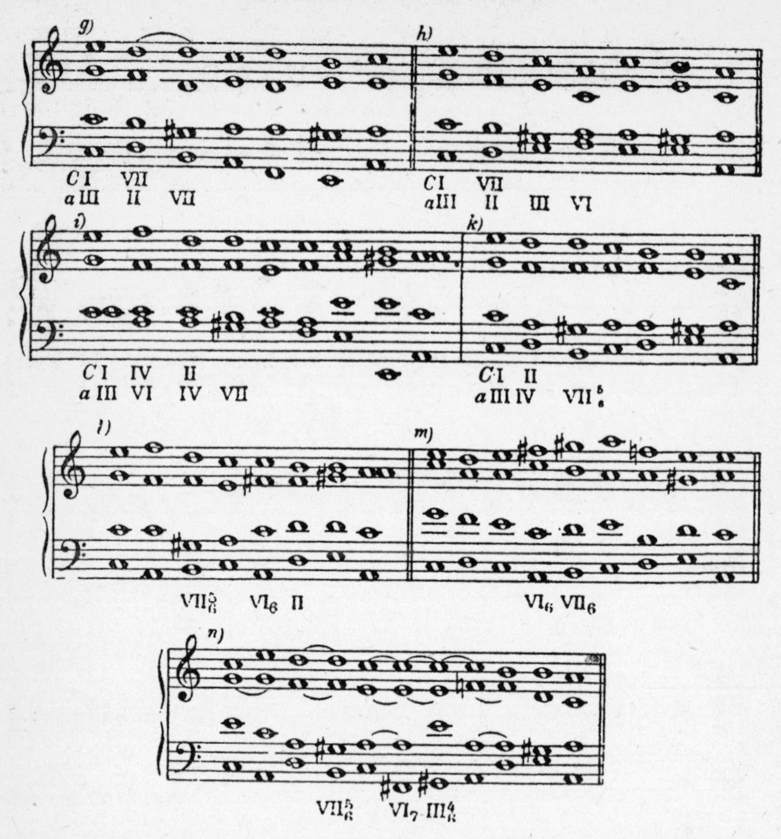

minor, is also here *E* minor II, which can be taken immediately after the *C* I (110*d*). The II does not necessarily progress to V, but may be followed by I or III, by which repetition is avoided. The forms of the altered II, III, VI and VII already used in *A* minor make here an even better connection. But also the altered IV is usable.

As in all these modulations, often after V a deceptive cadence should be used. As before, in the planning of the phrases the student will first write down the triad numerals and then determine the positions and inver-

sions. Under the old-key numerals of the first chords, there will be placed in a second line the re-numbering of these chords as of the new key. From the modulating chord on, the chords will be numbered only in the new key. Here the student must give closest attention to the fundamental progressions and follow carefully our directions given for them; otherwise he may write many strange things and fail to gain fluency through practice in the use of all the materials. At all events he can as well through planning as through many decisions let his feeling for form hold converse with good taste;—but only for control and correction, not for dreaming.

Modulation one fifth downward on the Circle of Fifths (as from *C* major or *A* minor to *F* major or *D* minor), strange as it may seem, is somewhat more difficult;—probably because the pull to the sub-dominant, of which I have often remarked, which every tone and every chord seems to have, is almost stronger than the artistic means that we would use to lead the tonality in that direction, a direction into which it tends to slip by itself. In other words, it is more difficult to do something about it because it almost happens by itself without one's doing anything. The tonic itself, following its inclination toward the subdominant, is already a means of modulating to the sub-dominant. This first degree triad (*C* major I) is already the V (of *F* major) with which we would modulate. Since proceeding to the key of the sub-dominant happens almost by itself, there is little feeling of accomplishment for one who wishes to employ this modulation. Hence it will be necessary later to construct this modulation more artistically, so that we may perceive that we have done something,—that we may seem to climb down rather than to fall down. For the present these modulations will seem very simple, but of course they are not bad on that account.

After the I in *C* (which is V in *F*) the I in *F* can follow at once. Since there is nothing to force this pro-

gression, it is advisable to interpolate the *F* V_7 (111*b*), in root position or an inversion. If one wishes to use some other chord to bring in the *b*♭, *F* II, IV or VII are possible. These chords make the modulation more varied, because often the I and V can be evaded and other chords can be substituted for them. Again the deceptive cadence should not be forgotten.

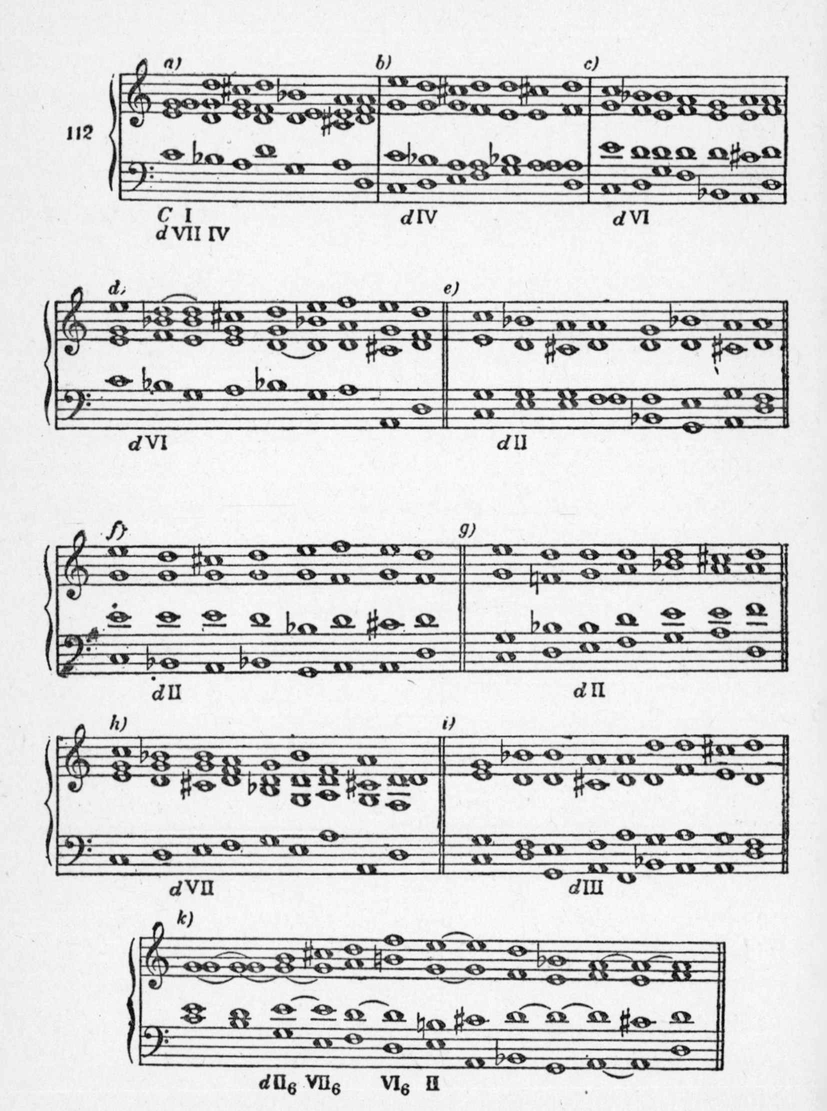

In the modulation from *C* major to *D* minor it is necessary first to satisfy the turning point *c* before using chords that have *c*♯. Suited to this purpose are *D* minor IV, II and VI. These can also be used as modulating chords and the cadence can begin at once. If however it is desired to use V, III or VII, and the way has been prepared by one or more of the other chords just mentioned (IV, II, VI), then the rest is the same as in the earlier modulations. Since the *c* in the bass must be cared for as third turning point before raised tones can appear, some of the examples are not permissible (112*b*, *e*, *h*), while others, in which the *c*♯ comes only at the end, can still be tolerated. The use of the raised tones makes other difficulties, as shown in the examples. It is advisable to double the fifth (112*a*) or third (112*f*) rather than the root.

Now the modulations from *A* minor: to *C* major, to *G* major or *E* minor, to *F* major or *D* minor. *A* minor is a *C* major that begins on *a*. The *a* (I) can be regarded as the sixth degree (VI) of *C*, and the modulation constructed from there as before.

113

a minor to *C* major

The modulation from *A* minor to *C* major is apparently nothing but a cadence in *C* major beginning on VI. One could hardly find a stranger means of modulation.

The modulation from *A* minor to *G* major, like that from *C* major to *F* major, can well be very short, because one of the neutral chords is lacking (*A* minor III),

and *A* minor I is best followed at once by *G* V. However VII or III can also be used.

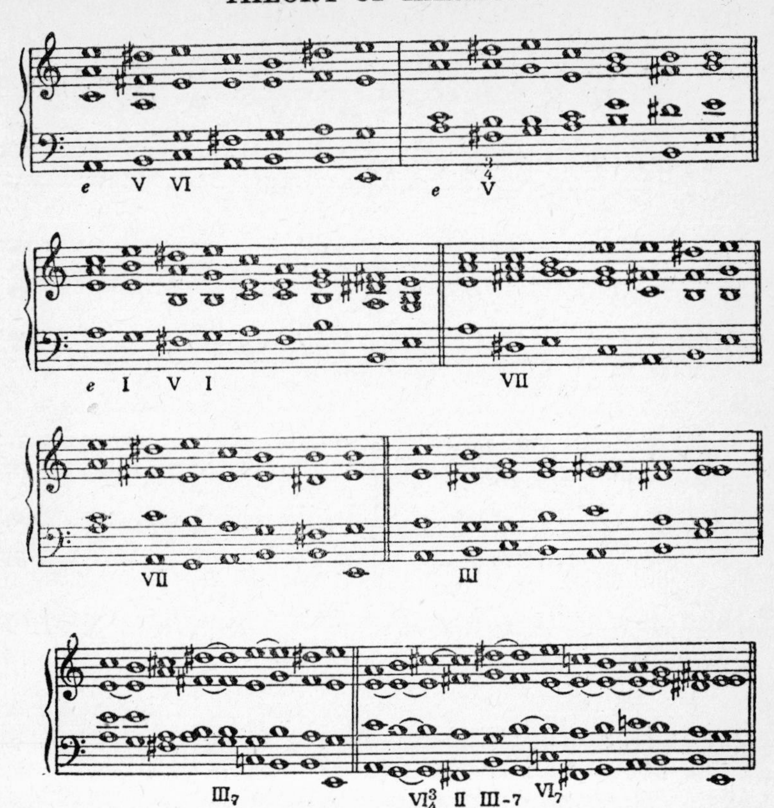

From *A* minor to *E* minor the modulating chord may be used immediately (II, V or VII).

A minor to *F* major. Either the V at once or the II, IV or VII inserted first (116).

A minor to *D* minor. First care for the turning point *c*; hence use chords with *b*♭ or *b*♮ which are also modulating chords (*D* minor IV, VI, II); then begin the cadence, or use first a V and then the cadence (117).

We have regarded the minor key as a variety of the major key, since to a point the two coincide. If one recognizes that *A* minor, in the form which uses no

raised tones, is so little different from *C* major that one can use them interchangeably, then one can capitalize on this possibility in order to interchange them, and can therefore, if he has to go to *A* minor, go first to *C* major, then rename (re-interpret) this *C* major as *A* minor, and make the cadence in *A* minor. Or if one has to go from *C* major to *E* minor, he can go first to *G* major and not express *E* minor till the cadence. Likewise to *D* minor: proceed first to *F* major; then make a cadence in *D* minor. The principle can also be reversed: if one wishes to go to a major key, the modulation may be made apparently to the relative minor, the tonic triad of this minor key renamed as VI of the relative major, and the major key brought in in the cadence. Thus for example from *C* major to *G* major: modulate first to *E* minor; *E* minor I = *G* major VI; cadence in *G* major. *C* major to *F* major: go through *D* minor, reaching *F* major in the cadence.

Here is of course a possibility of making the modulations more varied. However, while these modulations are somewhat richer, the others are not therefore less good. In one place these will be more suitable (or satisfying), in another place the others. For composition one should have simple as well as complicated possibilities at one's disposal. Whether one uses this or that is perhaps often only a question of taste, but also often a question of construction. In general: in modulating from major to major it is best to take as intermediate key the relative minor (*C* major through *E* minor to *G* major); in modulating from minor to minor, a relative major (*A* minor through *G* major to *E* minor). There is little need, in modulating from *A* minor to *G* major, to go by way of *E* minor, or from *C* major to *E* minor, by way of *G* major. Essentially we find in this enrichment two ideas to which we shall return later: (1) the intermediate key, (2) the possibility of using other chords than just those belonging to the old and the new key.

To keep in balance, the intermediate key must not be too firmly established. Otherwise the cadence must be correspondingly longer. In 118*a*, for example, *E* minor I appears twice, in 118*c* the dominant of *G* twice. Both of these might well demand a longer cadence. But in 118*a* the dominant of *E* minor appears only once, in

118*c* the tonic of *G* not at all. In this way the danger can be avoided.

The idea of the intermediate key can also be applied to the relative major or minor of the original key. As for example: *C* major to *G* major or *E* minor through *A* minor; *C* major to *F* major or *D* minor through *A* minor; *A* minor to *G* major or *E* minor through *C* major; *A* minor to *F* major or *D* minor through *C* major.

These modulations (especially 119*a* and 119*b*) are quite short and the new key is hardly made clear. Yet they are certainly not bad. Instead of the striving to reach a *definite* goal, there appears in these phrases generally the striving to reach a goal, perhaps not yet definite, or if definite, by a roundabout way. Such phrases have something that is certainly of value to the directional feeling of short modulations: they are, so to speak, *on the way* (*im Gehen*). That is, they have a forward drive which will surely find a goal, even though it may not be clearly indicated at the beginning. I must say that I regard this being "on the way" one of the most important traits of a living phrase, and that it sometimes seems more important to me than even goal consciousness. We keep moving, even without knowing the goal.

An extension of the idea would be to use two intermediate keys. As: *C* major—*A* minor—*E* minor—*G* major; or, *A* minor—*C* major—*D* minor—*F* major.

Finally the idea of the intermediate key can even be extended to the cadence. As: *C* major to *G* major, really establishing *G* major, then first a cadence in *E* minor or *A* minor, turning back then to *G* major.

SECONDARY DOMINANTS AND OTHER ALTERED CHORDS FROM THE CHURCH MODES

The old church modes brought variety into the harmony through the use of accidentals (sharps or flats temporarily altering scale tones). These alterations, however, were felt to be scale tones rather than chromatic tones, as we can still see in our minor scale, where the raised sixth and seventh tones in ascending are as much scale tones as the unraised tones in the descending scale. In the Dorian mode (the one beginning on the second tone of a major scale—in *C* major, on *d*), these tones occurred ascending: *a*, *b*, *c*♯, *d*, but descending: *d*, *c*, *b*♭, *a*. In Phrygian (beginning on the third tone, *e*) there would be *b*, *c*♯, *d*♯ (this was somewhat unusual) and *e*, *d*, *c*, *b*. In Lydian (on the fourth tone, *f*), beside the augmented fourth (*b*) the perfect fourth (*b*♭) could be used; in Mixolydian (on the fifth tone, *g*) its seventh tone (*f*) could be raised (*f*♯). In the Aeolian, our minor of today, we should find *e*, *f*♯, *g*♯, *a*, *g*, *f*. The seldom used Hypophrygian is without immediate significance for us. It is however of value to know something of the characteristics of the church modes, if we are to use their harmonic wealth to enrich our major and minor.

Through the use of accidentals we have the following chords from the church modes:

1. Triads with major third (as substitute for a leading-tone), where the scale tones would give a minor third. These are II, III and VI. (More rarely VII,

which is normally diminished, hence would require two altered tones.)

These are the dominants of the old church modes. They contain the raised seventh tone, the leading tone into the eighth (fundamental tone): II that of the Mixolydian, III of the Aeolian, VI of the Dorian, and VII of the Phrygian (this last was seldom used, as it is likely to confuse the relationship to the fundamental tone). Since these chords appeared in the church modes as dominants, on the fifth degree, but are found on secondary degrees in our scales, we call them Secondary Dominants.[1] Obviously they can be used also as seventh chords, extending the idea to the dominant seventh of the Lydian mode as a secondary dominant for our IV (127).

2. A major triad that does not have dominant character, *b♭-d-f* (from Dorian or Lydian), from which comes perhaps the Neapolitan Sixth chord, which will be treated later.

3. A minor triad, *g-b♭-d* (from Dorian or Lydian).

4. A series of diminished triads.

---

[1] *Nebendominanten,* lit. "neighboring" or "side" dominants; called also "artificial," "borrowed," or "apparent" dominants.—Translator's note.

5. Finally also some augmented triads.

The use of all these chords is very simple, if the student observes at first the Turning Point rules. That is, every tone foreign to the scale is considered as the sixth or seventh tone of an ascending or a descending minor scale. Raised tones belong to the ascending, lowered tones to the descending. According to whether the tone is sixth or seventh tone, it is followed by a whole or half-step progression. For example an *f*♯ can be considered the seventh tone of a *g* scale, which should be followed by *g* (or sometimes *e*, but never *f*♮), or as sixth tone of an *a* scale, which should be followed by *g*♯. But it is also possible for such a tone to be understood as a sixth tone, and then, by re-interpretation to be treated as a seventh. The *f*♯ could for example be introduced as the sixth tone of an *a* scale, and then be led to the triad *g-b-d*, suggesting a mixolydian (*g*) origin.

To keep things in balance, the student should not use too many of these altered chords,especially at first. The use of many such chords would demand an elaborate and extended cadence. For that the means are not yet available. One thing more: if the student wishes to use these altered chords in modulations, he must avoid placing them where they will work against the key aimed at. For example the use of the secondary dominant *c-e-g-b*♭ to bring in the chord *f-a-c*, will injure the effect if the intended modulation is from *C* major to *G* major. To be sure one could yet overcome this injury by following the *f-a-c* with *e-g♯-b*, which will lead to *a-c-e* (II in *G* major). However, as long as the student is not in a position to weigh minutely these fine points, he will do well to use only those chords which, if they do not compel the reaching of the goal, at least will not hinder it. On the whole it will be best to use these chords in the cadence, where the tonality is already well established.

In 130 is decidedly a distortion to be avoided. The *b* causes surprise; one would rather have expected *b♭*; we have learned that our modulations should glide gently and lead clearly.

Better is the second solution. On closer examination we notice that we could really have done it following one of the earlier suggestions; namely, the one about using intermediate keys (here *A* minor). I have given this explanation about intermediate keys only reluctantly, for it is false to distinguish different keys in so short a phrase. So, as we call a certain secondary triad III, and not *e* minor, we also prefer to speak here, not of keys, but of triads introduced by secondary dominants. A triad can sometimes be treated as a key, but it confuses the picture, blurs the view of the whole and the coherence of its parts, if every triad preceded by a dominant is called a separate key. 131 gives several modulations with such altered chords (*i.e.*, chords having tones foreign to the key).

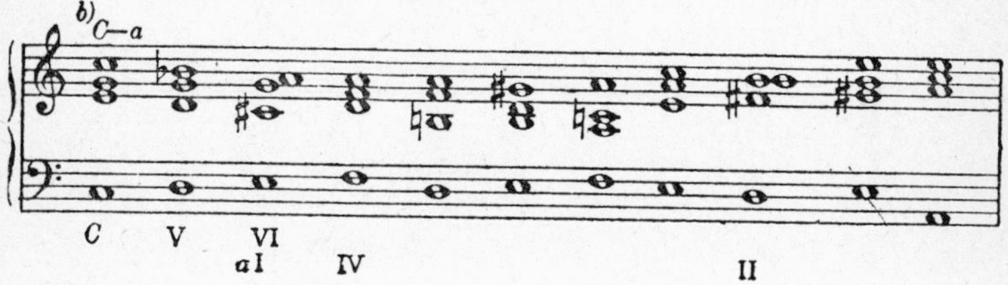

d) C—e e) a—C

C III 3/4 VI III C II I
e I

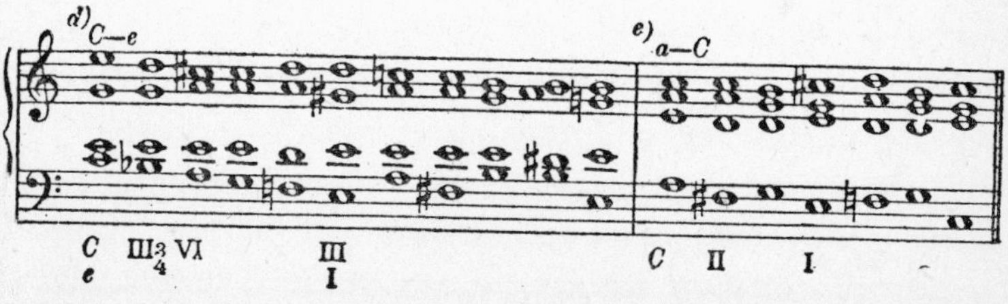

In 131*c* at X a secondary dominant (on the second degree of *F*; obviously *F* major is already to be understood here) is resolved deceptively (as in the deceptive cadence). This secondary dominant on the second degree has the name Changing Dominant (*Wechseldomi-*

nante). It is not clear to me how the name originated or what it means, but its function is to replace the ordinary II in the cadence;—usually in this manner, that the chord succession is II—I^6_4—V—I; however, the changing dominant is often followed directly by V—I.

The Changing Dominant is most often used in the $\frac{6}{5}$ or $\frac{4}{3}$ position, but the root position also is often used. The only new thing here is the resolution of a secondary dominant in the manner of a deceptive cadence (II—I). Such progressions are naturally possible also from other secondary dominants, but the student will do well to handle these sparingly, for otherwise he may write much that, while not unusable, is yet unusual and will mar the style of the whole. It is true only on the average, but it is hardly too much to say, that deceptive cadences after secondary dominants will have a smooth effect if the modulation is not brought about by the deceptive cadence. They will sound more abrupt when they bring in a modulation that has not been prepared. These deceptive cadences are in good use, but care is needed; they often sound far-fetched, and they often lead too far afield. 133 shows what devices for safeguarding the tonality such progressions demand.

In 131*a* the second chord ($\frac{4}{3}$ chord over *a*) can be regarded as Changing Dominant (on the second degree of *C*). Then the following chord over *g* is *C* V. But the

latter could also be *G* I; in that event a modulation has taken place and the preceding chord is *G* V, a real dominant rather than a Changing Dominant. Then the fourth chord would have to be V with lowered third (in *G*), the next VI with raised third. *G* would then be an intermediate key, a conception which will prove inexpedient. With equal right one could name the sixth chord (6th chord over *c*) as in *A* minor. This would then be the second intermediate key. So it is better to drop the explanation by intermediate keys and to indicate secondary dominants in the original key until a series of chords establishes a new key. In 131*d* it would hardly be possible to indicate such intermediate keys. The second chord, a $\frac{4}{3}$ over *b*♭, could belong only to *D* minor. The fifth chord, 6th chord *f-a-d*, would of course bear this out; but *f♯-a-d* (133*g*) would do as well, and then the explanation by intermediate keys would be possible only by very complicated interpretations.

Secondary dominants are well suited for extending a cadence (134).

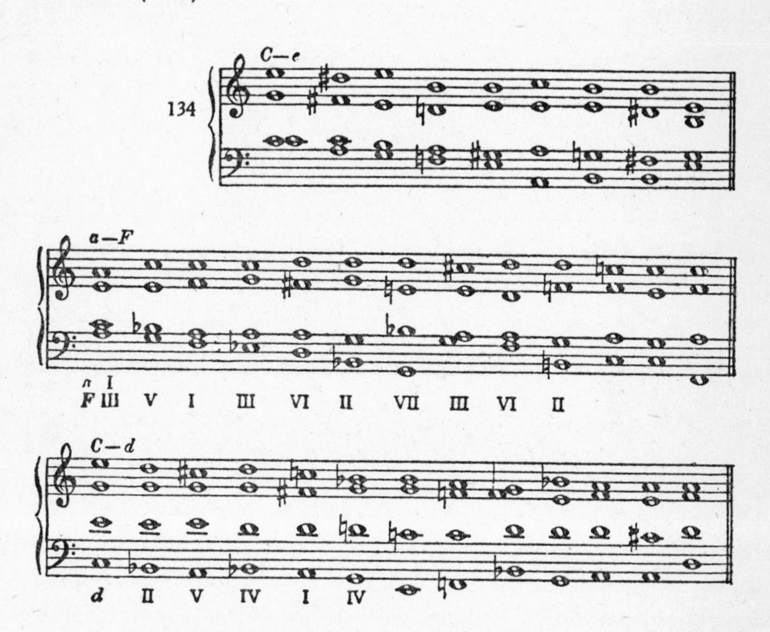

The modulation then is better short, with some direct means.

It is clear that the secondary dominants are likewise available in minor, and that no new rules are needed. One practical suggestion should be made, explaining also why in major a secondary dominant cannot be used on the fourth degree. The secondary dominant derives its existence mainly from the fundamental progression up a perfect fourth, imitating the V—I of the cadence. From IV (*C* major *f*) this would be an augmented fourth (*f*—*b*), unless one moved to a triad on *b*♭, which is out of the key. At this stage we would hardly know what to do with a chord on *b*♭, and the progression to *b*♮ does not carry out the principle of the upward perfect fourth. For the same reason we do not, for the present, build a secondary dominant on unraised VI in minor keys (*f* in *A* minor) since it would tend toward *b*♭. Also on the raised sixth and seventh degrees in minor the secondary dominants are not practicable. For such a chord as *f*♯-*a*♯-*c*♯-*e* (or *g*♯-*b*♯-*d*♯-*f*♯) wanders farther from the key than we dare to go at present.

I shall not cease from warning the student against excessive use of secondary dominants. We are not yet so well equipped but that roughness could creep into our work, and it is always tasteless to sacrifice the smoothness of the exercises in order to bring in a great many altered secondary chords. In general I advise, in an exercise of ten to fifteen chords, that hardly more than three or four secondary dominants be used.

Several secondary dominants can be joined together or with other altered chords. Only one must take care not to go too far from the key. 135*d* shows the bad results possible from too great use of these chords.

All seven chords in this exercise can be construed in *C* major; but from the third chord (if not from the beginning) they could easily be called *G* major, or from the fourth they could all be located in *D* major. There are three faults here: 1. Both of the secondary dominants used progress to dominants (*C* major V and *G* major V). 2. Both (the third chord as well as the sixth) are themselves brought in as if they were dominants; the third chord is preceded by what could be II in *G*, the sixth by a possible II in *D*: this is the man-

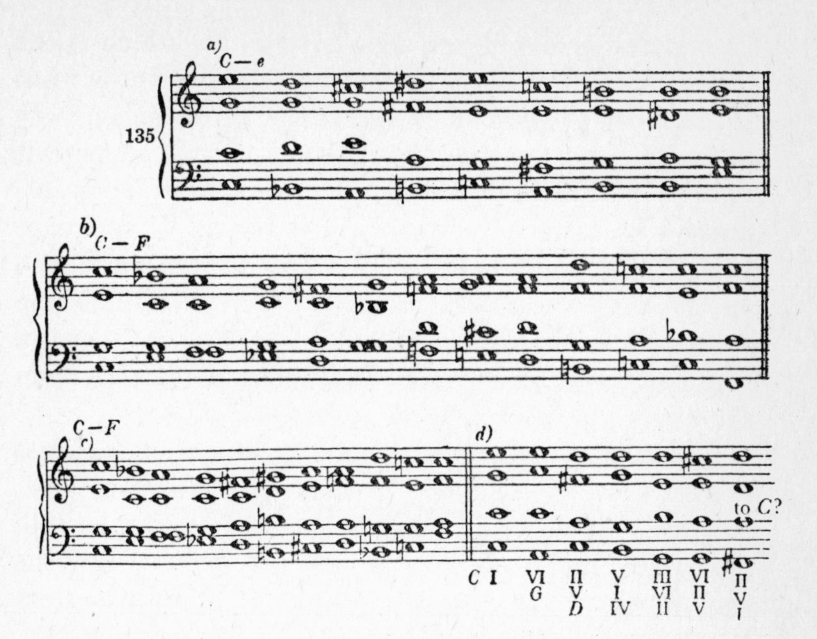

ner in which one modulates or confirms a key. 3. In joining two secondary dominants there is a danger in that they are both major triads; the second can as a result have a strong tonic suggestion. A major chord, as a more complete imitation of the chord of nature (the harmonic series), has a stronger tendency to locate itself as a tonic than has a minor chord, which through its natural incompleteness gives less sense of finality. This difficulty can be removed only through the chromatic use of secondary dominants, which will be discussed later. The following may serve as a guide rule for avoiding faults of this kind: When secondary dominants bring us too near to the key of the dominant, it is well, since the use of secondary dominants has easily an effect on tonality, to seek at once the region of the sub-dominant. For example: if V or III has become too prominent, one can lead to a II or a IV through a VI. Or vice versa, if one has come too close to the region of the sub-dominant (II, IV) one should then try to return to the region of the dominant.

After the student has used secondary dominants without chromatic progressions, *i.e.*, like scale chords in minor, he can proceed then to build them with chromatic alterations. Then their possibilities become much greater. The following principle should be carefully observed: the purpose of each chromatic alteration is to make a leading tone, rising or falling. Melodically a raised tone should always proceed upward, a lowered tone downward. Rarely would I permit a leap from it, —possibly when bad voice leading can thereby be avoided, or a complete chord placed, and the tone in question is in an inner voice. Otherwise the purpose of any such alteration should be visible in the voice leading. For the same reason the raising or lowering should be obvious as such, by its following immediately the unaltered tone in the same voice. If in the preceding chord two voices have the tone in question, it is of course sufficient to have the alteration in one of them; the other voice may leap. It is now possible, to a certain extent, to evade the Turning Point rules in minor. Through the richer materials that we have now, secondary dominants and the like, equilibrium can be restored in the cadence.

136*a* shows the chromatic use of altered chords. There are no especial difficulties. Progressions like those at +) and ++) we shall omit for the present. The following rules are recommended: I. Melodically clear chromatic progressions as rising or falling leading tones in chromatic scale passages. II. Since they have melodic value, it is recommended to use them in the outer voices, soprano or bass. The bass especially can profit from them, as otherwise it must often stand still. The latter can also be avoided by a change of position (to another inversion). III. The purpose of chromatic progressions is no other than that first learned in connection with the Turning Points. The chromatic progression offers the advantage that the danger to the tonality is less because a tone thus approached can hardly be perceived as a scale tone, as we have already implied when we established that a dominant should never be approached chromatically. Thus the chromatic progression from *c* to *c*♯ in VI in *C* major hinders the perception of the following II as a tonic (*D* minor). Even if this II is given a major third, it could at the worst be only a dominant. A danger like that shown in 135*d* is therefore easy to remove.

Again the student is advised here not to overdo the matter. Sparingly used, these materials have excellent effect, but it is tasteless to push them to extravagance, since they can not yet offer sufficient variety.

Of the other chords derived from the church modes the diminished are especially effective. For example *e-g-b*♭ (or still better the seventh chord *e-g-b*♭*-d*) as III in *C* major recalls II in *D* minor. Hence it moves easily to *a-c*♯*-e* (V of *D* minor), VI in *C* major. One of the minor chords can have the same effect. For example *g-b*♭*-d* recalls IV in *D* minor; V or VII of *D* minor follows naturally, resolving to *D* minor I, which is II of *C* major. The student must not, however, consider that other keys really appear in such a passage. I mean only to show the suitability of these chords to bring in secondary dominants (here, *a-c*♯*-e*).

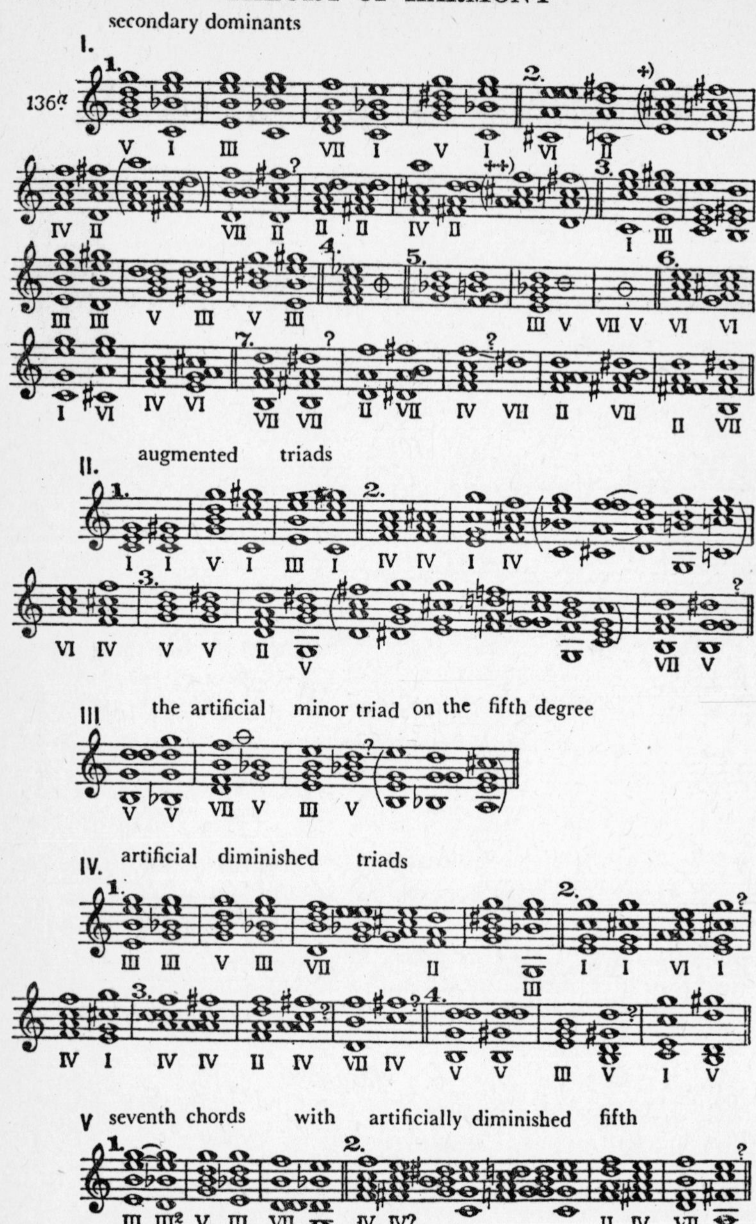
secondary dominants
I.
136a
augmented triads
II.
III the artificial minor triad on the fifth degree
IV. artificial diminished triads
V seventh chords with artificially diminished fifth

For the use of these newly learned materials there follow some general suggestions to add to those on page 77.

Guide Rules

I. *Secondary dominants* can be used wherever the scale chords (on same roots) can be used, provided the fundamental progressions permit. Naturally they are best *where the fundamental progression resembles dominant function; hence resembling the pattern* V—I, V—IV and V—VI. For their main purpose is *to support the tendency to a dominant-like progression, through an artificial leading tone.* The progression to a chord a third lower is also often usable, but does not add greatly to our resources. The progression to a chord a fourth lower is also possible, but can hardly fill any but a passing function (*i.e.*, melodic, in the sense of a change of position). The progression a third higher is almost entirely useless, especially as it often leads to chords that have not yet been explained, for which reason also several progressions already mentioned are excluded, as the example shows, where the seventh chords are treated (see 137A).

II. *Secondary dominant seventh chords* can be used wherever secondary dominants are permissible and the dissonance can be properly treated. In general they serve the same purpose better, because the seventh gives an additional urge in the same direction, demanding according to rule a dominant-like progression.

III. *Artificial augmented triads* are to be used in the same manner as the natural augmented triad (III in minor). The latter, to be sure, can precede or follow any chord, but its most important functions are: III—VI, III—I, III—IV and III—II; this last is seldom used because of the complicated voice leading. Obviously the same chords can follow the artificial ones as the natural: secondary dominants, artificial minor triads, artificial diminished triads, seventh chords with artificially diminished fifth, artificial diminished seventh chords. *Their main purpose is to give direction to a progression through an artificial leading tone* (see 137B).

IV. *The artificial minor triad* on the fifth degree is especially suited, as the examples show, to lead into the region of the sub-dominant (IV and II). It also leads well to VI (unaltered) or III (with raised third), as shown in 137C under *a*) at the V—II etc., also under *c*) at the V—VII. One will best conform to good usage if one considers this chord, in the progressions V—I and V—IV, as if it were II in the key of the sub-dominant (*F* major), or in V—VI as if it were IV in a minor key (*D* minor) (see 137C under *a*) and corresponding places in the following examples).

V. *Artificial diminished triads* can be treated like VII in major, or, much better, like II in minor keys (almost exclusively as a chord of the sixth [137D]). But for nearly every purpose, by addition of the seventh,—

VI. *Seventh chords with diminished fifth* are to be preferred, because for the modern ear the seventh always gives a stronger directional urge than the diminished fifth. The one on the third degree, being close to the key of the subdominant (137E1), leads very easily into the cadence. The most usual forms lead to II (III—II, III—VI—II), progressing like II_7 in minor (*D* minor). Less convincing is its progression to IV, where it is used like a VII_7 in major (VII—I!!). On I and V we cannot use them as yet with minor seventh; of the diminished seventh chords on both (E 2*b* and 4*b*) more will be said presently. That on IV recalls a II or V in minor (*E* or *A* minor) or a VII in major (*G*).

It is best in the cadence when it is treated like a VI in (*A*) minor; like a II in (*E*) minor it leans too closely toward the dominant; like a VII in major it is not very convincing, for reasons already suggested (VII—I!).

In addition we draw from these new materials two observations concerning chords already used.

I. *As dominant in the cadence* (next to last chord) we will use only a major chord (not an augmented) on the fifth degree, whose major third does not result from chromatic alteration. If it is preceded by the lowered seventh tone of the scale (as *b*♭ in *C* major), that tone, having sub-dominant character, must first be resolved downward, like the sixth tone of a minor scale. Contrary practice is of course to be found in the literature, but we have now no occasion to follow it.

II. For good reasons we will impose upon ourselves some restrictions on the use of certain diatonic secondary seventh chords. In the following the student will realize more and more that every chord can have different functions corresponding to its various tendencies, that it has more than one possible meaning, and that its meaning is definite only through its context. If I now restrict somewhat the use of the secondary seventh chords, it is in the effort to use them in accordance with their strongest tendency. To this effect the following principle may be laid down: *Every chord* (if the context does not prevent) *will demand a continuation like that of any other chord* (consisting of different tones) *which it resembles in interval structure*. Thus the seventh chords on II, III and VI in major have identical interval structure. Since II has a known definite function (II—V—I, II—I_4^6—V), the ear expects from the similarly constructed III_7 and VI_7 similar continuations (137F *a* and *b*) and it can be seen at a glance that these cannot easily be kept within the tonality. It does not absolutely follow that only this continuation is possible, as I show in several examples, proving that the tonality is not thereby doomed. However, these other progressions are less characteristic than that which follows the pattern of II. And so we see that in example *c*), in place of III, the secondary dominant on VI is more effective; in *d*), that on I or III; in *e*), that on II; in *f*) there is danger of a modulation to *G* major, which, to be sure, can be easily overcome. Since these chords in their characteristic progressions are doubtful, in others uncertain, I recommend—and this corresponds also to the appearances in the literature—very sparing use. At the best they have a certain melodic value when used with passing seventh. Otherwise they are better replaced by the altered chords on the same degrees, with which we have just become acquainted: secondary dominant seventh chords, artificial diminished triads, etc. [compare *c*) with *g*), *d*) with *h*)]. Of the remaining secondary seventh chords I and IV are similar. These too are best used with passing seventh. It is clear however that in practically every instance the secondary dominant seventh on I will have a more precise effect than the unaltered seventh chord [compare *i*) with *k*)]. The secondary seventh chord on VII recalls so closely II in minor that it can hardly be used in any other sense (*m* and *n*). The student can easily apply these same fundamental principles to the secondary seventh chords in minor keys, and he will accordingly confine himself to the characteristic behaviour of these chords, avoiding the uncharacteristic as unsuited to his purpose.

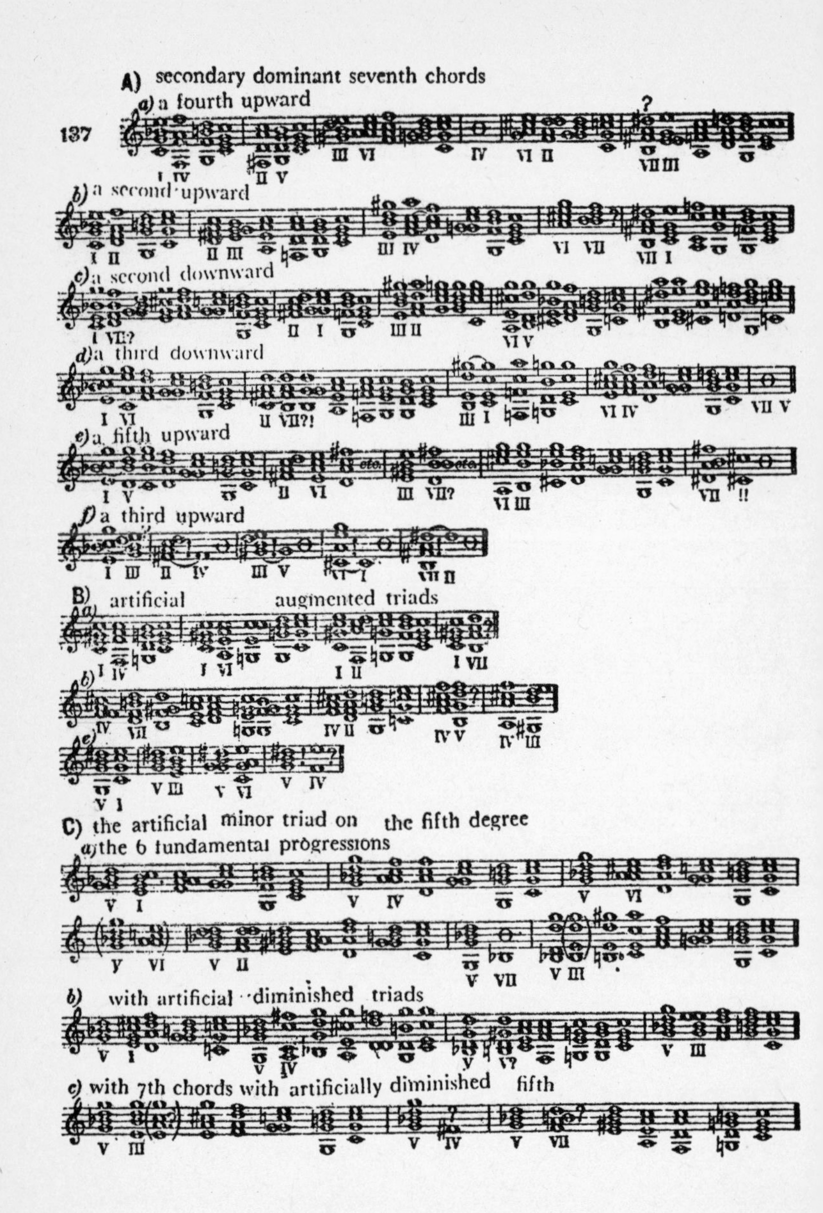
A) secondary dominant seventh chords
a) a fourth upward
137
?
I IV
II V
III VI
IV
VI II
VII III
b) a second upward
I II
II III
III IV
VI VII
VII I
c) a second downward
I VII?
II I
III II
VI V
d) a third downward
I VI
II VII?!
III I
VI IV
VII V
e) a fifth upward
etc.
etc.
I V
II VI
III VII?
VI III
VII !!
f) a third upward
I III
II IV
III V
VI I
VII II
B) artificial augmented triads
a)
I IV
I VI
I II
I VII
b)
IV VII
IV II
IV V
IV III
c)
V I
V III
V VI
V IV
C) the artificial minor triad on the fifth degree
a) the 6 fundamental progressions
V I
V IV
V VI
V VI
V II
V VII
V III
b) with artificial diminished triads
V I
V IV
V V?
V III
c) with 7th chords with artificially diminished fifth
V III
V IV
V VII

d) with artificially diminished 7th chords.
e) with artificially augmented triads
D) artificial· diminished triads
E) 7th chords with artificially diminished fifth
F)

The Diminished Seventh Chord

The diminished seventh chord is a ninth chord with root omitted. For example, on *d* as a root a (secondary) dominant seventh is *d-f♯-a-c*; the minor ninth is *e♭*; on *g* the ninth chord would be *g-b-d-f-a♭*; on *e*, *e-g♯-b-d-f*, etc.

If the root (*d*) is removed from any of these ninth chords a diminished seventh chord remains (*f♯-a-c-e♭*). If this chord progresses (*quasi* VII) to *g-b♭-d* (*quasi* I), or, as a secondary dominant, to *g-b-d*, then, considering the *d* as the real root, we still have in principle the progression to a chord a fourth higher (*d* to *g*).

Likewise diminished seventh chords can be built, by alterations, on every degree of the major or minor scale. To be omitted *for the present* are those from which the upward perfect fourth from the (omitted) root would not strike a scale tone for the chord of resolution. For example on IV in major (*C* major *f*), it should move to *b♭*, but actually goes to *b*. Or in *A* minor the IV (*d*) would tend toward VII (*g♯*).

The diminished seventh chord can be used without preparation. It is good, of course, to approach the seventh stepwise or by a chromatic progression, but this is not absolutely necessary. It has the following peculiarities:

It consists of three equal intervals, dividing the octave into four equal parts, minor thirds. If above or

below it another minor third is added, no new tone has been introduced, as the added tone doubles one already present an octave higher or lower. A chord dividing the octave in this manner can be built on any tone of the chromatic scale; but any three successive tones of the chromatic scale so used will give all the diminished seventh chords that exist. For example, *f-a♭-c♭-d*, *f♯-a-c-e♭*, *g-b♭-c♯-e*; trying another on *g♯* (*a♭*) gives the same tones as the first on *f*, namely, *a♭-c♭-d-f*; on *a*, *a-c-e♭-f♯*, etc. By sound and interval, therefore, there are only three diminished seventh chords. However, since there are twelve minor keys, each diminished seventh chord must belong to at least four minor keys as VII_7. The chord *f-a♭-c♭-d* can be (139*b*): VII_7 in *G♭* (*F♯*) minor if *f* (*e♯*) is taken as the root, VII_7 in *A* minor with *g♯* (*a♭*) as the root, VII_7 in *C* minor with *b* (*c♭*), VII_7 in *E♭* minor with *d*; or it could be regarded as the dominant ninth in these same keys with the root omitted. (Obviously in the written notes *a♭* may have to be changed to *g♯*, *c♭* to *b*, etc.) Hence each tone of this chord could be its root; likewise each could be its third, its diminished fifth or its diminished seventh. If the chord is inverted we do not receive a new impression of its structure, as we do with a major or a minor chord; —we still have only minor thirds (or augmented seconds). Therefore if this chord appears without context, or in a vague context, it is not clear to what tonality it belongs. Its *g♯* could be an *a♭*, its *b* a *c♭*, etc., and only from what follows can one tell whether one tone is a leading tone, falling or rising. Since the ear cannot make this decision sooner, and any of the possible resolutions can be satisfactory, it is possible to approach this chord in one sense (or key) and leave it in another. For example a diminished seventh chord containing a *g*♯ can follow a chord containing a *g*. even if the *g* ought not go to a *g*♯. The ear is prepared to accept the *g*♯ as *a*♭; hence permits the progression, even though what follows may treat the tone as *g*♯ and lead it to *a*. The rule about cross (false) relation can be relaxed to a certain extent in treating the diminished seventh chord. One should not however make unnecessary leaps, but write in melodic fashion (*i.e.*, nearly scalewise), as will always be possible.

The chord *b-d-f-a*♭ can be a ninth chord with root omitted:

in	*C*	major on			III	V		
in *C*♯	(*D*♭)	major on	I				VI	
in	*D*	major on		II				VII
in	*E*♭	major on			III	V		
in	*E*	major on	I				VI	
in	*F*	major on		II				VII
in *F*♯	(*G*♭)	major on			III	V		
in	*G*	major on	I				VI	
in	*A*♭	major on		II				VII
in	*A*	major on			III	V		
in	*B*♭	major on	I				VI	
in	*B*	major on		II				VII
in	*c*	minor on				V		VII
in *c*♯	(*d*♭)	minor on	I		III			

in	*d*	minor on		II			(VI)	
in	*e♭*	minor on				V		VII
in	*e*	minor on	I		III			
in	*f*	minor on		II			(VI)	
in *f♯*	(*g♭*)	minor on				V		VII
in	*g*	minor on	I		III			
in	*a♭*	minor on		II			(VI)	
in	*a*	minor on				V		VII
in	*b♭*	minor on	I		III			
in	*b*	minor on		II			(VI)	

Later it can also be VI (parentheses) in *D* minor, *F* minor, *A♭* minor and *B* minor, even IV in *D*, *F*, *A♭*, *B*, major and minor. For now we have 44 meanings at our disposal. It will be shown later that this chord has even more key connections, that it cannot be definitely located in any one key. It is at home everywhere but settled nowhere, a cosmopolite or a vagabond. I call such chords *wandering*[1] chords, as I have suggested before. They belong to no key exclusively, but can without change of form (even inversion is not necessary, only the choosing of a new root) belong to many keys, in fact nearly all keys.

We use the diminished seventh chord, not for the construction of modulations to distant keys, but for an easing of the way and a smoothing out of connections that might otherwise sound rough. However, attention must be given to one point: the diminished seventh chord, though its effect can be very definite, is also capable of giving to a phrase a certain weak, sickly impression; for its decisive effect as a modulatory force arises not so much from an urge to turn this way or

---

[1]Or *vagrant* (*vagierende*).—Translator's note.

that, as, much more, from its seeming to be indefinite, hybrid, immature. In itself it is undecided, has many inclinations, is easily won over. Therein lies its usefulness: a mediator must not be a partisan. Sparingly used, it is of excellent effect.

One thing we wish to emphasize: we should not use the diminished seventh chord, as it is commonly used, like a panacea from the household medicine cabinet, like aspirin, to cure everything. It is for us, as ninth chord with root omitted, just a special form of one of the chords of the scale. Only where this chord can be placed according to the principles we have hitherto followed—unaltered, as secondary dominant, or otherwise altered—only there can we properly place a diminished seventh chord. The deciding factor is still the fundamental progression, approaching and leaving. The student should plan his exercises with this requirement in mind; the decision as to whether a certain progression will be better with this or that form, with a secondary dominant or a diminished seventh chord, or otherwise, may require some deliberation.

In 140A diminished seventh chords are joined to all the triads of the key. Here much is worthless, much superfluous. The student will notice several augmented and diminished interval skips (140A*). There is no need to avoid these, as they are often practically unavoidable, and they are made harmless by the enharmonic possibilities of the diminished seventh chord.

In 140B the chord *f♯-a-c-e♭* (or *d♯*) is used in four different ways, followed each time by a different chord. In *a*) it is VI progressing to II; in *b*), V to I; in *c*), III to VI; in *d*), VII to III. But in *a*) at †, the diminished seventh chord on the second degree of *F*, *b-d-f-a♭*, goes to *F* I. This diminished seventh chord is of course indicated as a II (*g* understood as the root), and leads to I^6_4. But the *a*♭ goes to *a*♮, acting more like a *g*♯, according to our previous conceptions, in which an *a*♭ should go to *g*. If, however, ignoring the derivation of the chord, we write *g*♯ instead of *a*♭, and assume that we have a ninth chord on the seventh degree of *F* (root omitted), then the progression is VII—I^6_4;—an unlikely idea, for

VII is unsuitable (p. 194) for bringing in the I_4^6 of the cadence. Obviously it is not VII but II, and the problem is made clear in this way: if the diminished seventh chord is followed at once by V, with the I_4^6 omitted, there is then no doubt that it is a II, as is even clearer if we consider the same progression in the like-named minor, *F* minor. In minor its meaning as a II is indisputable, even if it leads to a I_4^6. Supported by these three analogous situations we must admit this to be the fundamental progression; writing the *a*♭ as a *g*♯ is explained by the inherent ambiguousness of all the tones of the diminished seventh chord and their resulting susceptibility to enharmonic changes. The *a*♭, as ninth of II, is the same to the ear as *g*♯, and can behave accordingly, as if derived from VII in *F* major. From its true derivation it acquires the right to the fundamental progression II—I_4^6; from its ambiguous actual sound, the freedom of a melodic progression.

141*a* shows the three most commonly used progressions: a fourth higher, a second higher, a second lower (from the understood root). Whether one or another takes place can be recognized from the movements of the separate voices; going to a chord a fourth higher all four voices move (the chord of resolution has entirely new tones); a second higher (like deceptive cadence), one tone is common, the others move; a second lower, two tones remain stationary, only one tone is new. Thus they are not difficult to distinguish. The student should realize what roots he is joining. For the best construction of fundamental progressions, directions can be given, judgments on their function and effect. If we ignore the connection with the real root, then each chord is unique, requiring special consideration and judgment. Aside from all theory, the student will never realize the value of the consciousness of fundamental progression until he is in a situation where he must give a good account of himself in harmonic variety in the construction of a certain form.

In 141*a* the resolutions which would result in chromatic chords are omitted. These are not usable at present.

In 141*b* are given progressions and deceptive cadences using inversions. All this is good and will be used even more freely later. Only two progressions should be avoided. These are shown at ⊗ and †. The explanation will be given later (p. 194). At ∮ a leap is made to the $^6_4$ chord. This progression is justified by the often mentioned cliché principle, and is especially useful for the I^6_4 in the cadence.

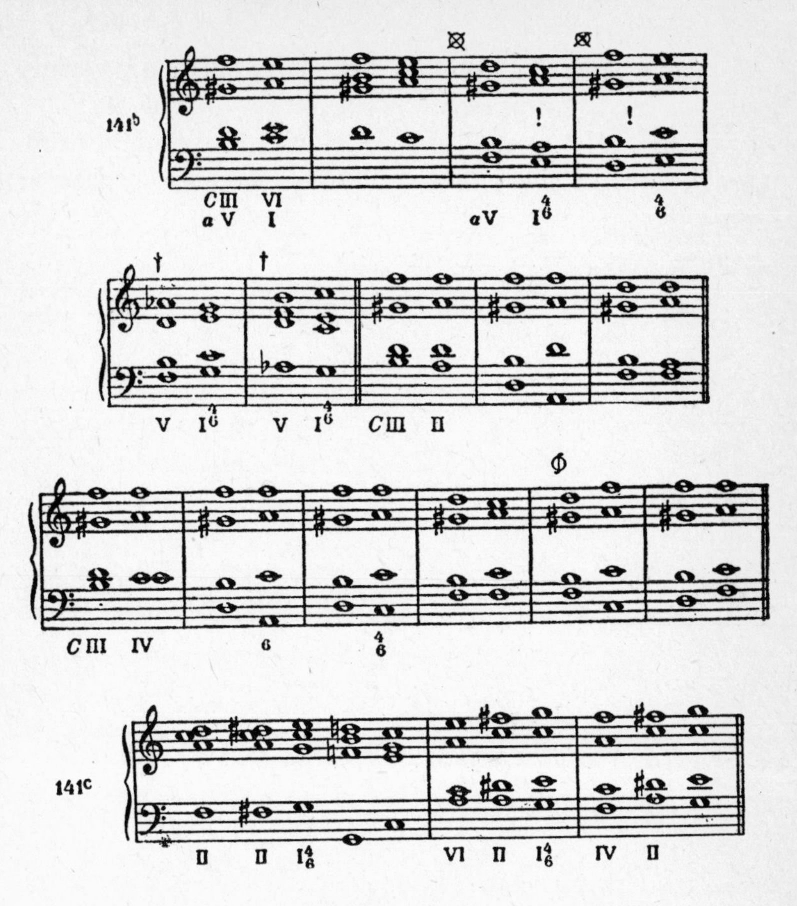

Guide Rules

For the Use of the Diminished Seventh Chord

I. The diminished seventh chord can be used only where the ninth chord from which it is derived (root omitted) could be used, and where its chromatically altered tones can progress in accordance with their natural tendencies as leading tones. (This is in apparent contradiction to the freely wandering privilege that this chord ordinarily has; but the contradiction is only apparent and calls attention to the fact that the fundamental progression may be different from what the student supposes when it is impossible to follow the natural tendencies of the leading tones. We shall permit ourselves enharmonic notation, for the present, only in the progression last mentioned: the diminished seventh chord on II (II_9) to I_4^6 in major.)

II. It may replace dominant seventh chords or secondary dominant seventh chords in all the functions of these chords, as long as the following chords remain within the key (see 141*a*). For the present that is its most important function. It is of great value for this purpose, improving many rough details, especially in the danger of cross relation and ignored turning points. Deserving of special mention is the progression in140A under 3 at **), where, following the cadencing I_4^6, it suggests a deceptive cadence by resolving to a VI or IV. Also where it brings in this same I_4^6 chord (141*c*), fulfilling the function of a II. Both of these progressions are in good use.

Little needs to be said about the laws of rhythm; it will be sufficient to point out two precepts which were still valid in the nineteenth century and may help in the effective form of our exercises. One concerns *organ point* (or *pedal point*), which will be introduced in the next chapter. The other concerns the $\frac{6}{4}$ chord *in the cadence* as a device for delaying the appearance of the dominant seventh chord. This should appear only on a strong beat of the measure. The dominant seventh comes then on "two," the final chord on "one." (To be sure, the last chord is often on a weak beat.)

In this and other instances of rhythmic shifts and alteration of accent, where the measure is no more than a means of counting, it often happens that the $\frac{6}{4}$ chord appears on a weak beat. The rule is not therefore universally valid, but it is nearly so, as the $^6_4$ chord is generally used in modern music—that is, the $^6_4$ chord in a cadence. The other $^6_4$ chord, used in passing, is naturally free to appear on a strong or a weak beat. Yet it is advisable for the student, in the interest of simplicity, to use also the passing $^6_4$ on the first beat. Without further admonitions, the student can now write his exercises in measures. It will be best to use half notes—since we are concerned with harmonic rather than rhythmic effects,—placing two half-note chords in each $^4_4$ measure.

Since modulation to a key two removes distant on the Circle of Fifths touches on a more remote relationship than to the third and fourth removes, it is more complicated. We shall therefore postpone it for a while, taking up the others first.

From *C* major and *a* minor the keys three removes upward are *A* major and *f*♯ sharp minor; four removes upward, *E* major and *c*♯ minor; three removes downward, *E*♭ major and *c* minor; four removes downward, *A*♭ major and *f* minor.

Modulation to Keys Three and Four Fifths Higher on the Circle of Fifths

Here the simplest modulations make use of the *relationship of like-named keys* (*a* minor—*A* major, *e* minor—*E* major, etc.). This relationship rests upon the sameness of key-note and of the dominant chord; under certain conditions this common dominant can cause an ambiguity. For example, *e-g*♯*-b* is dominant of *a* minor and of *A* major. When this chord is struck alone, minor or major key can follow equally well; when it proceeds from the minor key (as V of *a* minor), it then becomes necessary to neutralize or liquidate the conditions of the minor key, and to place the chord in such manner that it possesses the freedom of movement to turn to minor or to major. The possibility of going to the major key is helped by the tendency of every triad—especially a dominant—to progress to a major triad a fourth higher, thus giving the impression that it is leaving the one scale because of its natural affinity for the other.

This transformation of a minor key (*a* minor) into the like-named (*A*) major, can be used also in modulating *from the relative* of this minor (*C* major to *A* major), and also *to the relative* of this major (*a* minor to *f*# minor). For *C* major can be regarded as *a* minor in its natural form (without raised tones), and, if its fifth and fourth tones are treated as seventh and sixth according to the turning point rules, it can soon be given the raised (sixth and seventh) tones which will stamp it as definitely *a* minor. Likewise *a* minor, changed to *A* major, can be further transformed to *f*# minor. Obviously this modulation from *C* major to *A* major or *f*# minor, or from *a* minor to *f*# minor, can be explained as from *C* major through *a* minor to *A* major, through *a* minor and *A* major to *f*# minor, or from *a* minor through *A* major to *f*# minor. It is not necessary, however, to touch upon the intermediate key, and I advise, as I have explained before, that the *C* major (or *A* major) preceding the *a* minor (or *f*# minor) be regarded as *a* minor (or *f*# minor) in its natural or uncharacteristic form, and that careful attention be given to the turning-point tones and to the change from unraised to raised tones, as has been done before in going from *C* major to *a* minor.

Modulation to keys four fifths higher on the Circle of Fifths (*C* major or *a* minor to *E* major or *c*# minor) follows the same principle, changing *e* minor to *E* major. Here the taking of an intermediate key (*e* minor) is more justified; the whole problem is then resolved into a modulation up one fifth on the Circle, plus a modulation up three fifths (1 + 3 = 4). Of help also is the fact that the dominant triad of *e* minor (and of *E* major) appears also as secondary dominant on VII in *C* major or on II in *a* minor, and also that the feeling for *e* minor can begin at the first chord (I of *C* major is VI of *e* minor; I of *a* minor is IV of *e* minor).

Our problem then falls into three parts:

1. The introduction of V of the new key first as V of the like-named minor. The neutralizing of unraised tones may be necessary.
2. The transformation of this dominant of a minor key into that of a major key; preparation for the new interpretation of the same chord.
3. The proceeding into the major key, and perhaps on into its relative minor.

A cadence should follow, as usual.

Let us consider first the *transformation of the dominant*. This is most simply accomplished if it is so long sustained that its minor-key source is forgotten, as with a *fermata* (hold). This very simple device is in fact often used in classical works to eliminate some tonal obligation. The effect of the General Pause rests upon the feeling of suspense, as if one asks, "What new thing will come now?" Yet this means is not practicable for us, because its relative tastelessness (it is tasteless today because of its triteness) is exceeded only by the scant possibilities for surprise with the materials now at hand, also because we choose to gain our effects not through tricks of performance but through purely harmonic means. We shall use two forms of a similar expedient: (1) the *stationary voice*, particularly its special case, the *organ point* (or pedal point), where as a substitute for a sustained chord one tone,—the most important tone,—*the root*, is sustained, while the other voices move in suitable chords; (2) *repeated progressions through the dominant*.

The *stationary voice* differs from the situation so often found in the simplest progressions where one or more voices are stationary for a time, in that here the other voices can build chords into which the sustained tone cannot well be placed, or may even be dissonant with it. Usually it is the root or fifth of the Tonic or Dominant (or a secondary dominant) which is stationary, but in some circumstances it could be the third. The sustained tone is called *organ point* when it is in the bass (usually —for our present purpose always—it is then the root). The most important rules, for us, governing sustained tones and organ point have to do with the beginning and end. 1. The sustained tone should begin on the strong beat, on "one" of the measure. 2. The sustained tone should be a consonance at *beginning* and *end*. 3. It should be left on a weak beat. 4. The chords in between should of course build logical progressions and be closely related.

We shall not write any greatly extended organ points; it will suffice to indicate its function. Most important for our purpose is the appearance of the dominant which is to be reinterpreted, at the beginning and again at the end of the organ point. By placing the dominant at these points we can best fulfill the condition that the sustained tone should be consonant at beginning and end. This repetition of the dominant is a strengthening, which helps us to forget its derivation from the minor key by stressing its value in itself, thus favoring its native tendency to turn to the major key. Meanwhile the sustained tone preserves the continuity so that the ear does not for a moment lose the sense of what is going on. In general we shall place just one connecting chord between beginning and end of the organ point, which then will be three half notes long.

On "one" then (see 144) place the V, on "two" the connecting chord, on the next "one" the V again, but if possible in a different position. In choosing the connecting chord we shall avoid those which would hinder the reinterpretation of the dominant: those which are more akin to *a* minor than to *A* major, as those which contain the minor third of the tonic (*c*), I, III and VI of *a* minor; also those that lie so close to *C* major as to require chromatic progressions (144*d* and *e*), for a dominant should not appear through a chromatic progression.

As will be shown in the next chapter, the relationship of the minor sub-dominant is such that it always yields to the tonic; also the tendency of the dominant to turn to the major key is so strong that I and VI cannot much hinder. It is better, however, to choose chords that can belong equally well to *a* minor or *A* major, such as secondary dominants, artificial diminished triads or artificial diminished seventh chords; namely: II as changing dominant (*b-d♯-f♯-a*) and as diminished seventh chord (*d♯-f♯-a-c*). Here of course the minor third *c* does no harm; but also II, IV and VI of *a* minor with the raised sixth tone are suitable; even with the *c*, which is here a dissonance and must resolve to *b* (144*k*). 144*b* is ruled out by its fundamental progression (III—V); at 144*c* (VII—V) VII is a diminished triad, hence demands other treatment.

The fundamental progressions must now be considered. Only IV and VI will give strong progressions (145*e-h*: V—IV—V and V—VI—V); with I and II we have falling progressions (145*b*, *c*, *d* and *i*), which of course are not bad (VII and III are useless). Of course the I is in poor taste, as will become evident when we reach the major key. In 145*e*, *f*, are difficulties in voice leading which make unavoidable a diminished or augmented melodic interval. The downward direction of the seventh and sixth tones of *a* minor (in 145*g* and *h*) is freely explained on the theory that here *A* major already appears. This theory is especially justified when the changing dominant and the like are used. The most suitable forms are those in which the chord tones of the V are brought in by the treatment of a dissonance. When the connecting chord is a seventh chord, it cannot be complete. Care must be exercised to express the dissonance through the characteristic tones: root, seventh, sometimes the diminished fifth.

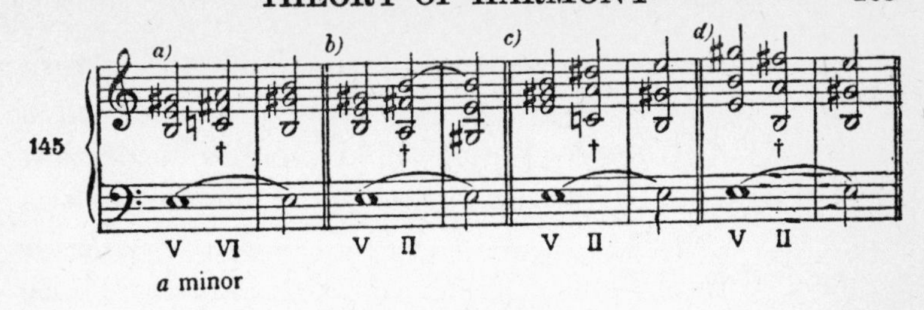

For carrying out this lingering-on-the-dominant procedure for reinterpreting (as to minor or major key), through a *sustained tone* in the *upper voices*, and for the so-called *passage through the dominant*, the same considerations are necessary as for the organ point.

The difference between these forms and the organ point is mainly that with the sustained tone (146 *a-e*) another than the bass voice is stationary, by which one will perhaps avoid too severe clashes of dissonance, and that with the passage through the dominant (146*f*, *g*) there is no stationary voice. Here scalewise voice leading is advisable, by which the connecting chord results in part from passing tones, from melodic movement. The V can here also appear as a 6th chord, either in the first or the second place. The changing dominant with its necessary resolution is of excellent service here, since it can give to the dominant almost the weight of a tonic—a very useful trait.

The considerations that we have indicated for the second placing of the dominant will obviously apply equally well to the first: the same chords will be suitable to introduce it. 147A shows a number of such possibilities. (The unusable chords were shown in 144*f-i*, and explained above.)

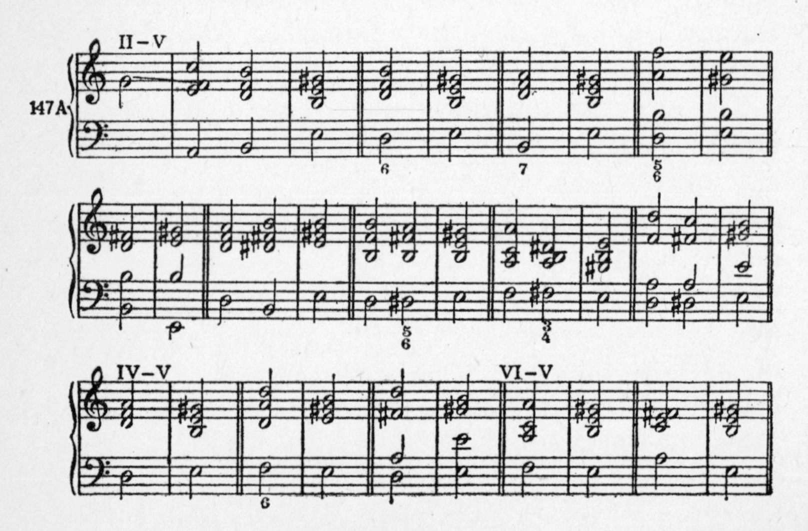

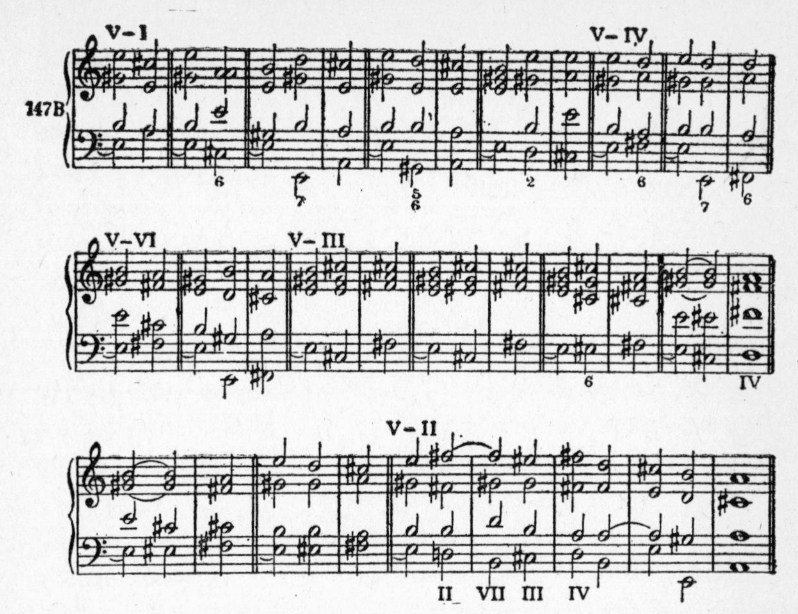

Here again we must remind the student that the turning points are important; whether the final key will be *C* major or *a* minor makes no difference. Naturally all of these chords and forms can be successfully handled through the use of secondary dominants and other artificial chords.

The leaving of the organ point must now be considered. The I is desired, but it may be delayed in different ways (147B). Our first thought is for the rising fundamental progressions (V—I, the two deceptive cadences V—VI and V—IV, also V—III, which is best carried out with the secondary dominant on III); but also V—II is conceivable, if well followed up. Change of position should be used when possible. The first chord following the organ point can be placed at once on "two" of the measure, but it is also possible to insert the V_7 chord or the diminished seventh on V, bringing the first chord to determine the major key on the first of the next measure.

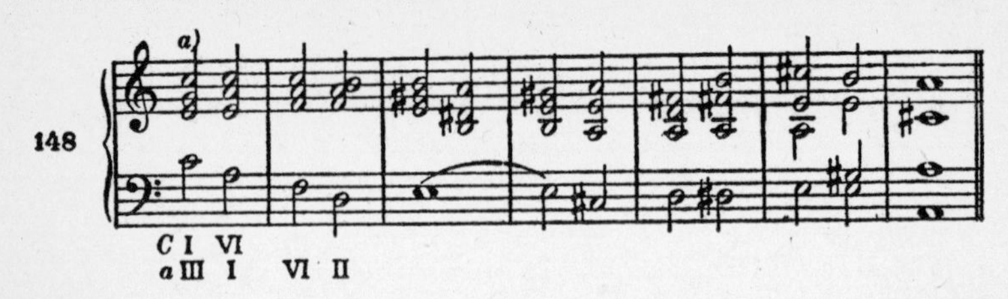

To avoid undue length, it is advisable to use not more than four to six chords before the dominant.

In 149 are modulations to *f*♯ minor, following the suggested course to the dominant of *A* major, then after the "lingering" on this chord, going directly through the cadence to *f*♯ minor. Here the secondary dominant and the diminished seventh chord on III of *A* major are very effective.

For practice the student may take each of the modulations here shown, as far as the cadence, then turn it in a different direction: those in 148 to *f*♯ minor, those in 149 to *A* major.

The modulations from *a* minor are treated in the same manner (150, 151).

In this modulation the student can use a few more secondary dominants, diminished seventh chords and the like, since they help in the reinterpreting of the dominant. It will be wise, however, in the first exercises to use few or no altered chords, in order to keep well in mind the sense of the fundamental progressions.

He must never relax his efforts to keep this clear, even when he feels sure in the handling of single chords, even when it may seem no longer necessary.

The student, now for the first time writing exercises in rhythm, will be inclined to think of each two measures as a phrase, a very inadvisable procedure if he wishes to make something of the highest voice. Where motive repetition occurs in sequence style, obligations often arise which are almost impossible to meet. Hence

a melodically designed exercise is likely to be unsatisfactory.

As we have already indicated, *modulation to the fourth remove upward* on the Circle of Fifths rests on this same principle. Only here we go to the dominant, not of *a* minor, but of *e* minor. The relationship of *C* major (*a* minor) to *e* minor is so close that it is no more difficult to go there than to the dominant of *a* minor. The opening chord (*C* major I), instead of being regarded as *a* minor III, is now thought of as *e* minor VI. Everything else—the bringing in of the dominant, the lingering on or repetition of the dominant, the entering of the new key and the cadence—remain the same, so that the student can by simple transposition (with slight changes) transform a modulation three removes upward into one four removes upward, and vice versa. I recommend this procedure for added practice; in general he should work out the examples for himself.

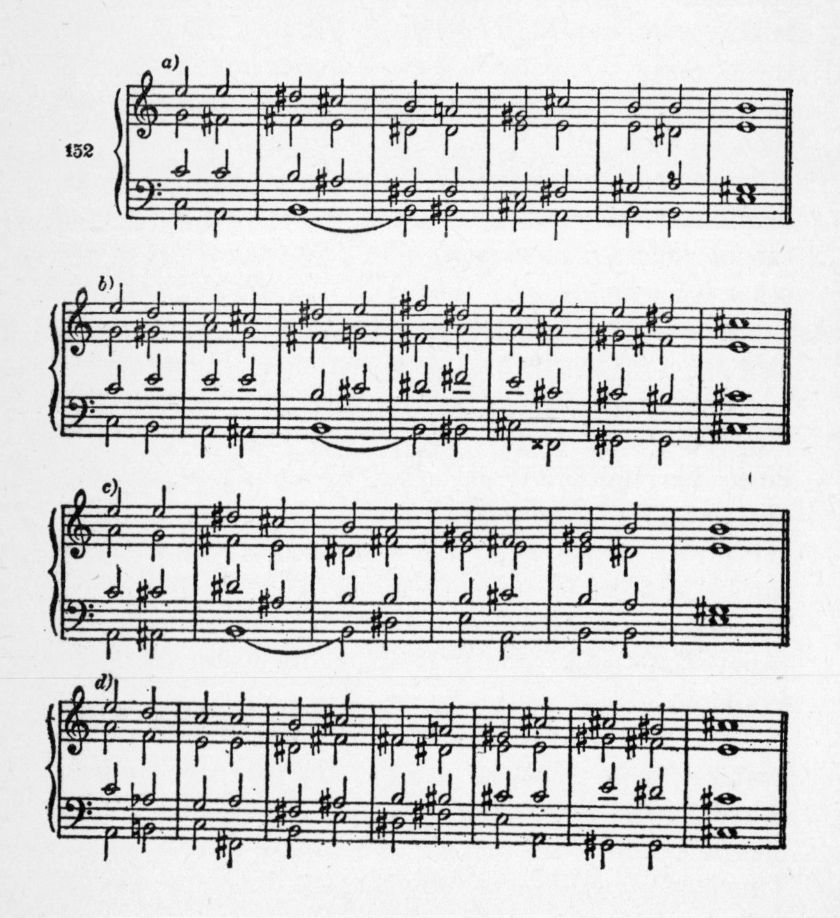

MODULATION TO KEYS THREE AND FOUR FIFTHS LOWER ON THE CIRCLE OF FIFTHS

From *C* Major and *a* Minor to *E* Flat Major and *c* Minor, and to *A* Flat Major and *f* Minor

For this modulation we use a similar means but less complicated than the preceding. We have seen how a dominant, arising from a minor key, hence following a minor tonic, can be followed by a major tonic. Here the situation is reversed: a I of a major key is regarded as a dominant (or perhaps secondary dominant), and then followed by a minor triad. In an analogous situation, the dominants (*g-b-d*) of like-named keys (*C* major and *c* minor) are identical; so that the same *g-b-d* can be followed at one time by a major chord, at another by a minor. If, then, the I of the original key, *C* major (in *a* minor the same chord will be brought in as a III), is looked upon as a dominant, it can be followed immediately, or perhaps after the addition of a direction-giving seventh (*b*♭), by a minor chord on *f*. Since this chord on *c* can be a dominant (V in *f* minor), or a secondary dominant (I in *c* minor, VI in *E*♭ major, III in *A*♭ major), the following minor triad, *f-a*♭*-c*, can be interpreted as I in *f* minor, II in *E*♭ major, IV in *c* minor, or VI in *A*♭ major. Thus we arrive in a region that could not be reached by means thus far available.

The result may easily be monotonous. When, for example, as in 153*a*, after *E*♭ II the new key is established in the most direct manner (V—I), the fundamental progressions are all to chords a fourth higher. This is inadvisable, not only because of the monotony, but also for another reason: perhaps it is *too* natural,

too obvious, to give any impression of something accomplished. Such progressions might with some justification be forbidden because they show so little imagination, because they provide so obvious, so cheap a means. In themselves they are obviously good, even too good. We do not like too much goodness. The student should try therefore to avoid too much of this sort of thing. The use of inversions, seventh chords, even diminished seventh chords, does not help much. One must then take care to bring in variety through deceptive cadences or through interpolation of other chords (153*f*).

In the *modulation to keys four removes down* on the circle, a deceptive cadence helps to reach the new key (153*d*).

The modulation from *a* minor is somewhat more difficult: the *a* opposes the *a*♭, soon due to appear (cross relation, as it might be called). To remove the *a* neatly, it is advisable to place it in a conspicuous voice (soprano or bass) and treat it as if it were the sixth tone of *c* minor, allowing it to pass through the *b* to *c* (154*a*).

The diminished seventh chord (*b-d-f-a*♭) is very useful here, since it enables *a* to move through *a*♭ to *g* (154*b*). Still better is the solution 154*e*, where this move is in the most conspicuous voice, the soprano, and the next progression brings in the *d*♭; thus the most important elements of *f* minor are prepared.

In 154*c* the diminished seventh chord is followed by the direction-giving seventh chord on *C* I. The tones of the diminished seventh chord are not necessarily approached through chromatic progressions (154*d*). Likewise we can here permit ourselves (at first only with the diminished seventh chord) augmented or diminished interval progressions.

THE MINOR SUB-DOMINANT RELATION

In the modulation to keys three and four fifths lower on the circle of fifths we have touched upon the relationship of a major tonic to its minor sub-dominant. We noted the tendency of the major tonic to act as a dominant to a minor tonic. Obviously this circumstance can be made use of, not only in modulation, but also for extending the cadence, and for enrichment of the materials within a key. This new relationship, established through the tendencies of primary triads, makes it possible to bring into the key, along with its scale-tone chords and those which we added by imitating some features of the church modes, also the secondary triads of those keys to which this minor sub-dominant belongs, the chords of the keys three and four fifths lower on the circle, thus significantly enlarging the tonality. For *C* major these would be:

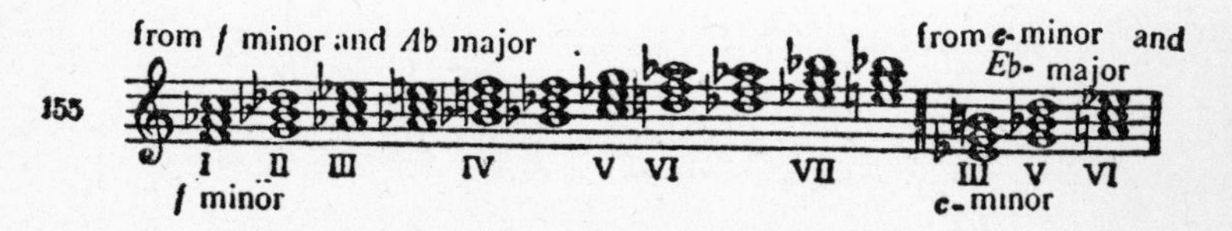

It is important to remember the derivation of these chords: from the region of the minor sub-dominant. They stand therefore in sharpest contrast to the secondary dominants, which belong mainly to the region of the dominant (only that on I leads to the sub-dominant; that on VI leads to the changing dominant—II). Hence some progressions between the two regions are too abrupt to be of use. In general these chords will serve to enrich and strengthen the sub-dominant region, and cannot always be joined directly with the dominant region. For the relationship of the two regions, it must be remembered, is not direct but indirect. *C* major VI and *f* minor I are related only through their common relationship to *C* major I; they are, so to speak, related by marriage.

156 shows the connections of all seven triads of *C* major with the new chords. Though some of these progressions are unusual, none is bad or useless. Each one may be, in some situation, the only thing for the purpose, to say nothing of its possible expressive value. In the light of these observations, the following

Guide Rules

are given, with some restrictions.

I. Progressions are not in good usage which cause difficulties in voice leading. Our harmony is for the most part derived from the combinations that resulted from the moving voices in polyphonic music; whatever made difficulties in voice leading was avoided and is still not in the best use. Such are for example II with VI (of *f* minor), III with VII, VI with III (at †) because of the danger of fifths, and also for another reason which will be discussed later; also III with IV, V with VI, VI with IV, and VII with VI (at ⊕) because of augmented and diminished melodic leaps. The student will do well to avoid these entirely. Whether he will ever make use of them will depend, not on the precepts of harmonic theory, but on the needs of an artist who is sure of his form. Whatever the latter does is right.

156
I
II of f minor III III V VI VI VII III of c-minor VI
II
I of f minor II III III IV IV V VI VI VII
III
III of c min VI I of f minor II II III III IV IV
or
V VI VI VII III of c-minor VI
IV
I of f minor II III
III IV IV V VI VI VII III of c-minor VI
V
I of f-minor II II III III IV IV V VI
VI
VI VII III of c minor VI I II III III IV
VII
IV V VI VI VII III of c-minor VI I of f minor II
III III IV IV V VI VI VII III of c minor VI

The recommendations of harmonic theory concern what is in good use and why it has a place in the system.

II. Readily eliminated are the diminished triads weakly approached (I—II, III—II, IV—VI [of *c* minor], V—VI [at ▽]).

III. *C* major IV with *f* minor IV ($\not{f}$). The IV of minor is the sub-dominant of the sub-dominant, and by the natural power that the sub-dominant has over the tonic, it is clear that the tonality might easily be lost. Of course we have now ample means to reestablish it. But here the means for the reestablishing would be more interesting than those by which it was lost. The tale becomes boring when the police are more exciting than the robbers. When we wish to stray so far from tonality, to carry on in so revolutionary a manner, we shall learn more entertaining ways to do it.

IV. One should consider carefully before joining III with I (of *f* minor), as can be seen readily in the reverse progression, *f* minor I to *C* major III (157 *a* and *b*). In this not-too-pleasing progression the ear will not perceive the chord *e-g-b* as *C* major III, but will hear it rather as a variant of 157*d*, which 157*c* resembles closely. Hence it is not so much that these two chords do not appear together in any key, as that in this aural similarity it lies too close to a more pleasing progression to be justified. Nevertheless 157*e* and *f* show that this 6th chord can be confirmed as a III by what follows.

V. Progressions which have an analogy in some not-too-distant key, where the same chords are built from scale tones, or with one of them a secondary dominant, will cause no difficulties, as long as cross relations are melodically removed (by turning point rules or by chro-

matic progressions). Here it is often possible to effect a reinterpreting of chords as to key.

VI. Likewise progressions in which chromatic melodic progressions are possible without necessitating augmented or diminished progressions in other voices.

VII. Decisively important, as always, is the fundamental progression.

In 158*a-g* are given the forms that can follow directly dominants, secondary dominants and the like. 158*a*, *b* gives progressions from I, 158*c*, *d* from V, 158*e* from the secondary dominant on II, 158*f* from that on VI, 158*g* from the diminished seventh chords on I, II, V, and VI. There is nothing new in these progressions. There are analogies to all of them (in *c* minor, *f* minor, *g* minor and *d* minor). The only difficulty is sometimes in the avoidance of cross relation, as is shown in 158*h*. This difficulty can be removed easily by turning point handling, chromatic and diminished seventh chords, which the student may now be trusted to use.

Close and easy to bring in are progressions from a major chord to a minor chord with the same root (156⊡). The student knows already how to proceed here, and also that the appearance of such minor chords through chromatic change has melodic more than harmonic significance, from the chapter on secondary dominants, where was discussed the dominant, *g-b♭-d* (as *C* major V), derived from the Dorian mode. In 159*a* the minor chord (6th chord on *e♭*) has no influence on what follows. In 159*b* on the other hand the minor V of *c* (over *b♭*) prepares for the region of the sub-dominant. In 159*c* the chromatically introduced *a♭* in the bass enables the inconspicuous entrance of the 6th chord *f-a♭-d♭*.

In these progressions that change a major triad to a minor, it is advisable to let the chromatic move of the third take place in the bass, so as to keep the bass moving;—not that it makes much difference, with so little change in the whole picture.

Of far-reaching effect are connections like: I of *C* major with III or VII of *f* minor (I or V of *A*♭ major), and likewise other degrees (156 ⊗). With the second degree there is one less possibility than with the other minor triads (160 Φ). The circumstances of the latter might be copied for the second degree, but not with

due consideration of the degree of kinship. Likewise there are only two possibilities with the major triads.

The measure of the harmonic value of these connections is always the fundamental progression. The strong progression to a chord a third lower requires no special motivation; the weak progression to a chord a third higher is to be judged as formerly.

For all such connections there is a device well suited to make them smooth and convincing: the chromatic progression. In our earlier work, using closely related materials, it was a scale passage of the principal or a related key that smoothed out the harmonic procedure. Here a single scale takes over such functions: the chromatic scale. It is easy to see why. As we recognized the scale as a simple melody, a musical form based upon a primitive but clear and easily understood law, we cannot now deny the same attributes to the chromatic scale. Its melodic force helps to join what is more distantly related: such is the purpose of chromaticism.

Somewhat difficult to handle (in voice leading) are the examples in 160 ⊕. Here it is not always easy to avoid an awkward skip. The student will do well at first to choose progressions that do not make this skip necessary (161). When he is sure of these, he may then risk augmented or diminished skips, at least in the inner voices. They are less objectionable now, for the melodic and harmonic proceeding rests less and less exclusively upon the pattern of the major or minor scale. And now it is no longer out of place to suppose the reinterpreting of a tone (enharmonic change), which will usually restore melodic equilibrium. Of course, the nearer the voice movement is to the major or minor scale, the more intelligible will the voice be. The student's efforts should still be in that direction. As a model for the skip of an augmented second I suggest the so-called "harmonic minor scale" (in which I recognize the true *melodic* minor scale).

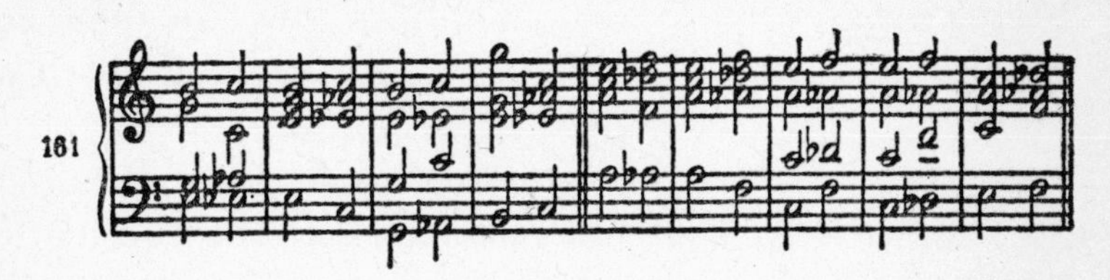

Some examples will show the usefulness of these progressions:

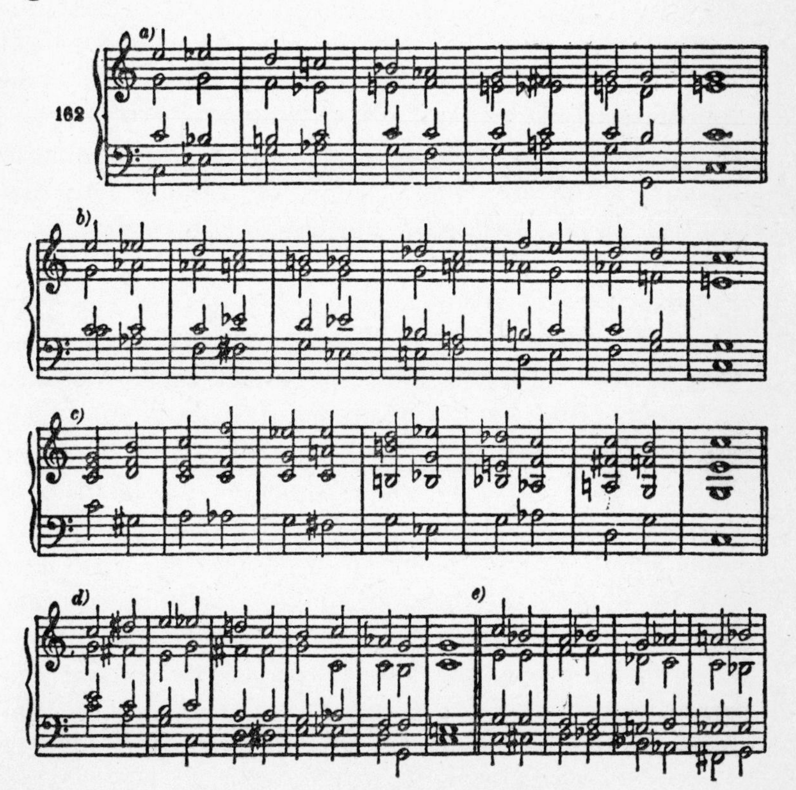

I have added a cadence to each. Doubtless most persons will feel these as modulations rather than as cadencing formulas.

Of the connections given in 156 those indicated with ○ have not yet been discussed. We shall now consider how to bring in each one, and how to proceed from it. Here again melodic voice leading is the best help.

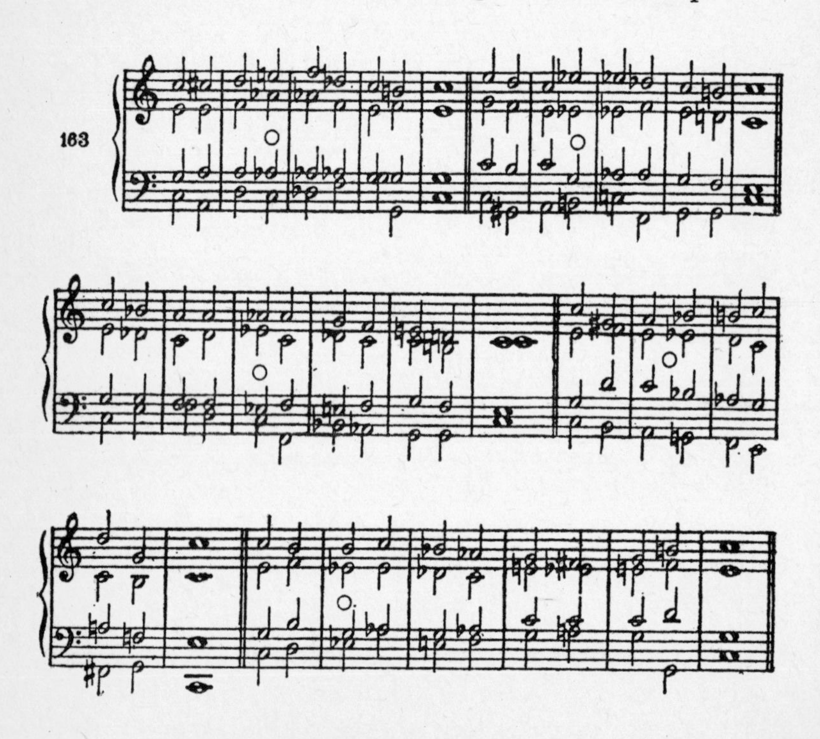

164 gives examples of the use of chords related to the minor sub-dominant. In a minor key I advise at first to use the relationship through the like-named major, thus: in *c* minor the chords related to the minor sub-dominant of *C* major. Later the student can go farther and use the relationship of the relative major (in *c* minor, that of *E♭* major), but at first this could bring him into difficult situations.

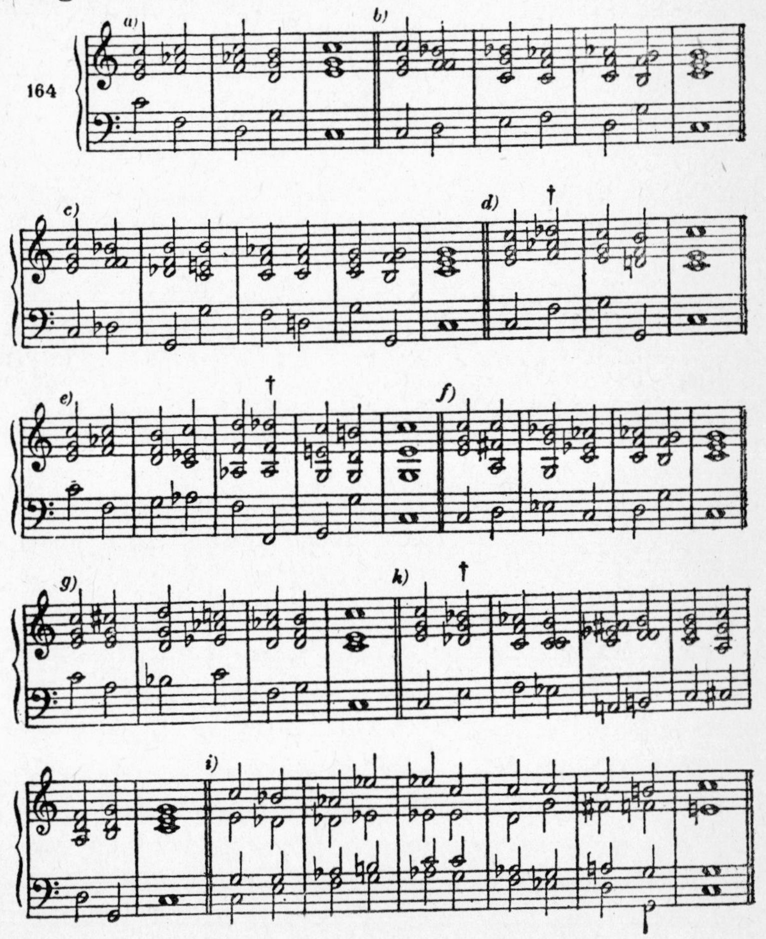

In 164*g* it would have been better to lead the *b*♭ in the bass to *a*♭; however, the continuation shows, as also in 164*k* where the *c* goes to *d* when *b*♭ might have been better, that the strong chords which follow can overrule such considerations.

165, in *c* minor, uses the sub-dominant relation of the like-named major key (*C* major); then, in *a* minor, the more remote relationship of the relative major.

Here the student must show taste and a feeling for form. He can no longer come at the multiple possibilities through precepts alone. I find it better when he is timid than when he is bold, when he hesitates to use rough progressions than when he decides upon them all-too-easily. He must discriminate! And even when one has gone far beyond what can appear here, to where nothing is bad in itself, perhaps also nothing good in itself, then that organ to be developed, the feeling for form, will be exercised by making choices, sooner than if it had no obstacles.

In 164*d* the so-called *Neapolitan Sixth* is used at †. This is a sixth chord reached through the minor subdominant relation, in *C* major and *c* minor *f*-*a*♭-*d*♭. As a diatonic triad it is found in *f* minor as VI (or in *A*♭

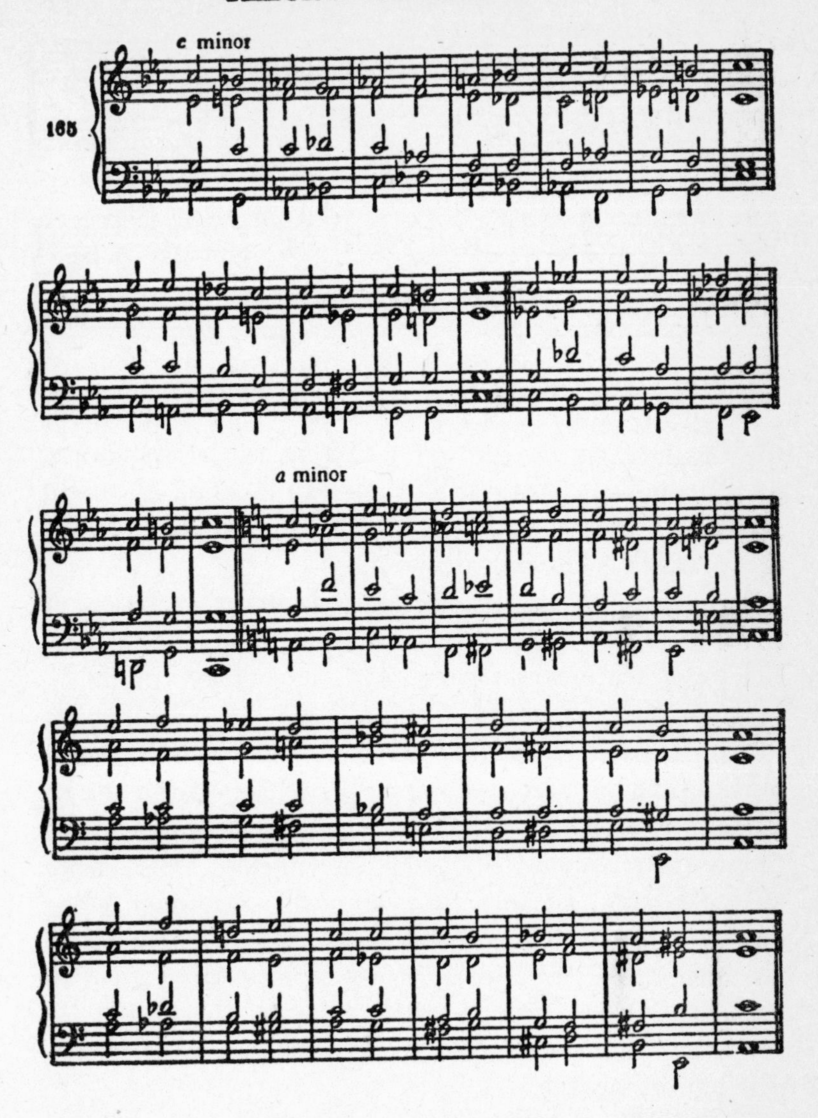

major as IV). In *f* minor its connection with V is not new (VI—V, 166*a*). Its typical appearance, however, is its use as a II in the cadence (166*b* and *c*). Hence the conception that it is a chromatic alteration of II.

More correctly, however, it should be called a substitute for II.

If we really accept that this chord is a chromatically altered form of II, it means that root and fifth are lowered. But the conception of the altered root is decidedly to be rejected. Aside from the fact that it is to be found in only one other instance (in the augmented $\frac{6}{5}$ chord, soon to be described), hence is certainly exceptional, it is the most irrational idea that one could have. The roots are in our conception fixed points, from which measurements are taken. The reliability of all discovered distances is guaranteed by the immovability of these points. Then one must not move them!

Against acceptance of the lowered root theory, is the manner in which the Neapolitan Sixth is used. It generally appears (167*a*, *b*, *c*, *d*, *e*) immediately after

I (but also after many other suitable chords), resolves generally to I^6_4 or V.

If the root were really lowered, it should frequently appear as in 167*f*, *g*. But of course these cases are not only exceptional; they are rare. That they ever appear proves, not that the root is lowered, but that anything can be good in the right place.

The Neapolitan Sixth is therefore best looked upon as a substitute for II in the cadence. In this sense it is often used as a $^6_4$ chord (168*a*), and also in root position (168*b*). Whether this chord, in cases where it does not have the typical function of the Neapolitan (substitute in a cadence), still deserves the name Neapolitan (168*c*), is doubtful but unimportant.

In 167*g* is shown the possibility of deriving the Neapolitan Sixth by the simultaneous lowering of root and fifth. If consecutive fifths are to be avoided, this approach is possible only when the offending voices are so inverted as to be a fourth apart, or through especially artificial voice leading (168*d*). Obviously this approach is neither bad nor forbidden. But in spite of the mediation of the minor sub-dominant, these two chords have

about the most distant relationship possible among chords. So if one joins them directly together one is close to that territory where any and all chords can be joined. Since, besides, this progression is hardly ever used, the student will for a time rule it out. For like reasons (as has been said) analogous connections from other minor chords are not available (III and VI, 156 at †).

The functions of the Neapolitan Sixth can be imitated by the sixth chord of any major triad, even I or V. These, to be sure, would not lead to scale chords (169*g* and *h*), hence are not now usable. If, however, we reverse the process, and seek, for the scale chords, such 6th chords as bear the same relation to them as the Neapolitan bears to I^6_4 or V, we have the forms shown in 169.

In these it must be noticed that the progression to the $^{6}_{4}$ chord, because of the cliché effect of the $^{6}_{4}$ chord, can easily lead astray the feeling of tonality. One can easily control this ambiguity, but it must be watched. Hence it is advisable first to use these chords in their other function, after the II—V pattern.

AT THE BOUNDARIES OF TONALITY

More observations on the *diminished seventh chord;* on the *augmented triad.* The *augmented* $^{6}_{5}$, $^{4}_{3}$, and 2 *chords* and the *augmented sixth chord* (on II and on other degrees). *Other alterations of II;* of other degrees. *Connections* of altered and wandering chords.

The chords described in the preceding chapter can be brought in much more smoothly, much less abruptly, through the use of wandering chords. So far, we know two of these, the diminished seventh chord and the augmented triad. It has been shown (p. 144) that the diminished seventh chord can appear in both major and minor, and if it is regarded as a dominant ninth with root omitted it can be built not only on V but (like a secondary dominant) on other degrees as well. Then when the two commonest deceptive cadences were explored (Ex. 141*a*), we found a possible connection with a large number of heterogeneous chords, thus demonstrating its eminent capability of bringing near what is distant, of making gentle what is violent.

In general the student will do well not to go too far at first in the use of chords from the minor sub-dominant region. For it is not always easy to restore balance with the panacea of the diminished seventh chord. Also the use of a panacea is very unartistic;—unimaginative and comfortable, profitless! Therefore I find Ex. 171 very bad.

I have explained why a gradually unfolding modulation is better for practice purposes. For the same reasons, however, I cannot favor extension of the cadence by similar means, as the latter problem is quite differ-

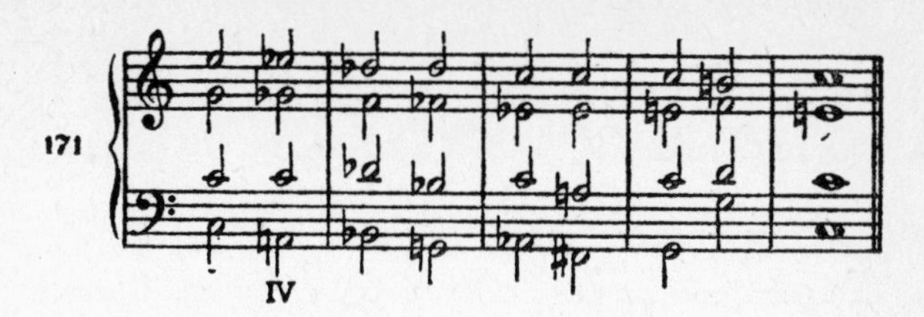

ent. The bringing in of so many relationships gives to the tonality an appearance of greater restlessness, in which more violent action is no longer out of place. Anyway, the diminished seventh chord can accomplish much, but not everything. The student should not, for example, use it every time he wishes to proceed from a scale-tone chord to one with alterations. The result may be abrupt; the abruptness is not necessarily unfortunate, but does not answer our present purpose.

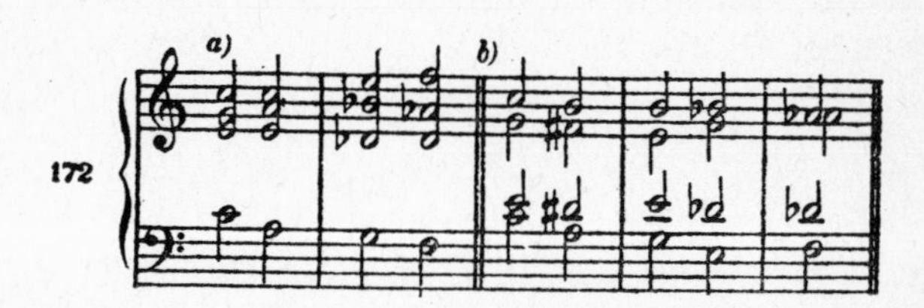

172 is naturally not absolutely bad. A good melody could lie above it; good leading of the soprano could perhaps save it. But in itself it is rougher, more abrupt than anything we have thus far allowed. Much depends here on the leading of the voices. It is best to plan each voice so that it resembles some closely related major or minor key. In 172*a* the tenor brings in a *d*♭ in a way in which a *d*♭ could hardly appear (as in *f* minor or *A*♭ major). Perhaps also the unremoved *a* natural in the bass; in 172*b* the alto and tenor voices.

In an earlier situation (p. 152) I have ruled out a

certain use of the diminished seventh chord which often appears in masterworks: the diminished seventh chord on V (ninth chord with omitted root) preceding a I^6_4.

The rule of the old masters seems to have been quite casual: the diminished seventh chord could be connected with any chord; hence also with I^6_4. But whether it is regarded as a VII (of *c* minor) or as a V, it weakens the following dominant, since it contains its weightiest elements: the rising and falling leading tones. Moreover VII is generally a substitute for V, so that the fundamental progression here is VII (=V), I, V, I, which is not very interesting.

The Augmented Triad

Similar in construction to the diminished seventh chord is the augmented triad. Its structure also is such that it returns upon itself; if we transpose its lowest tone up an octave, the interval between this tone and the former highest is the same as both the other intervals of the chord, a major third (174*a*). The minor third divides the octave into four equal parts; the major third, into three. We have seen that there are only three different diminished seventh chords; likewise there are just four augmented triads (174*b*). Hence, by reasoning analogous to that with the diminished seventh chord, every augmented triad can belong to at least three minor keys (174*c*).

174

If we take its two most important resolutions in each of the three minor keys to which it belongs, we find the following six possibilities: the same chord (to the ear), notated *e-g♯-c*, *e-g♯-b♯*, or *e-a♭-c*, has two good progressions from each of the three forms, one to a major chord, one to a minor chord. Namely:

175

in *a* minor to *a-c-e* (I) or *f-a-c* (VI)
in *c♯* minor to *a-c♯-e* (VI) or *c♯-e-g♯* (I)
in *f* minor to *f-a♭-c* (I) or *d♭-f-a♭* (VI)

Since its resolution to a major chord (III—VI in minor) is to a chord a fourth higher, we can use it easily to bring in a tonic, by building it artificially on the fifth degree of the desired major key. Then it is simply V with its fifth chromatically raised.

176

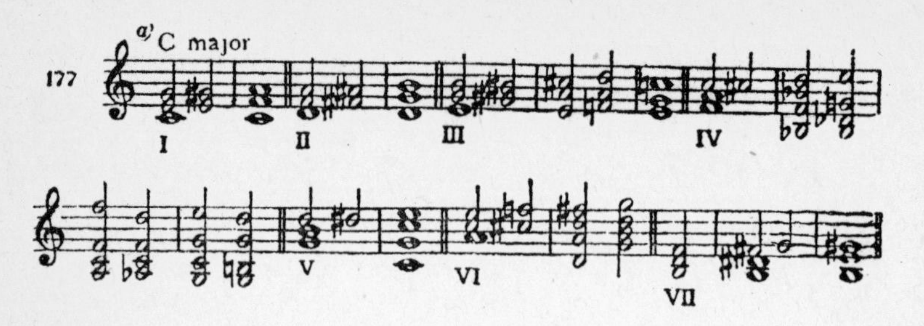

This can naturally be used also on other degrees, after the fashion of a secondary dominant; here sometimes the third too is raised (177). It can be approached from other triads by chromatic progressions (178*a*) or without them (178*b*). Finally, every triad can be joined with all four of the augmented triads (178*c*). For the augmented triad, by virtue of its constitution, as evidenced by its belonging to three keys, is a wandering chord, like the diminished seventh chord. While it has fewer resolutions than the latter, it is similar in that, because of its ambiguity, it can follow almost any chord. Augmented and diminished skips are good, since the sense of a strange tone at the moment it appears is not clearly established.

In 179 are some examples; the student may add more, if he wishes to try out all that has been suggested in the foregoing. With the augmented triad it is not necessary to discriminate between root position and inver-

sions. It is nearly always reinterpreted (as to root), hence can hardly ever have the feeling of a $\frac{6}{4}$ chord. To avoid unnecessary complication, enharmonic notation may be used. In 179*d*, for example, *a*♯ should perhaps have been written for the *b*♭; but in *C* major we prefer to avoid writing *a*♯.

The fact that the augmented triad resolves into a major key by the strong progression to a chord a fourth higher, even when it originates in the like-named minor key, favors its use in joining major to minor. The student can use this advantage in modulations, but I do not advise constructing a modulation with this chord alone (any more than with the diminished seventh chord).

There remain to be mentioned two more ways of handling the augmented triad, harmonically unimportant but by no means to be ruled out. By the lowering of any tone we have a major triad (180*a*); the lowering of any two gives a minor triad (180*b*).

These resolutions have more the effect of suspensions

resolved, since their fundamental progression would be a third upward, hence weak; but they are useful in preparing for a stronger progression to follow.

AUGMENTED $^{6}_{5}$, $^{4}_{3}$, 2 AND 6TH CHORDS AND SOME OTHER WANDERING CHORDS

As customarily derived, the augmented $^{6}_{5}$ chord is in major a II^{6}_{5} with root and third raised and fifth lowered; in minor a IV_7 with raised root; two chords with identical sound and similar function.

181

Both chords resolve equally well to I^{6}_{4} (182*a*, *b*) or to V (182*c*). Fifths occur in the latter progression, whence the position shown in 182*d* is preferable.

182

In the just mentioned derivation of the augmented $^{6}_{5}$ chord we come across again the idea of the raised root, which I consider incorrect in a system which measures from roots (which should therefore be immovable). I find it therefore more suitable to derive it from the ninth chord on the second degree in major or in minor, formed as a secondary dominant, *i.e.*, from the diminished seventh chord. Then, equally for major or minor, it can be derived by the following steps: II in (*C*) major or minor; secondary dominant; secondary dominant seventh chord; secondary dominant ninth chord; root omitted, diminished seventh chord; lowered fifth.

In the diminished seventh chord we have already accepted the idea of the alternative *e♭* or *d♯*; the chord derived from it may also make use of this enharmonic change. More important than the question as to how it is derived, seems to me the question, to what harmonic needs or possibilities it owes its existence. The answer to this question indicates also how it should be handled—how to approach it and how to leave it. It is usually found in the place of a II or a IV; namely in the cadence, preceding a I_4^6 or a V_7 (182). It can therefore be regarded as a substitute for one of these chords, preferably for II, since the progression from II to V follows the pattern of the authentic cadence, II to I that of the deceptive cadence. Hence its use is very simple: in major it is brought in like the chords of the minor subdominant relation; in minor, like a secondary dominant or a diminished seventh chord. In a cadence its moving to V or I is obvious, or sometimes to III (182*e*, *f*, *g*) is easily intelligible: II—V, II—I, II—III;—the authentic cadence pattern (a fourth upward), the two commonest deceptive cadence patterns (a second upward or downward): the three important rising (strong) progressions.

The question as to the needs and possibilities met by the augmented $^6_5$ chord is bound up with the same question concerning other wandering chords. Above all, such chords are good when they are suited to the surroundings, in that they are not the only such occurrences, and so are not incongruous with the style of the whole. Wandering chords appearing, so to speak, in company, usually give to the character of the harmony a certain coloring (*Chromatic Fantasie and Fugue* of Bach). Since nothing is bad in itself, it cannot be asserted that one of these chords appearing alone is necessarily bad. Yet it is evident that chromatic chords appearing in large numbers favor the establishing of a new *unifying concept*: the chromatic scale.

The augmented $\frac{4}{3}$ and the augmented 2 chord are to be regarded as other inversions of the same chord, the $\frac{4}{3}$ as the second inversion, the 2 as the third (184*a*);—or simply as inversions of the augmented $\frac{6}{5}$ chord. No new directions are needed for these. They can appear wherever the augmented $\frac{6}{5}$ can and the melodic line makes a different bass note desirable. The augmented 2 chord will sometimes cause a difficulty, as the repetition of the *c* in the bass (185*d*) is not very happy. Since this chord consists of four tones, there must be yet another position (184*e*). In my derivation from a ninth chord this would be the fourth inversion of the ninth chord. In the first mentioned derivation this would be root position—a good demonstration of how unnatural this conception is. Nothing special needs be said about this position. One should perhaps be very careful with the resolution to V_4^6 (184*f*), but the situation is not entirely new, as it recalls a similar one with the diminished seventh chord. The resolution to I_6 is much used (184*g*, *k*).

The so-called augmented sixth chord (184*b*) needs no further explanation, since it is nothing but the aug-

mented $^{6}_{5}$ chord without the ninth (or seventh), hence resembles the augmented $^{6}_{5}$ chord much as the diminished triad on VII resembles the V_7 or the seventh chord on its own root (VII_7). It is used where the augmented $^{6}_{5}$ (or $^{4}_{3}$ or 2) chord can be used, presumably for the sake of avoiding consecutive fifths (184*d*; see also 182*c*). Obviously other positions (inversions) of this chord can be used. It is not necessary to prepare the augmented $^{6}_{5}$, $^{4}_{3}$, 2 and 6th chords, after the manner of other seventh chords. The tone that is the seventh in my derivation is actually just a diminished fifth, since the root is omitted, and the ninth is actually a diminished seventh, both of which we have been treating freely. The illusion of a minor seventh, made visible by enharmonic change (184*c*), is given by the third of the supposed root, which as such certainly requires no preparation. The fact, however, that this chord is identical in sound (enharmonically) with a dominant seventh chord (*a♭-c-e♭-g♭*), will be made use of later.

major
a)
5
6 - chord
185
I
I 4 6
II
III
IV
V
VI
b)
I
V
II
III
IV
V
×
VI

c) 3 - 4 - chord
II
III
IV
V
VI
d) 2 - chord
e) minor
I
II

III
III
†
IV
V
f)
VI

As we expanded the dominant idea to include the idea of secondary dominants, as we built artificially diminished triads and diminished seventh chords, we proceed here likewise by suitable alterations, with the augmented $\frac{6}{5}$ on II as a model. On other degrees then we obtain the following chords (the student can construct for himself the other inversions, $\frac{4}{3}$ and 2, and the augmented 6th chord):

These chords may be brought in by using the minor sub-dominant relation in major, or through chromatic progressions. For the use of these chords on other degrees than II there are not many examples in the literature. I have certainly seen them in Brahms and Schumann. The examples here given show that they are usable, even though they may require strong means of reestablishing the tonality.

The enharmonic similarity (to the ear) of the augmented $\frac{6}{5}$ ($\frac{4}{3}$, 2, or 6) chord to a dominant seventh chord can now be used readily in this way: that the one is used (approached or resolved) as if it were the other. For example, an augmented $\frac{6}{5}$ chord on any degree is regarded as a dominant seventh chord, which it resembles

187
I
III
IV
V
VII
in minor
I
III
III

exactly in sound, and is resolved accordingly, on a pattern of V—I, V—VI, or V—IV (188*a*); or a dominant (or a secondary dominant) seventh chord is regarded as an augmented $\frac{6}{5}$, $\frac{4}{3}$, or 2 chord and resolved accordingly (188*b*). In combination with the idea of Neapolitan 6th chords on various degrees, this treatment effects a great enrichment of the tonality.

It is evident that there are chords here that could be understood differently. But, since we are not studying analysis, we need not be greatly concerned. We are working with a system which attempts to include as many occurrences as possible within a single idea. It is superfluous to say that there is not much purpose in racking one's brain to decide whether to write *c*♯ or *d*♭, *g*♯ or *a*♭, because of the harmonic significance. One uses the simplest notation. The fault lies in our inadequate system of notation, nowhere else.

Before I proceed to indicate the connection of these various wandering chords with each other, I wish to call attention to two other wandering chords.

The one (189*a*) is best derived from II_7 in major or minor, by raising the third and lowering the fifth. The raised third becomes a rising leading-tone; the lowered fifth a falling leading-tone. Here we have a combination of the secondary dominant principle with the minor sub-dominant relation. The other of these chords (189*b*†) is already known to us through the minor sub-dominant relation; it is identical with II_7 of *c* minor or VII_7 of *E*♭ major. But what follows it shows it in a new light; the *d* is really felt as an *e*♭♭. This enharmonic change would be especially necessary if one thought of it as derived from an inversion of an augmented $^6_5$ chord (189*c*). To be sure, the first chord can take the same resolution (189*d*). Thus the idea is suggested that the root of both chords is not *d* but *a*♭ (189*e*, *f*). This assumption seems to be favored by the circumstance (189*g*) that the second chord resolves also to a minor chord on *d*♭, as can be done also with the first (considering *f*♯ the equivalent of *g*♭) (189*h*). The *d* would then be the lowered fifth, the *f* (as *g*♭♭) the lowered seventh. On the other hand the most usual and direct resolutions of these chords are those in 189*i*, allowing them to be construed as II, with the progres-

a)
b)
c)
189
d)
e)
f)
g)
h)
i)
II
V
II
V
II
(VI)
III
II
(VI)
III
II
(VI)
I
II
(VI)
I
k)
major
I
IV?
V
*
VI
*
VII
minor, besides the foregoing
l)
m)
n)
o)
p)

sions II—V, II—III, II—I; while the conception of *a♭* as the root (VI of *c* minor) gives VI—II (fourth higher) for the progression to *d♭*, or VI—I (third higher) for that to *c*. The latter is of course possible, but not convincing.

In the first place it is simpler to build these chords, like so many others, on the second degree; the derivation from VI is far-fetched and impractical in actual use, though it may seem harmless enough in theory. In the second place, the *d* in 189*i* is the root of II; in VI it would have to be a mis-notation for *e♭♭*, hence a tone foreign to the key, as the lowered fifth on an *a♭* root (naturally the scale-tone fifth would be *e♭*). This same foreign tone must now suddenly become, in the chord of resolution (V), a *scale* tone (*e♭♭—d*)! Such a paradox is not impossible, but it is complicated. With the other conception it is not necessary; the only progression that could cause difficulties in explanation when treating this chord as a II, is that to a *d♭* chord (major or minor). Here we join a II with a II. There appears to be no fundamental progression. But this situation is not new to us. In the first place we have joined two chords before, where there was no fundamental progression. For example, when a triad was followed by the seventh chord on the same degree, or a secondary dominant by the secondary dominant seventh chord, the diminished seventh chord (ninth), etc. Secondly, a very similar example has come to our notice, when we joined the augmented $^6_5$ chord (II) with the Neapolitan sixth (II). It is certainly consistent to assume the same right here.

Now we come to the same advantage that we have gained before when we applied the alterations of a chromatic chord to other chords of the scale. So we have the chords in 189*k*, of which those marked, as well as one on VII, are already familiar. Several others are perhaps a little difficult to bring in, but not too difficult for the means now available. It is especially clear from this shifting of these chords to various degrees of the scale how "wandering" they really are and how incorrect analysis is which places them in this or that key.

Not much needs really to be said about these chords, for they are not especially complicated. Only the fact that they play a large role in Wagner's harmony, and that much has been written about them (I am not familiar with these essays except by hearsay), prompts me also to take a stand in the matter. The chord at 189*b*, transposed a minor third higher and enharmonically changed (189*l*), is universally known as the "Tristan chord." It resolves, analogously to 189*b*, to a major chord on *e*, which then should continue as in 189*l*, hence in *e*♭ minor, but is handled by Wagner as the dominant of *a* minor (189*m*). There has been great argument about this chord, as to which degree of the scale it belongs to; I feel that I can best contribute to the clearing up of this question if I refrain from proposing a new derivation. For anyone who has come to realize how rich are the relationships with even distant keys, the moment these wandering chords open up new channels of trade and supply new currency for exchange, it is immaterial whether the *g*♯ (189*m*) is regarded as an appoggiatura resolving upward to *a*, giving the chord the form in 189*a*, or the *a* as a passing tone through *a*♯ to *b*, or whether even the worst possibility is chosen, namely: that the chord belongs really to *e*♭ minor (189*n*) but, being a wandering chord, is reinterpreted and drawn into *a* minor. (This last relationship seems extremely remote, but is not really, for *a* minor and *e♭* minor have not only that chord, but other and simpler chords in common: for example, *e♭* minor VI is identical with the changing dominant, the secondary dominant on II, of *a* minor; the Neapolitan sixth of *a* minor is V in *e♭* minor; also the Neapolitan sixth of *e♭* minor is V in *a* minor.) Of course I am not really going to say that this chord has anything to do here with *e♭* minor. I only mean to show that even this conception has some justification, also that little has been said in merely giving a derivation for the chord. It might be derived from anywhere. But essential for us is its function, which is clear when we know what it can do. And why must the allegiance to a key be especially established at any price for these wandering chords, if we calmly refuse it for the diminished seventh chord? To be sure, I have related the diminished seventh chord to a key, but not with the idea of narrowing its circle of effective use, but only to present to the student its possibilities in a systematic way, so that he may discover through the various combinations what the ear has long recognized intuitively. Later the student, without referring these wandering chords back to a key or a degree, will best take them simply for what they are: homeless apparitions roving about between the domains of tonality, incapable of standing alone, but extraordinarily adaptable; spies seeking out weaknesses and using them to cause confusion; deserters whose main object is the giving up of their own identity; trouble makers in every situation; but, above all, highly amusing fellows.

If we are willing, then, to forego an exact derivation

for these chords, their effect becomes much clearer. We see then that it is not necessary for such chords to have a function resulting from their derivation, since the climate of their homeland has no influence upon their character (it will be shown later that many other chords act in this manner, though they may not seem to at first). They thrive in every climate, and it can be shown how another form of this chord in *Götterdämmerung* is resolved (189*o*) and led to *b* minor, providing another Wagnerian confirmation of my first derivation (189*b*); for 189*p*, the scheme of the citation 189*o*, is certainly a transposition of 189*b* a half-step lower. Even so, I do not say that such must be the derivation, for this chord appears in Wagner with the greatest variety of resolutions:

etc., and many could easily be added. These examples show that chords arising from chromatic progressions, and other wandering chords, have no need of a clear demonstration of origin and resolution in the voice leading.

As a guide in finding resolutions for such wandering chords it may be suggested that, since the control over chord successions through watching the fundamental progression is often difficult to apply, the control through melodic moves may be used as a substitute,—as has often been said. That is, in general the best connections of simple chords with wandering chords, or wanderers with each other, are those in which the second chord consists entirely of tones that have appeared in the first, or can be recognized as chromatic alterations of tones of the first. In the first examples these tone derivations should be expressed in the voice leading; an *e*♭ in the second chord should actually be in the same voice that had the *e* in the first. Later, when the function of these phenomena is clearer to the student, it will no longer be necessary to show their derivation through the voice leading.

In the following connections of wandering chords we shall still think in terms of tonality and build them so as to stress the key and the relation to the degrees of the scale.

1. Diminished seventh chords together (191); diminished seventh chords with augmented triads (192), with augmented $^6_5$, $^4_3$, and 2 chords (193), with Neapolitan sixths (194), and also (195 and 196) with the last described wandering chords (p. 209).
2. Augmented triads together (197); augmented triads with augmented $^6_5$, $^4_3$, and 2 chords (198), with Neapolitan sixths (199) and with the other wandering chords (200).
3. Augmented $^6_5$, $^4_3$, and 2 chords with Neapolitan sixths (201) and with the other wandering chords (202).
4. Neapolitan sixths with the others (203).
5. The other wandering chords together (204).

The connection of diminished seventh chords together is very simple, can take place through chromatic progressions in all voices, or even by leaps (191*b*); the only possible difficulties are in spelling. It is sometimes difficult to decide, for example, whether to write *e*♭ or *d*♯,

g♯ or *a*♭. For such problems it is best to be governed by the apparent key of the passage itself, rather than that indicated by the key signature, and to try to spell the chords in conformity with that key. One should not, however, be too pedantic; I prefer to avoid the use of double sharps and double flats, and find that the best notation is that with the fewest accidentals. It is well to notate each chord in a way that recalls a more familiar chord. Also, all progressions should be so treated melodically that at least fragments of three or four consecutive notes in any voice belong to some one major or minor or the chromatic scale, and the transition from one scale to another should conform to some recognizable scale. This notation has the advantage of being easily read, while the other does not even serve its supposed purpose, to show the derivation. Against the use of too many diminished seventh chords, it may be remarked that, while their effect is strong, there is little gain in this strength; it is too easily acquired for one to have much pride in using it.

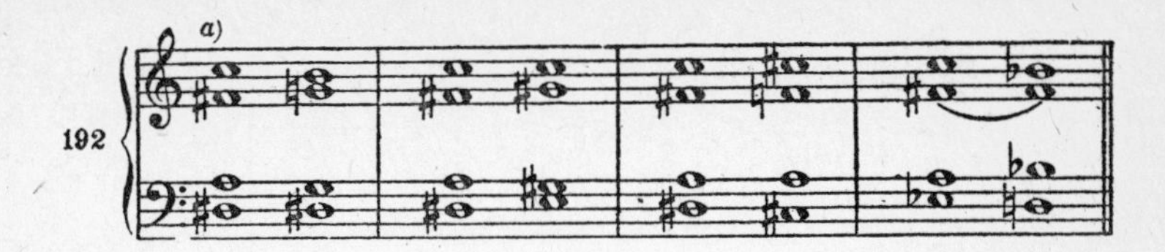

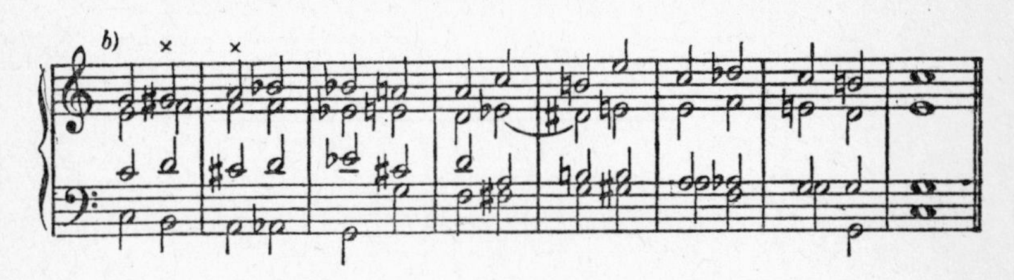

The connection of diminished seventh chords with augmented triads is illustrated in 192*a*. In 192*b* it is used in a phrase in *C* major.

In 193 we have the diminished seventh chords joined to the augmented $\frac{6}{5}$, $\frac{4}{3}$ and 2 chords on II. Those on other degrees can also be tried by the student, after the pattern in 193*b*.

The connection of the Neapolitan sixth chord (II) with two diminished seventh chords (194*a* and *b*) is

especially important. The one at *a* is to be regarded as on VI, that at *b* as on I of *c* minor (minor sub-dominant relation) or *C* major, giving a good fundamental progression. The third could only be considered as a V; to lead it to a II is hardly advisable—a falling (weak) progression. It is weak further because of the two stationary voices, with only one chromatic progression and the remaining voice, if correctly written (as *b*), making an unlikely move (to *d*♭). Admitting that this progression is harmonically worthless, we have still said nothing concerning its possible use as a means of expression; —witness the *Rhine-Gold motive* (194*d*), which rests upon the same fundamental progression (see also 173).

In 194*e* are Neapolitan sixths on other degrees.

Especial difficulties are caused by the augmented triads at 199*b*. There is hardly a position in which augmented or diminished interval progressions can be avoided without enharmonic changes. The student will do well to omit such progressions.

195
etc.
etc.
a)
196
etc.
etc.
b)
III

a)
b)
197
a)
198
b)
a)
b)
c)
199
etc.
hardly?
etc.
d)
e)
f)

The connection of the augmented $\frac{6}{5}$, $\frac{4}{3}$ and 2 chords with the Neapolitan sixth rests upon the fact, already mentioned, that these chords sound exactly like the seventh chord (and its inversions) that might be considered the dominant of the Neapolitan sixth. The $\frac{6}{5}$ chord is then usually so written, in our example *g*♭ instead of *f*♯. Very effective is its repetition following the Neapolitan sixth, leading then to the I_4^6 (201*a*). This repetition is well calculated to reestablish a tonality that is beginning to totter.

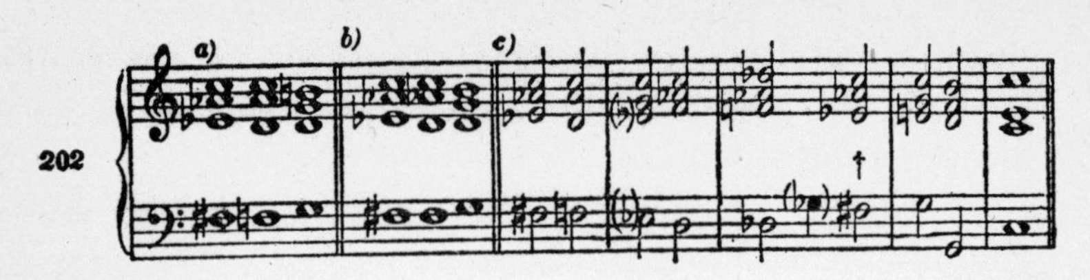

Their connection with the other wandering chords on II appears often enough, though the one in 202*a*, where the *f*♯ moves to *f*, does not exactly call for a V in root position (with *g* in the bass). While the I_4^6 is no better here, 202*c* is possible. The bass progression at†, also at 201*b* (†), *d*♭—*f*♯, is of course usable only if we think *g*♭ with an enharmonic change. Surely no trouble here!

In all these examples the voices have been led, wherever possible, as demanded in our first directions. That is, augmented and diminished interval progressions, consecutive fifths, etc., have been avoided. In the more difficult progressions naturally augmented intervals could not always be eliminated. At such times they are justified. Necessity knows no law. But when, as here, the relationship of such chords to each other depends upon widely distant keys, then it is pedantry to keep the voice leading in one key, especially one major or one minor key.

In closing we shall add a few more resolutions of the diminished seventh chord.

In 205*a* is shown the transformation of a diminished seventh chord into four different dominant seventh chords by the simple process of lowering any one of its tones a *half step* to become the root (actually our supposed root of a V_9!). If instead one tone (any one) is kept as the root, and the other three raised a half-step (205*b*), we have then one of four other possible dominant seventh chords. Or by a similar process it may resolve to a major or minor triad, by sustaining any one of its tones for the root (205*c*). If any two tones not consecutive in spelling (hence a diminished fifth or an

augmented fourth apart) are held stationary while the other two rise a half step, then we have two forms of the altered chord mentioned on p. 209 (205*d*). If three tones are held and one rises a half step, we have a seventh chord identical with a VII_7 in major or a II_7 in minor (205*e*). If any two tones consecutive in spelling are held and the other two rise a half step, we have a seventh chord similar to III_7 in major (205*f*). When any three tones descend a half step while the fourth remains, the result is the same as when three are held and one rises, but in different keys (205*g*) (VII_7 in major or II_7 in minor).

This sort of progression I mention only in a supplementary way, (1) because it is not always based on good fundamental progressions; (2) because this practice of making alterations in a chord is not consistent with our general practice; (3) because these progressions have usually only pseudo-harmonic significance; they are found mostly as so-to-speak melodic treatment of the harmony, where they give rhythmic interest to the flow of a principal voice. They are doubtless often used in modulations, but usually without consciousness of the fundamental progressions, hence rather senselessly.

MODULATION TO KEYS TWO, FIVE AND SIX TIMES REMOVED ON THE CIRCLE OF FIFTHS; TO KEYS SEVEN AND EIGHT TIMES REMOVED AND TO CLOSER KEYS, BY SUCCESSIVE STEPS AND INTERMEDIATE KEYS

For the first exercises in these modulations it will be best for the student to refrain from using the harmonic enrichments just learned. He should at first construct these modulations working again with the simplest means and making use of the simplest relationships. Naturally they could be worked out very quickly through the use of the materials presented in the preceding chapter. It is important, however, that the student should also know the simple, fundamental means and learn to achieve his purposes smoothly through them alone, so that he may develop a sense of form, before he ventures upon the others, for which no exact directions can be given because of the enormous number of possibilities. Then with the latter his sense of form will be a guide to correct procedure.

Modulation to keys twice removed is accomplished most simply by dividing the process into two steps. The original and the new key have few chords in common. From a major key to a key two fifths higher, these are in the dominant region, III and V, with the III closer to the new key. From a major key to a key two fifths lower they are in the sub-dominant region, II and IV, with the IV closer. A modulation is not impossible, to be sure, through the use of these common chords alone, and in most textbooks it is so indicated. In the upward modulation the succession I—III—V gives only falling progressions, but I—V—III is good (206).

Downwards, a useful and fairly quick modulation can be constructed from I—IV—II.

However, when one is not sitting in an examination, where one must hurry, one may have time to construct a real modulation. He can then use a process based upon essential, not accidental, relationships. He can then employ appropriate means for an appropriate end. Modulation to distant keys through a simple series of triads, as recommended in most of the textbooks, is absolutely bad. Such proceeding does not follow the pathway of art, though it does serve the purposes of many examinations, where the sheep are separated from the goats, for the protection of the latter from the former. This purpose it also accomplishes: to place in the student's hand an easily grasped and retained scheme that seldom misses—not even when he is a victim of the nervousness which is the most conspicuous result of examinations. There is seldom occasion for a quick modulation; certainly not where only simple harmonies are employed. Modulations to distant keys appear in the literature only where elaborate means of modulation are available and used. To be convinced one need only examine the scores of Bach. He will find that distant modulations occur through a series of steps, or if sudden through the use of the strongest means. These are usually diminished seventh chords, as other strong means were not known to Bach, but also, and this is very important, through passing tones and embellishments tending in the direction of the new key. Actually, a seemingly sudden change of key is almost without exception forewarned, either by a certain loosening (*Aufgelöstheit*) in the harmony or in the melody through alterations—usually enlarging the melodic progressions;—in the polyphony by characteristic augmentation or diminution; in the dynamics; in short in all possible ways. Very often, in the harmony, the suitability of the chord that is to be used to turn to the new key is indicated in advance. After this chord has been once used in an ambiguous sense, its reinterpretation comes as the fulfillment of a necessity. The student then is expected to accomplish the same results through harmony alone, with only triads and dominant seventh chords permitted, using as a plan for the whole nothing more than the accidental possibilities of a casual relationship. "Because you are the nephew of my father's brother-in-law, I am your friend." I belabor no aesthetic principle; I do not say, "That is not beautiful;" I do not forbid something as ugly because I do not understand it; but, if there is anything which is utterly lacking in artistic symmetry, it is this way of modulating.

It is certainly possible to modulate as these textbooks recommend. I prefer, however, especially in the province of simple harmony, the method of the old masters, who did not push a modulation along a straight line to its goal, but made breaches at several points in the tonality, allowing at least two or three main streams escaping from various points to join at a certain point for united action.

Keys twice removed on the circle of fifths are less closely related than those once, three times, or four times removed. With one remove there is always at hand the direct relation between I of one key and V of the other; I of *C* major is IV of *G* major or V of *F* major. With three or four removes the use of V of a minor key to lead to a major triad seems like the fulfillment of a necessity of this V. With two removes, *G* major I is *D* major IV, and *F* major I is *B*♭ major V, but *C* major I is not in *D* major or *B*♭ major. The reinterpreting can only be as follows: *C* major I (V) = *G* major IV (I); *G* major I (V) = *D* major IV (I); and: *C* major I (IV) = *F* major V (I); and *F* major I (IV) = *B*♭ major V (I). Thus is shown the necessity and the combinations. For an intermediate key the simplest is the key once removed in the same direction; then we add up two successive modulations, each to a key once removed: 1 + 1 = 2. Later the student can choose other (perhaps several) intermediate keys. For now we have:

from *C* major through *G* major or *e* minor to *D* major
from *C* major through *G* major or *e* minor to *b* minor

from *a* minor through *G* major or *e* minor to *D* major
from *a* minor through *G* major or *e* minor to *b* minor
from *C* major through *F* major or *d* minor to *B*♭ major
from *C* major through *F* major or *d* minor to *g* minor
from *a* minor through *F* major or *d* minor to *B*♭ major
from *a* minor through *F* major or *d* minor to *g* minor

The intermediate key is of course not so firmly established as the final key; otherwise it would demand a cadence. It is held together loosely enough to make possible the further shift, but still must be clear enough to remove the feeling of the original key. As long as the stronger modulating means given in the preceding chapter are not used, the student will do well to handle difficult tones in the manner of the sixth and seventh tones of a minor scale. Obviously two intermediate keys can be used; for example: *C* major through *G* major and *e* minor to *D* major. A few examples follow; the student is now in a position to construct a wide variety of modulations to the most nearly related (one remove) keys.

In the cadence the student can use secondary dominants and other altered chords, but it is advisable to use them sparingly, since the first part of the modulation is very simple. In 208*b* secondary seventh chords are used without preparation. Later the student will use these as freely as triads, even without the "passing seventh" which appears here. Obviously the deceptive cadence plays an important role in these modulations, as a means of preventing the two parts of the modulation from being too much alike. Also it is advisable to express one of the keys through other chords than just dominant and tonic (208*d*). If several intermediate keys are used, they should not all be minor, nor all

208
a)
C—G—D
b)
C—e—D
c)
a—G—D
d)
a—e—D
e)
C—e—G—b
f)
a—G—e—b

major. In 208*f* the bass, moving from *b* through the sixth and seventh tones of *e* minor, prepares for the *c*♯ of *b* minor,—a very smooth effect.

In modulating to a key two fifths lower it will be especially necessary to vary the structure of the two halves of the modulation. Perhaps here the student can make sparing use of secondary dominants and diminished seventh chords. Of course the cadence will then have to be more elaborate. In 209*a* at † we have again a secondary seventh chord with a passing, but

unprepared, seventh. In 209*c* the diminished seventh chord at † is to be figured in *F* major, despite the following $^6_4$ chord over *f*. The chord at ∮ enters as a Neapolitan sixth, but is then treated as *B*♭ IV. Obviously all these modulations could be made shorter, but they should not be, especially by the student. He needs to learn how to make use of the materials that have been given to him, and here is a splendid opportunity. I have purposely worked out these modulations in rather long phrases; to gain as much practice as possible is a main object. From the feeling for form the student will soon observe that, when he has made one part rather lengthy, the continuation comes under a certain compulsion. It cannot then be long or short according to whim, but makes an absolute demand: the employment of something special in the harmony, or perhaps in the melody; at any rate it is not free, but obligated—not through law, but through the feeling for form. The student will do well to keep these considerations well in mind; if he lightly ignores them he may stifle his sense of form.

When he has sufficiently practiced these simple ways, he may then go ahead with the use of more complicated means. I recommend that the materials be introduced into the exercises in about the same order in which they appeared in the foregoing chapters. Thus what has been learned can be reviewed and the number of possibilities increased.

In 210*a* two quarter notes are used in the alto to bring in the seventh of the dominant seventh chord. The student may do likewise occasionally, but he may also,

especially with the dominant seventh chord, use the seventh freely without regard to cross relation.

In 210*a* at the sign ⊕, the triad numerals II—I—II appear, although the chords have little resemblance to the corresponding chords of the scale. But of course we recognize in this II an inversion (actually root position) of the Neapolitan sixth chord. Here and in similar situations, for the sake of a simpler view of the fundamental progressions, we may adopt the temporary expedient (*Hilfsvorstellung*) of looking upon the Neapolitan sixth as a tonic, calling it a I for the moment. Then the following diminished triad must be its VII; hence we have I—VII—I, a quite familiar progression. Since however the Neapolitan is actually on the second degree, the passage that appears to be I—VII—I in *C*♭ major is really II—I—II in *B*♭ major with the Neapolitan treated as a momentary tonality (*tonartmässig ausgeführt*). The student should not label the passage as *C*♭, but just consider that he has used a temporary expedient in so thinking of it.

Keys Five and Six Times Removed

Modulations to these keys also are most easily accomplished in successive steps. They should be a combination of two or sometimes three separate modulations (such as those to keys once, three times and four times removed). Going to a key five times removed, the combination can be 4 + 1 or 1 + 4; *i.e.*, first to a key four times removed, thence to a key one remove beyond, or, vice versa, first to a key once removed, thence to a key four removes beyond. To a key six times removed it would be 3 + 3. Since this key is the same, whether considered six fifths higher or six fifths lower on the circle of fifths (*C* major to *F♯* major or *G♭* major), there are two ways of making the 3 + 3 combination, upward or downward. The six could also be a combination of 3 + 4 — 1, 4 + 3 — 1, — 1 + 3 + 4, — 1 + 4 + 3, or even 4 — 1 + 3, 3 — 1 + 4, etc. The five could also result from other combinations, as 3 + 3 — 1, 3 — 1 + 3, 4 + 4 — 3, etc., but is often done as 3 + 2 or 2 + 3, in which of course the 2 is 1 + 1. What has been said regarding the establishing of the intermediate key in modulations to twice removed keys applies also here. Secondary dominants, diminished seventh chords and other wandering chords will be very useful, but here again the student is advised to practice first with simple means. The following modulations are to be worked out: from *C* major and *a* minor to *D♭* major, *b♭* minor, *B* major, *g♯* minor, *G♭* major, *e♭* minor, *F♯* major, *d♯* minor.

In the examples much use is made of recently mentioned, more elaborate means of modulation. Thus in 211*c* the modulation *C*—*G* is brought in by the Neapolitan sixth; in 211*f* the Neapolitan sixth of *f* minor is introduced by the corresponding augmented $\frac{4}{3}$ chord. These means make it possible to omit the "pausing on the dominant" in the third and fourth modulations. I should like to call attention to a certain difference, if anyone should compare the "quick" modulations which I have censured, with these. It might be asserted that I place together chords so unrelated that the result is equivalent to those same "quick" modulations. But the difference is here: in the others these chords are supposed to bring about the modulation; with these they only introduce it, prepare for it,—cause the tonality so to waver that modulation is possible. Thus the goal is kept constantly in view and the means well suited to reach it.

e) C— Gb (3+3)
f) C — cb (3 + 3)

g) C — F♯ 3 + 3)
h) C· d♯ (4 - 1 + 3)
i) a — D♭ (4 + 1)
k) a — (1 + 4)

l) a–B (1 + 4)
m) a- g♯ (- 1 + 3 + 3)
†
†
n) a–G♭ (4-1+3)
o) a–e♭ (3–1+4)

p)
a—F♯ (4 - 1 + 3)
qu)
a-d♯ (1+4+1)

Upon this preparation of the final key rests the most satisfying effect of modulation. For example, in 211*a* the second chord, the augmented $\frac{6}{5}$ chord over the bass *e*, is a pointer toward the *g*♭ of *D*♭ major; the resolution to the $\frac{6}{4}$ chord is another hint in the same direction. They are not actually *D*♭ major, but just a step toward it. A similar example is in 211*b*; in 211*c* the third measure, which could be called *b* minor, points toward the *B* major at the close; in 211*k* the Neapolitan sixth over *b*♭ (third measure) points toward *b*♭ minor, etc. The student will find many other such in these examples. Of course he should try to do likewise. If the result is not especially good, it is no misfortune (my examples, to be sure, are no outstanding "artistic triumphs;" they should be taken as suggestions, by no means as models). The main thing is to keep striving for something. Whether one attains it is not so important.

A device recommended in most text books and appearing occasionally in 211, is the *sequence*. The sequence is a kind of repetition well suited to gain unity. Repetition, sometimes felt as monotony, rightly used gives a strengthening, a lifting. There are many kinds of repetition, useful one way or another in developing form (*formbildenden Zwecken*); a discussion of them, since they encroach upon the province of work with themes and motives, belongs properly to a treatise on form. Hence only the following general remarks are needed here. The sequence is an exact repetition of any part of a phrase. In the harmonic sequence a chord succession (at least two chords) is immediately repeated, but (and here it differs from simple repetition) beginning on a different degree of the scale, hence higher or lower by a major or minor second or third, or a perfect or augmented fourth. The harmonic sequence is a favorite means toward effective form, since it assures continuity and unity, and helps greatly in listener's comprehension by its broadly contemplative construction (since it repeats what might have been missed on first hearing). Beside these advantages, the composer does not need to exert his powers of invention for new ideas any more than is necessary to join closely and evenly the two similar forms of his thought. Since it is good in itself, the sequence has been much used; since however there is little real gain in such easy space-filling, excessive use of it must be forbidden. I have no objection to the student's using it occasionally. For him it is surely sufficient if he can bring it off, if he can work out the smooth tying together of the sequence unit in its repetitions. I have also no objection if he uses it as recommended, to make a modulation, so to speak, in two jumps (*in zwei Anläufen*). I do not recommend too free use of it; its construction is too mechanical to be very sympathetic.

The transposed repetition of a melodic fragment is to be regarded as a sort of sequence, even if the harmony is not in sequence. I find this kind of sequence more desirable because it is less mechanical. An example is the soprano in 211*m*; also 211*p*.

The student should choose for himself other combinations. If for a modulation of five removes he plans it as 4 + 3 — 2, it might be, for example, from *C* major through *E* major to *C*# major, then back (through *F*# major) to *g*# minor (212*a*).

A design of this sort (212*a*) might become too complicated; if one were to work out each part very fully the whole would be very long. With each part treated

briefly we have those quick modulations that I can approve only with some strong means of modulation. The student must decide for himself. If he chooses so complex a way, he must know that the example will be very long or that the distance between the successive resting places must be erased by the strongest of modulating means. 212*b* shows another solution of this same problem, with a less complex plan.

Modulations to keys as remote as five or six times removed, will not frequently appear in a phrase with

simple harmony, because a composition which modulates so intensively will require stronger means of modulation. The working out of such practice exercises with simple means will therefore never give so smooth a result as in the modulations to closer keys. Still more difficult are the keys seven, eight or nine times removed, which are more easily reached as five, four or three removes in the opposite direction. Thus modulations from *C* major to *C*♭, *F*♭, and *B*♭♭ major, taken in the other direction become modulations to *B*, *E* and *A* major. Nevertheless the more complicated route must often be travelled, so the student may well practice it.

For so great a change of key in so small a space as

in 213, examples in the literature can be shown only since Wagner. There of course the object is not to reach a new key but to avoid staying long in any one key. The harmony also is melodically treated; its richness, its active movement, its sudden twists and turns, correspond to like traits in the principal melody, to which it is suited like a countermelody. That this sort of thing can hardly come off well in examples and exercises, is indicated in my example 213,—indicated, though perhaps not proved, for I could certainly do it better. Nevertheless the student should also try it, as otherwise he will not become acquainted with his means of modulation.

HARMONIZING THE CHORALE

Like every art form, the chorale is clearly articulated (*gegliedert*). The articulation is shown by the holds at the ends of the musical phrases (corresponding to the ends of the poetic lines), which divide the thought into parts.

Characteristic of the chorale are the cadences (*Abschlüsse*) which close the phrases. They provide contrast, though contrast with coherence: those contrasts which are necessary in a tonality; those contrasts through which the tonality is made clear. With a slight exaggeration, which I shall explain presently, the entire chorale, or any larger composition, can be regarded as a more or less rich and elaborate cadence, and the chords,—perhaps not all, but at least those which close the phrases,—can be thought of as parts of that cadence. Herein lies the exaggeration: these chords would have had to be *ordered* toward an effective cadence. If such a cadence seems less rich than the circumstances which called forth its component chords in one piece, there is nothing to wonder at;—the outline is simple, the details more complicated. If one is satisfied with the simplicity of such a plan, then it becomes apparent that even the simplest cadences must be considered; perhaps even a cadence consisting of just one chord, the tonic, could suffice. Such simplification is unlikely, however, as I have indicated in discussing cadences, because the tonality can hardly be expressed effectively unless through its contrasts that motion is set going, that contest for superiority, in which the tonic will remain the victor. It is clear then that, for the building of this supposed cadence as an extract from the whole, the same triads are used, even though they appear also in other connections. Especially, however, I, then V and IV: tonic, dominant and subdominant; also the dominant and sub-dominant regions, hence III, VI, and II.

A slight discrepancy in this comparison: in a cadence, especially if it is short and simple, there is rarely a chord repeated (except I); in our hypothetical cadence the repetition of V or VI (or even others) is by no means ruled out.

An essential feature here, new to the student, is the treatment of various triads of the key as separate tonalities (*tonartmässig ausführen*), through the cadences. This causes no difficulty, as it is somewhat similar to the intermediate keys in modulations, where episodes appear in a foreign key, the characteristics of the former key are neutralized, but also the feeling of the episodical key is worked out of the structure by definite means. Here the phrase can end on a triad—and usually will—as if this triad were the tonic of another key. If for example a phrase were to close on *C* major III, the cadence should be constructed as a modulation to *e* minor, and this modulation should be prepared by what precedes it.

With a chorale melody before him, the student can recognize the phrase endings by the holds (*fermate*—𝄐) and can determine the possible triad for each close. (We assume that in general a new harmony will appear with each half note. Obviously two or more chords could be placed under one half note, but we shall not do so unless there is some special purpose.)

The *b♭* at the first close can be I, VI, or IV; the *f* at the second, I, V or III; the *c* at the third, V or II (VII will of course not be usable); the *e♭* at the fourth, IV or II, likewise at the fifth. The close of the entire chorale, the sixth phrase, must of course be I. The following considerations will determine which triads should be given the preference. The most important is the expression of the tonality. The strongest for this purpose, as we know, is the tonic, with the dominant and sub-dominant next. Hence the student will try to close the first phrase with the tonic. If the tonic is not possible, then V or IV may be considered, or as last resort III, VI or II. For the other phrase endings triads will be chosen which offer a good contrast with the first, if the melody permits. If the first ends with I, use V, IV, III, VI or II for the others. The repetition of a triad is not necessarily ruled out, for sometimes the melody gives clear indication of such a repetition. Quite otherwise, however, are those instances where a fragment of melody is repeated exactly or with slight variation. If possible the student should then try for a variation through different harmony. To avoid undesirable chord repetition a deceptive cadence can sometimes help (more on this later), but this necessity will not often arise. The last tone of the phrase is not sufficient in determining the cadence; the note preceding it, often two notes, must be taken into account. Since many chorale phrases have only six or eight notes, it could almost be said that they should be worked out backwards from the close, from the cadence. However, the beginning of the phrase must also be considered, in itself surely, but especially in its relation to the close of the preceding phrase. This relation should be carried out as if there had been no break at the hold, as if the harmony proceeded uninterruptedly past the hold. The two chords to be chosen here must stand in logical succession; the first of the new phrase cannot be chosen without a look at the last of the old. The student will have to determine first whether the two or three melody notes just before the last permit the use of triads which can build a cadence ending in the chosen chord; for there must be a cadence. Though it is only a partial close, not a complete close, it is still a close, and should be indicated as such in the harmony. So far, we know no other means for this indication than the cadence.

We examine first the first phrase. It appears from the numerals under the last three notes that a tonic cadence is possible. The *c* can be harmonized by V, the *e*♭ by II or IV, the *d* by I, VI or III, giving the following cadencing formulas: I—IV—V—I, VI—IV—V—I; also, to be sure, III—IV—V—I, but only with some caution, since between III and IV (a progression in the shape of a deceptive cadence) there is less direct relationship. Also the progression in the shape of a deceptive cadence, the "overstrong" progression, if it is used in accordance with its character, must have a sufficient occasion for its "overstrong" action. It involves (as does the deceptive cadence) a change of direction; hence one should first see whether the state of affairs demands anything of the sort, whether the deceptive cadence is a necessary solution, as in the following situation: when there is danger of losing coherent connection by going too far in one direction, a sharp turn the other way will help keep to the middle of the road.

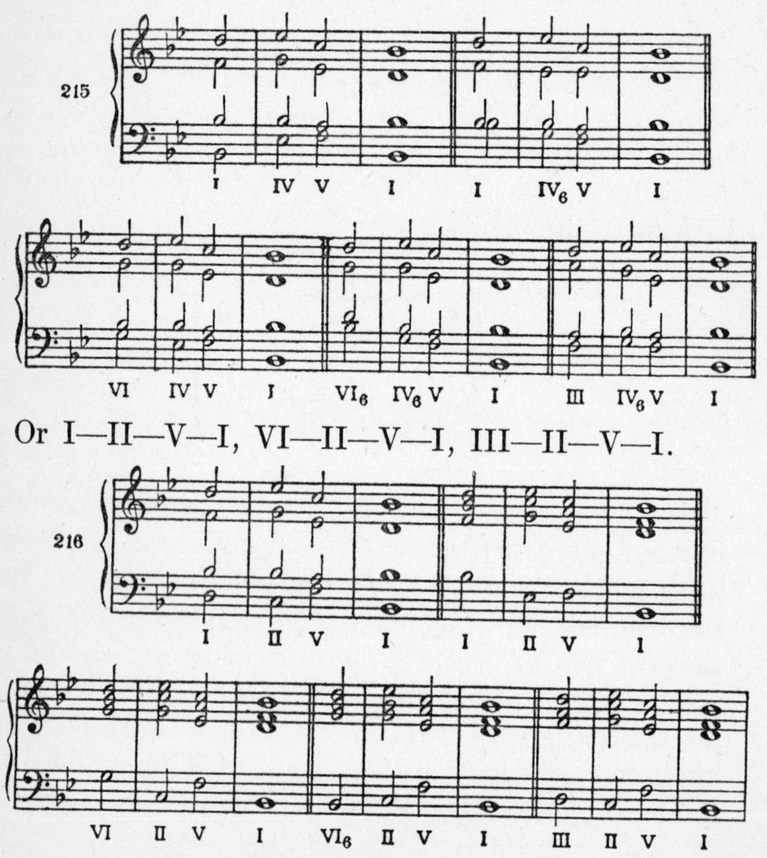

Or I—II—V—I, VI—II—V—I, III—II—V—I.

All these cadences are usable; since the tonic cadence is so satisfactory and can be constructed in so many ways, one might say that it is definitely suited to this melody. However, a cadence closing with VI would also be possible (217).

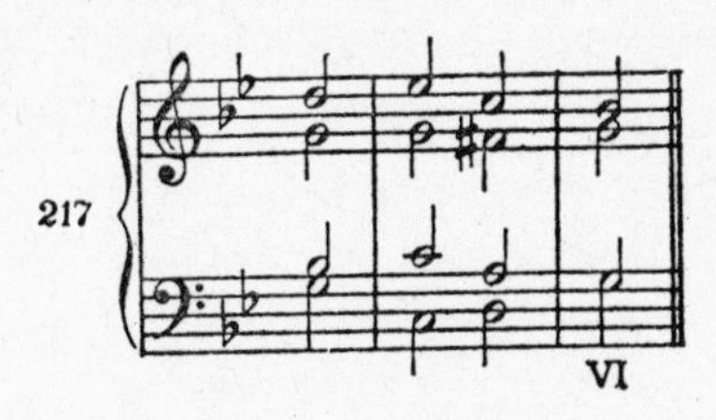

Most unlikely would be a cadence closing with IV, which cannot be carried out without bringing in the sub-dominant relationships. It is inadvisable also (218) because the phrase could then too easily be taken for *E*♭ major;—if possible, the tonality should be clearly expressed (through I).

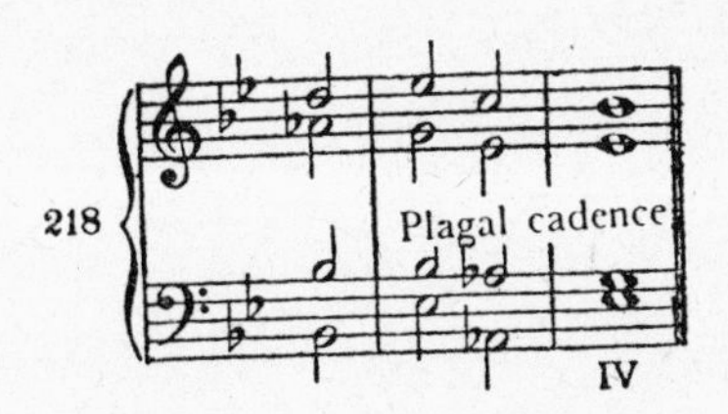

The VI cadence, which is certainly possible, should be used only when really necessary; perhaps when the same phrase is repeated, as it might be in place of the third phrase. In fact it is generally true in chorales that the root or fifth of a chord is more often found in the melody than the third. There is a historical reason for this preference: the third was discovered last, allowed only sparingly at first, and probably avoided in prominent places long after that. The student may give preference to root or fifth, but there is no need to avoid the third entirely. In Bach there are many phrases closing with the third of a chord in the melody.

If the student now examines the other phrase endings in the same way, he will discover the following possibilities for the second phrase:

It is evident that II appears here as (secondary) dominant for V. Why the chord just before this cannot be a V^6_4 (219*c*) is clear when we notice that the preceding *c* in the melody does not permit a chord that can be well joined to a V. For the same reason this close will not turn toward a III. In the turning to a V a difficulty is interposed also by the "unresolved" *e*♭ just before the *c* (because the *e*♭ does not go to *d*). Since the *e*♭ is left by a skip, hence not "resolved," before the region is reached where *e*♮ is possible, one should take care to place it in another voice, preferably the bass, where it can be "resolved" to *d*. It will be well if the chord under the *c* has an *e*♭, as in 219*b*, *e* and *f*. But then there is so little time left for the turning to the V that the cadence is in danger of being weak. Anyway, if an *e*♭ appears under the melody *c*, a V^6_4 cannot be placed under the *f*, because then the *e*♭ could not be resolved. Of course a tonic cadence could be used, but we have just used it in the preceding phrase; besides, it would be a type of cadence that has not yet appeared among those which we have studied, the Plagal cadence (as also in 218), to be discussed later. It will hardly be possible for the student to find any other harmonizing for this close. In Bach's *St. Matthew Passion*, from which this chorale is taken (simplified by the omission of passing tones and embellishments), this phrase is harmonized as in 219*g*. Since Bach has used in this place two chords to each half note, he is in a position to arrive at a richer and clearer cadence. The student may use quarter notes occasionally,—*but only for this purpose*: namely, *when through the use of quarter notes a richer harmonizing and a clearer cadence* are made possible, and especially when without them a satisfyingly strong cadence is not available. (We write the chorale melodies in half notes; Bach wrote them in quarter notes; I have transcribed the citation in our notation.) But only for this purpose! The student should omit entirely the adornment through passing tones and embellishments. At this stage we cannot look upon them as harmonic material. Later consideration will make clear in what sense they are. In 220 are closes for the third phrase. Not much else is possible here. The forms *a*, *b*, *e*, *f*, *g* and perhaps *c*, are relatively satisfying. The form at *d* is not impossible, but it will sound a little rough because of the scant preparation for the e♮, which has a challenging effect in so undistinguished a chord;—we seem to hear nothing else ("*als ob nichts dabei" wäre*). The (Plagal cadence) form at *g* is good in itself, but in consideration of the tonality rather doubtful, as will be clear if it is compared with the harmonizing of the first phrase in 218.

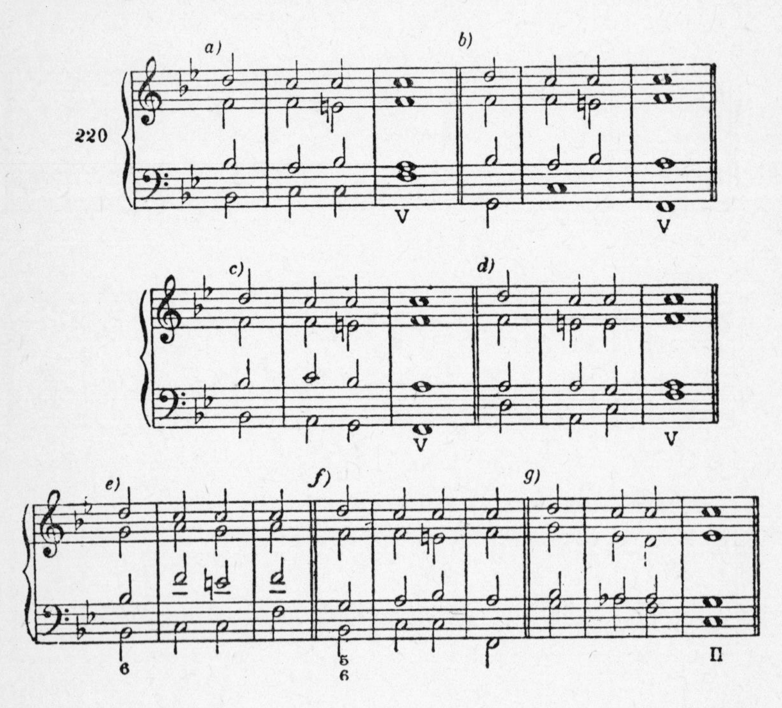

An interesting problem is presented in the fourth and fifth phrases (221), which in our simplification have the same melody notes (in Bach there is some variation through the ornamental notes). Here it will be necessary to harmonize the two phrases differently, and also to give an increase in intensity to the repetition. For the close II or IV is possible. There is therefore a pronounced turning to the region of the sub-dominant.

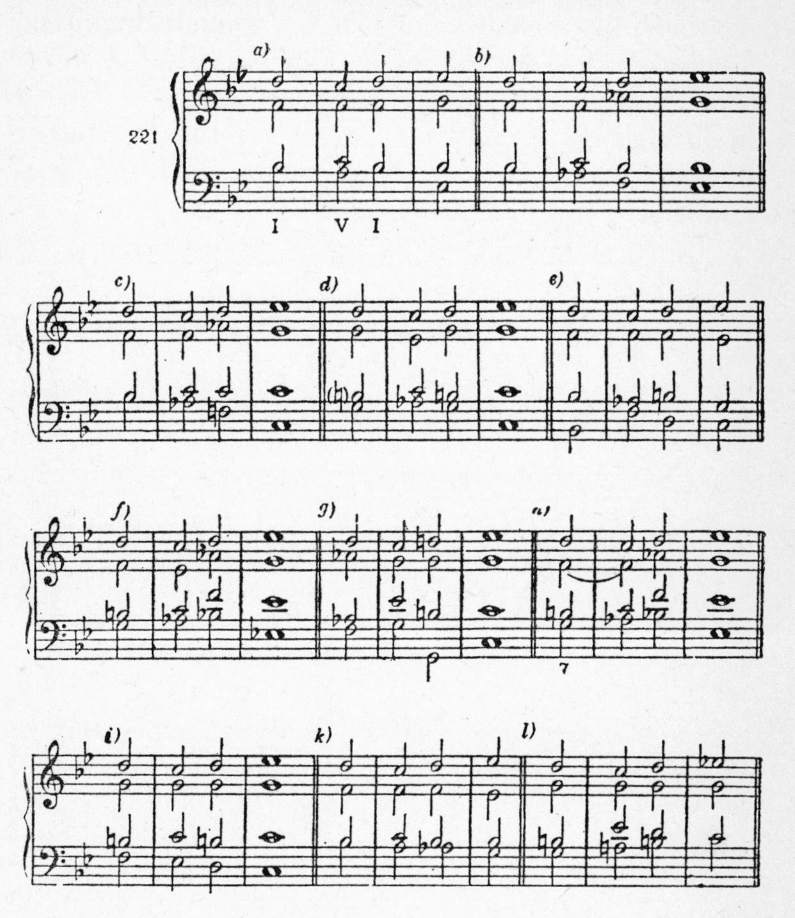

In 221 are several possible harmonizings for either of the two phrases; 222 shows several combinations for the two phrases together.

The simplest form is of course 221*a*, which the student will not miss for anything. The other forms reach the

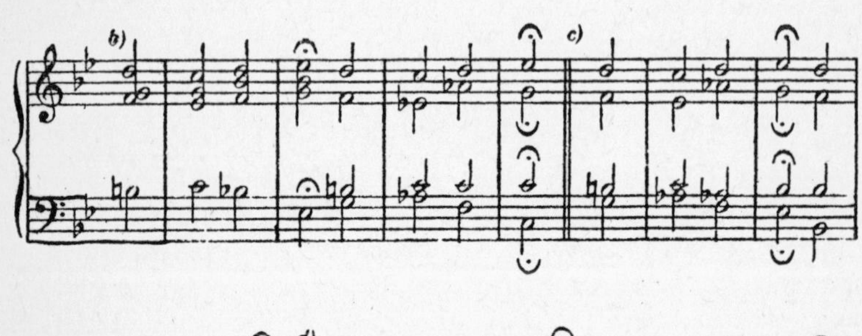

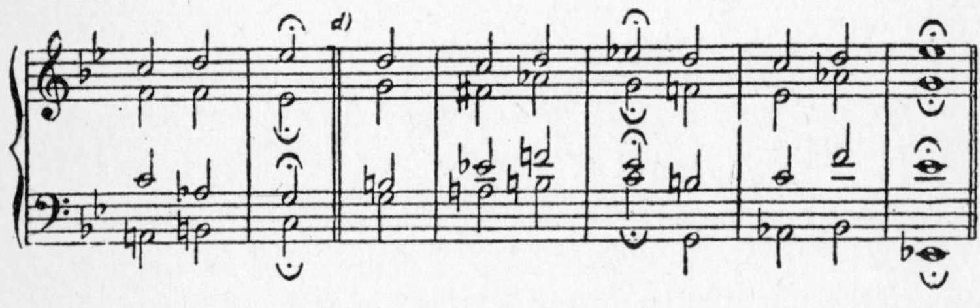

sub-dominant region through the rising leading tone *b* or the falling leading tone *a*♭, prepared in many ways. 221*i* is probably too simple, using only II and its dominant (secondary dominant). In general this tonic-dominant harmonizing is seldom used in chorales. When it is unavoidable here and there, the student should write it simply rather than to make it unnaturally complicated; the chorale is possibly based upon a very simple harmony, with any other ill suited to it. Here however the situation is otherwise; there can be ample harmonizings both suitable and interesting. Also

221*k* is not something that the student should use frequently. It appears in Bach, to be sure, but on the whole rarely; and then never from necessity, as it probably would with the student, but for a certain effect which the student has not at present the means to produce. For the succession of the two forms, the deciding question is whether it is better to close first on the *E*♭ chord and then on the *C*, or the reverse. Bach uses this form:

First II, then IV. Usually, however, the reverse would be more effective, depending upon the context. In general it is certainly better to use the II *after* the IV, because then it is easier to pass through V to I. Thus we recognize the strong triad progression, which here is transferred from chord succession to phrase succession. Only it is not absolutely stronger; for there is a very compelling effect in the succession II—IV, in that a minor chord is followed by a major,—a tentative, so to speak, by a decisive. After this IV the Bach harmonizing does not use the II or IV again (the II is used again only at the end as a secondary dominant, in which form it belongs almost to the dominant region), but proceeds toward the final I with clear preference for VI and chords that go well with VI. It cannot absolutely be said, perhaps, that this cadence results from the compelling force of the progression II—IV, but yet this tendency is very striking.

224 shows several possibilities for harmonizing the last phrase. Here there is not much choice; the close is too definite.

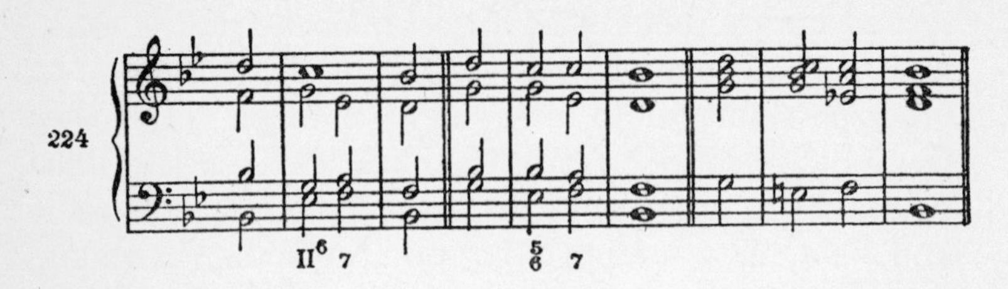

Many chorales, and sometimes separate phrases, begin on a strong beat (without a "pick-up") and have a "feminine" close, *i.e.*, on a weak beat. Generally then the last melody note is the same as the preceding. Here the cadence is always to be completed on the strong (first) beat, and then the entire chord is repeated on the weak (second) beat. Sometimes a suspension can be used on the first beat in one or more voices, and resolved on the second, to keep up the movement. When the note on "one" is different from that on "two," it must then be discovered whether both may belong to the same chord (the final chord, which then is to some extent determined by the melody). Then between them is only a shift in position of the same chord. A little more difficult is the less usual situation where a feminine ending consists of two different notes that cannot be in the same chord. I recommend then that the two last notes be increased to whole notes. Usually the first whole note gives an opportunity to begin a cadence, which is then completed on the second.

When the student has investigated thoroughly the possible cadences (perhaps without writing them out, if he is sufficiently practiced to discover them by just marking them), he must decide upon the closing triads, with the following in mind: 1. The final close must be definitely on the tonic. 2. The first or at least the second phrase should also if possible close on the tonic, with perhaps one of them ending on V; if there is no other possibility both may end on V or on I, but then the tonality must be very clear and some variety must be sought in other ways (different positions of soprano and bass, close or open position, different harmony, etc.). 3. III and VI are good possibilities for the phrases lying in the middle; IV for those near the end, II likewise, because then the rising from the sub-dominant region to the dominant region has a powerful effect. However, other combinations often appear. 4. It would make things needlessly difficult to insist that, beside the necessary repetition of I in the first and last phrases, no closing chord should be repeated. However, while such a requirement would be exaggerated and practically unworkable, one should come as near it as possible. 5. Necessary repetitions of the same closing chord should be separated by other cadences in between. This requirement, too (like all the laws of art), is exaggerated. The opposite can also be good and the repetition can have a strengthening effect. 6. The most important thing is so to harmonize each phrase that no violence is done to the melody. This is a matter of *feeling* and therefore *talent*; but we certainly know much that can help. An example is the heeding of such individual traits of a melody as I have pointed out in the second phrase, where the *e*♭ should first be neutralized before the *e*♮ can appear.

With the closes decided upon, the openings of the phrases can be chosen. The main deciding factor is that each opening should follow well after the preceding close. As has already been said, this connection should be the same as if there had been no stop. Then the opening should also prepare for the chord which will close the phrase. Thus the first chord should be at least in the neighborhood of the key represented by the closing chord. This kind of preparation is nearly always good but is not always possible. When it is not possible at the opening, it can take place gradually during the

phrase, even between widely different closes. Also a sudden turning in the midst of a phrase can often have a very strong effect.

While Bach (225*d*) in another chorale in the *Matthew Passion* ("*Was mein Gott will*"), which is in *b* minor, after the cadence on *b* (I in *b* minor), brings at once on the first bar the dominant (*E*) chord of the closing chord (*A*), 225*a*, *b* and *c* take more time and lean toward the sub-dominant region of the closing chord (*A* major or *f*♯ minor), *i.e.*, toward *e*, *D* and *b*. 225*a* and *b* make the change gradually, while *c* makes a sudden change of direction. In general the method is to be preferred which indicates the intention at the first step, as Bach does here. However, he himself does it often enough with a sudden change. For example, in the fourth phrase of the chorale, *Ich bin's, ich sollte büssen*, in the *Matthew Passion*, which is in *A*♭ major, a sudden turning to the dominant (226*b*) would be very agreeable.

Bach, however, chooses here a close on III as a major chord (identical with the dominant of the relative minor), even though the e♭ at the beginning seems to stand in the way, and brings it in as a surprising change. A comparison of the two forms will show, although mine could have been better done, how much more interesting Bach's version is. The difference will be especially apparent if each is placed in its context in the chorale. Then we see that in this chorale less usual triads have been chosen for the third and fourth closes, because these phrases are repetitions of the first two phrases. Such are the reasons which justify a skilled designer in writing abrupt changes. In this style variation is one of the most important requirements.

In 227 is an attempt at harmonizing the first phrase. This melody is not too easy to work out; it is fairly long but uses few degrees of the scale, as the student will realize when he comes to writing in the chord numerals and deciding on good progressions. It will be especially difficult, with the *e*♭ and the *c* each appearing twice, to avoid a repetition of II or V (with their appurtenances). Probably the best is the solution 227*b*, although it is unpretentious and the repetition of the *f* in the bass (toward the end) is not very happy. The Bach solution is truly marvelous (228). This would

hardly be possible, to be sure, without the use of passing tones and embellishments, which are treated here not as ornamental but as essential tones, not as non-harmonic but as necessary chord tones. In general the student must be especially careful to avoid repetition of chords, and especially of what I have just called their "appurtenances:" along with a triad an accompanying dominant (or secondary dominant) or one of its substitutes (a diminished triad, quasi VII) can easily be smuggled in. As has been said, such repetitions cannot always be avoided; hence a good solution is not always easy.

If the student notices some things here that do not agree with the directions and explanations which I have given, he need not be disturbed: art never agrees entirely with the laws of art. Art is broad; the laws of art are narrow. Even so, I believe I have given the directions broadly enough to include these instances. If it appears that at ∮ the interval between alto and tenor (an eleventh) is greater than that recommended in our directions, the purpose of this direction should be remembered: "a uniformly smooth harmonic effect." It is clear that the purpose is fulfilled here, in spite of the wide spacing. Or if at † the *e♭* is not resolved in the alto, the direction as given suggested "it is better," not "it must." Also it will be noticed that the *e♭* is resolved almost immediately in the bass.

The student should practice chorale harmonizing as much as possible. I recommend especially the working out of each chorale in at least two or three different ways. He should of course strive for the ultimate in smoothness. Seldom will he realize this ideal. The value of this practice is only in the thorough working of the materials; it is a gymnastic exercise that strengthens certain muscles; as in all training of that sort, the object to be striven for is not the perfection of each separate exercise but the development of certain abilities.

Cadences

In example 218 a Plagal cadence was used. This is often necessary in chorale harmonizing, as in 226*a*, where a Plagal cadence must be used unless the *g* is to be the third of a chord on *e*♭. The Plagal cadence is a formula which is capable of closing even large works, but is less clear, less strengthening in its effect than the authentic cadence. The most conclusive close is the complete cadence (*Kadenz*), but a conclusive close is not always desired; sometimes just for contrast other cadence forms must be used. Also from another point of view the exclusive use of a strong cadence can do harm: the articulation (phrase structure) can be overemphasized, *i.e.*, too often emphasized. While the melodic needs of a musical sentence hardly demand more than one or two complete closes, the necessity for keeping the phrases distinct but not too sharply separated gives occasion for the incomplete closes such as the half cadence and the deceptive cadence. While the authentic cadence uses the rising progressions, here a falling progression is in order.

I. We shall divide cadences into two groups:

A. Those in which the last three chords give the succession IV (II)—V—I (*authentic cadence*) (the succession VI—V—I, where the overcoming of the sub-dominant region is imitated outwardly by the strong progression VI—V, is to be counted in this category for lack of a better classification).

N. B. The cadence formula IV—I_4^6—V—I is regarded as a variety of IV—V—I: IV—(I_4^6—)V—I.

B. Those that do not close with that succession.

II. In both groups variants can be formed by:

a) Varying the chord positions (inversions);

b) Using the seventh or ninth chords on the same degrees;

c) Using altered tones (secondary dominants, minor sub-dominant relation, etc.).

III. Important alternative forms appear in both groups when the primary triads (I, V, IV) are replaced by their substitutes; in these forms the variants mentioned under II a, b, c can also be used.

IV. An enlarged series of cadences results from the transposition of the above mentioned forms to other degrees of the diatonic scale, or even, in the sense of widened tonality, to all degrees of the chromatic scale. The following transpositions can be used:

1. Inexact.
   a) Using scale tones only.
   b) Partly with foreign tones.
2. Exact (in the key of the closing triad).

I. The cadences in group A (IV—V—I and II—V—I; II as substitute for IV) are *complete cadences* only

1. When they lead to the tonic (not transposed);
2. When V is the dominant and is built from scale tones;
3. When I and V are in root position.

II. All transpositions of the authentic cadence to other degrees, whether using scale tones or implying the key of the closing triad, we call *quasi-complete cadences* (*ganzschlussartig*) and reckon them among the half cadences. *E.g.*, V(♭)—VI(♯)—II(♯), VI—VII($^{5\sharp}_{3\sharp}$)—III, V(♭)—I—IV, I—II(♯)—V, etc. (next-to-last chord in dominant form).

III. All forms of the authentic cadence formula that are not complete cadences (because of inversions, etc.), also all closes based on other chord successions, we call *half cadences*. The following are especially important:

1. The *Plagal cadence*, which is characterized by the complete absence of the dominant (V) in the closing area, while the sub-dominant region (IV, II) is usually well represented; the essential succession is IV (II)—I. It is usually looked upon as a complete cadence, with this seeming justification, that it is often used for a final close. However, it can easily be shown that many undoubted half cadences, when tricked out with all the rhythmic, melodic, dynamic and other closing devices of the composer's technique, can make a very satisfying final close. Therefore, to keep some consistency in the idea of the complete cadence, it is more correct to group the Plagal cadence with the half cadences.
2. The *deceptive cadence* (IV—V—VI, II—V—VI, VI—V—IV, etc.).

IV. The other half cadences ending on the tonic we divide into:

1. Those which replace the characteristic chords of the authentic pattern, IV(II or VI)—V—I, with less characteristic chords: IV—III—I, II—III—I, VI—III—I, IV—VII—I, II—VII I, VI—VII—I, III—V—I, VII—III—I, etc.

2. Those which
   a) Use a different series of chords; *e.g.*, V(♭)—IV—I, V(♭)—II—I, V—VI—I;
   b) Replace characteristic chords in these different series with less characteristic chords; *e.g.*, III($^{7}_{3}\flat$)—IV—I, VII($_{7}$)—II($^{7}_{5}\flat$)—I, III—VI—I, etc.;
   c) (As far as not already included) use other chords entirely.

V. Half cadences not ending on the tonic:
1. Strictly in the tonic key. These are merely transpositions of the two last chords of the closes already given, to other degrees of the scale. Many of the possible forms are unusual and useless.
   a) Those closing on V are especially used. Gently recalling the inconclusive closes of the church modes, they have always been useful for punctuation, for emphasis of the phrase structure of longer sentences. IV—V, VI—V, II—V, I—V and even III—V. Why IV(II)—V is a half cadence is easily seen by comparison with IV(II)—V—I; it is in fact an interrupted, half completed authentic cadence.
   b) VI—V and I—V transposed to I give II—I and IV—I: Plagal, hence half cadences. Not all transpositions of these patterns to other degrees are in good use.
   c) The half-cadence character is evident in those following the IV—V pattern: VII—I, I—II, II—III, III—IV and V—VI (already familiar as the deceptive cadence).

d) A frequently used close is II—III, called the Phrygian cadence; the II is usually in the 6 position, and the III generally has an artificial major third.

2. Closing as if in the key of the last chord (*tonartmässig ausgeführte*). Here the widest latitude is allowed in the combinations, because the means of modulation which we have learned, when used with due regard to appropriate style, will give a smooth and satisfying close. This kind of cadence has already been mentioned as a 'quasi-complete cadence." It may be varied by the use of the alterations of II which we have learned: secondary dominants, diminished seventh chords, augmented $^{6}_{5}$ and $^{4}_{3}$ chords, Neapolitan sixths, etc. Also the augmented triad, the artificial minor and diminished triads, as well as chords from the minor sub-dominant relation, may be used here as they are used in the authentic cadence.

Since the authentic cadence has already been illustrated, 229 shows only half cadences not ending on the tonic.

The half cadence can be used often in chorale harmonizing, especially where melodic or harmonic de-

mands make it necessary, but also as a variant to make a softer outline. Occasionally, but not too often, the student may use a deceptive cadence, which is found here and there in Bach. The phrase will move toward a I, but after the V a VI or a IV will appear instead.

NON-HARMONIC TONES

SUSPENSIONS, PASSING TONES, EMBELLISHMENTS, ANTICIPATIONS

Suspensions and passing tones grow out of the simplest of melodic patterns, the scale, or the scale fragment.

A suspension (*Vorhalt*) is a delay in a step-wise progression of one voice during a change of harmony. It is most characteristic when it makes a dissonance, but apparently it is not absolutely required to do so, for the *a* in 238 is an undoubted suspension, if the I comes in as the final chord in a cadence.

Most suspensions really do make dissonances; only then are they sufficiently striking. Besides, we are vitally concerned with dissonances as a means of introducing the more distant overtones. The suspension can be prepared or unprepared. The student should prepare it at first, but later may use it unprepared, as a free suspension or appoggiatura (*freien Vorhalt*). The preparation takes place as with other dissonances; the tone that makes the dissonance is in the preceding chord in the same voice. If the suspension makes a dissonance, it can be a second, seventh, ninth or fourth above the root of the chord with which it appears. The resolution of the suspension is a melodic move one degree up or down.

A rising leading tone will in general not become a downward suspension, nor a falling leading tone an upward suspension, but exceptions sometimes occur.

There is a rule which forbids the appearance of the tone of resolution along with the suspension.

Exceptions to this rule are so numerous that it is hardly taken seriously today. In close position it does not sound very well on the piano, but in the choruses of Bach it appears very often (and also in piano and other works).

From the motet, *Komm Jesu, komm* (Soprano I and Alto II at *sf*). An exception to the strictest form of the rule occurs in the bass of 241 *c*, *d*, *e*.

Suspensions may occur in two or more voices at once.

The harmony may change as the suspension resolves, so that a different chord appears with the tone of resolution from that appearing with the suspension.

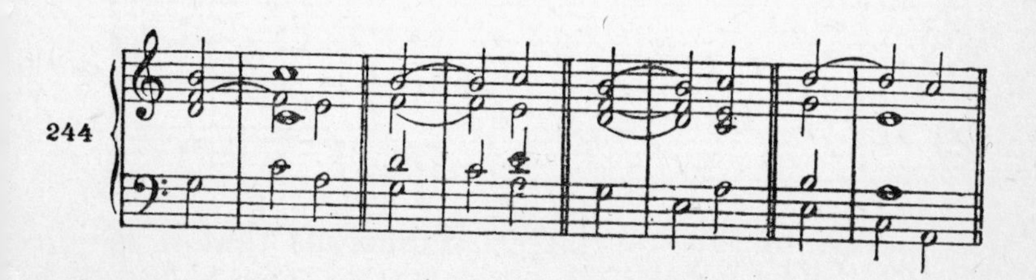

Obviously nothing should arise through the suspension that would otherwise be forbidden; hence no consecutive octaves or fifths. A suspension may be left by a leap, in the so-called ornamental (or interrupted,—*unterbrochen*) resolution, in which one or more notes appear between the suspension and its resolution. Without knowing all the recognized ornamental forms, one can use freely in this way any form that is remembered.

The ornamental tones will usually weave about or circumscribe the tone of resolution; they will lie melodically very close to it or else will belong to the chord; or they may be a mixture of both (245*c*).

I wish to call attention to a few well known forms, in which the turning point rules in minor are partly set aside (245*d*, *e*, *f*). As can be seen, the progression of the seventh tone to the eighth is interrupted or delayed while the sixth is interpolated.

The free suspension approaches the embellishment. For the prepared suspension there was once the rule that it must come on the strong beat. Only exceptionally could it appear on a weak beat. In the end the exceptions appeared almost more often than the rule. Obviously free suspensions can also appear on a weak beat. Then it is really hardly different from an embellishment. Either way, the resolution is important. But even in popular waltzes there are such instances as in 246, where the *d* leaps directly to the *b♭*.

The *d* and the *b♭* are embellishments (*Wechselnoten*) to the *c*, but the *c* is itself foreign to the harmony. With the same right suspensions can of course be left by a leap. Thus the dissonances in Schumann's *Ich grolle nicht* (247 +, †, ⊕) are either unresolved seventh chords or unresolved suspensions. They can be as well one as the other; it suffices to call them sevenths. The student will do well at least to indicate the resolution, though the resolution may be ornamental.

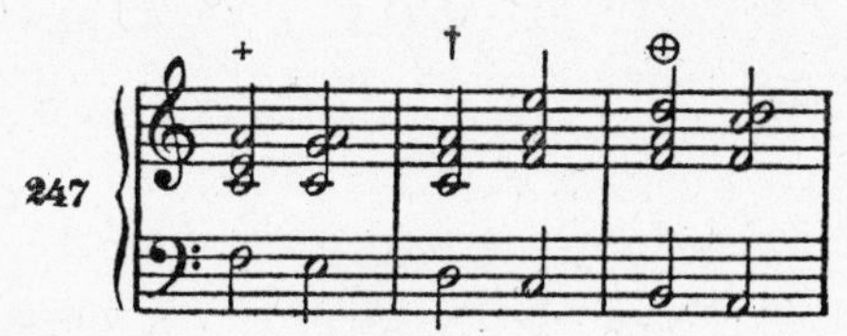

The passing tone (*Durchgangsnote*) we have often mentioned. It is the scalewise melodic joining of two melody tones at least a third apart, by filling in the intervening tones of the scale. If the two tones are a fourth apart, two passing tones would be inserted.

It is apparent that the first and last tones of the group will be consonances (chord tones). If passing tones join notes a fifth apart, then of course not all three can well be dissonances.

The *e* (249*a*) is a consonance; the two passing tones joining a fourth can both be dissonant (249*b*). Passing tones can appear in several voices at the same time.

Consecutive fifths and octaves arising from passing tones are just as objectionable as others.

In the older theory these consecutives were not ignored in passing tones, or sufficiently covered by suspensions. The theory was right; they are just as bad, or just as little bad, as anywhere else. The student may often wish to use a passing tone to prepare a suspension. This practice was not allowed by the strict, all too strict rule; but there is really no valid objection to it, as it appears everywhere in masterworks.

Accidental harmonies sometimes result from the simultaneous appearance of passing tones. These can be regarded as actual chords, as well as combinations of non-harmonic tones.

Passing tones can obviously be taken also from the chromatic scale. No difficulty needs arise here, if we recall our secondary dominants and keep in mind the idea of passing tones as a simple melodic form (scale fragment).

An outstanding service is given by passing tones in the use of wandering chords, where for example a reinterpreting is brought about through the use of a passing tone, causing two different turns of phrase, as 255*a* and *b*, to be united as at 255*c*.

255

An outstanding means of modulation; see also 256*a*.

256

The same thing can occur without wandering chords, as at 256*b*, where the transition from major to minor is greatly favored by the chromatic appearance of the *e*♭ and the passing tones *b*♭ and *a*♭.

The following is often seen:

257

And these likewise:

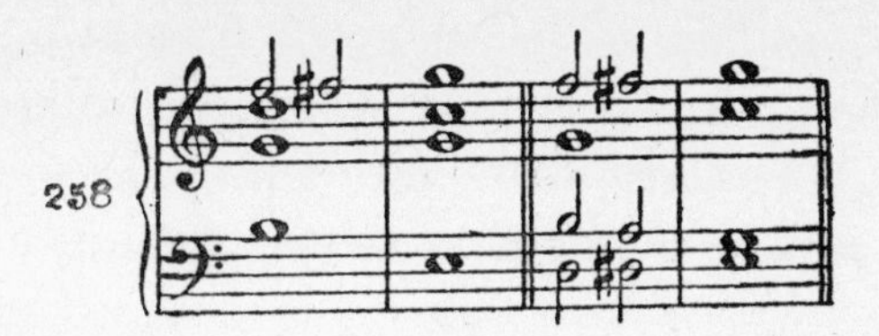

It is obvious that the student can write more daring combinations, the more closely he keeps to the oldest melodic form, the scale, especially the chromatic scale.

With altered or wandering chords the effect will nearly always be very smooth. Very often wandering chords can be led through passing tones to unaltered chords and vice versa, an excellent device in modulation, excellent also for enriching the cadence.

Here and in many other instances passing tones give rise to chords which are already known in more stable forms.

To list everything that could possibly appear would of course be impossible. The student will do best, as I have already said, if he will follow the oldest melodic form, the scale fragment, including of course the chromatic scale. An assignment that appears in nearly all the textbooks gives a musical sentence in half or whole notes, to be ornamented by the addition of suspensions and passing tones; of this I must heartily disapprove. This assignment is laughable; unartistic in the highest degree. This decking out with ornaments, this "tattooing," as Adolf Loos calls it, is childishness. I have no objection if the student occasionally makes corrections in a completed passage, in which appear passing tones and suspensions *which occurred to him at the same time as the melody and the harmony*, if he for example improves an awkward progression with a passing tone or revives a stagnating rhythm with a suspension. But the student needs to develop the ability to *conceive these non-harmonic tones along with the rest of the harmony*. This is not as difficult as it may appear; a preliminary process is entirely superfluous. The student must not use too many passing tones and embellishments, unless they occur to him naturally. I recommend rather that he do much experimenting, on paper or at the piano, seeking new combinations and progressions, then working them over into musical sentences. Working them over: here we have a better exercise than decorating; thus we develop the ability to bring in and handle these details in a natural way.

The embellishment (*Wechselnote*; lit. "changing note") is best explained as a fully notated trill (*Manier*) or as a motive. Usually, at least in its simplest form, it belongs to a figure in which one or more non-harmonic tones circumscribe or play about a chord tone (261).

Such an embellishment is, if you will, a trill (*Triller*) or a trill with afterbeat (*Nachschlag*), which would usually appear as in 262.

In the old ornaments (*Manieren*)—those given here are from Heinrich Schenker's *Ein Beitrag zur Ornamentik*—the student will find many examples which, played slowly, are certainly embellishments, even if one does not wish to recognize them as such in fast tempo. In nearly every instance, a principal tone is embellished by the *next* tone of the scale. The embellishment usually acts likewise, but not necessarily, as we know from the ornamentally resolved suspension, where a suspension is combined with embellishments. Among the much used forms of embellishments are the following:

Obviously chromatic tones can also be used as embellishments, at first perhaps with some caution.

The anticipation (*Vorausnahme*) is, in a way, the opposite of a suspension. In the latter one or more voices delay during a change of harmony; in an anticipation they move too early, so to speak.

In 265 a suspension (*a*) and an anticipation (*b*) are placed side by side for comparison. Like the suspension the anticipation can occur in one voice or in several.

When the student has developed some assurance in the use of non-harmonic tones, working in the manner that I have recommended, he should have little difficulty in realizing their possibilities, and he will have no need of the kind of exercise to which I object: to try to give an illusion of flesh and blood by draping a skeleton with rags. On the contrary he will soon be able to plan these non-harmonic combinations with the same foresight with which he constructs his harmonies. They will then cease to be accidental occurrences and begin to be governed by law, only a law that he cannot put into words. That a real master never does anything so unartistic as that other type of exercise, even under the excuse of harmonic sketches to be worked out later, will certainly be recognized by anyone who examines carefully a Bach chorale. Here is the one already cited from the *Matthew Passion*:

A first glance will show that we have not here a poverty stricken or uninteresting harmony set right by external adornment. Take each separate voice; all are pure melody, often as good as the chorale melody itself. A different purpose here, surely, from that other proposition! Then try to remove any unnecessary embellishments. For the most part it will be nearly impossible, or at least will leave things so rough that it never could have been Bach; perhaps not entirely impossible; though nearly all that seems to be ornament was born with the rest, there is still more that is good. One can live after losing a little toe, but one has no longer a well formed foot. In the first phrase are passing tones in bass, tenor and alto. It is clear that these are chords; their harmonic purpose lies in the problem of harmonizing a melody that appears three times (note the repeat and the next-to-last phrase) in such a way that the harmony, which might easily have very few chords, will yet give with a few powerful strokes the main features of the key (I, IV, V), but still will not be so rich as to prevent the last repetition from being richer and more interesting. Thus the triads of the sub-dominant region are relegated to the weak beats of the measure, where they have less force; but moving faster they appear oftener, equalizing that weakness. So it is that unequal forces are brought into equilibrium, by applying them to unequal lever arms. The second phrase returns to the principal key in hesitating fashion. Nearly at the last moment (*) the *a* in the bass still suggests the major key. The reason is clear: the chorale hovers between *D* major and *b* minor, as the cadences show; it would hardly be satisfactory to have *b* minor too firmly established in the beginning. The decision comes later. The *a* has therefore a definite function: to postpone the decision! It is therefore no ornament! In the third phrase the eighth notes which appeared at first as an imitation of the first four notes of the melody, have become a smaller but important motive that governs the figuration of the entire middle portion; hence they are not ornaments but essential constructive material. The next phrases are so complicated that I prefer not to go into them; it would be impossible to discuss them briefly. The relationships of the chords, regardless of whether their fundamental significance is more or less apparent, or whether they enter forcefully or are brought in by voices moving ornamentally,—these relationships are so firmly established in any true work of art by the essential structure, that the voices that build them, however they may also enrich the whole with decorative detail, however active and involved their melodic lines may be, can never really be looked upon as mere decoration. They can no more be omitted than parts of a steel structure. The audacity that supposedly leaves beauty (the essential function) to be added later, should be applied by one of these ornamenters first to a steel construction job as a practical experiment before he recommends it to a student. If he stands underneath during the construction, he will never recommend it again. Only in art are people so conscienceless,—in art, where there are no falling steel girders to take over the guidance of the enfeebled intelligence. It might be argued that these are only practice exercises, that later the student will do differently. Then these are immoral exercises; one cannot learn morals by practicing immorality. The teacher's example should be a good example. A good example is too often demanded of the student, too seldom of the teacher.

SOME OBSERVATIONS ON NINTH CHORDS

It is not necessary to have special rules for the treatment of ninth chords. The careful student can apply the rules for seventh chords; *i.e.*, let the dissonance move one degree down, progress to a chord a fourth higher.

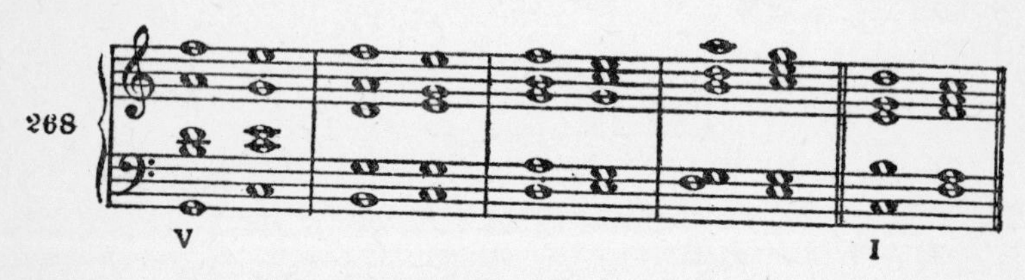

Caution: fifths!

The deceptive resolution must also be just as good, or so it would seem, as in the seventh chord; for if the seventh can remain stationary in resolving, surely the ninth can do the same, while the root ascends (269).

All of this results from situations in voice leading, is hence justified (for example, by scalewise moves), and it follows from my statements that the system of dissonances satisfies all requirements if it accounts for all the situations arising in voice leading. To leap from a dissonance, however, would be going considerably farther.

To prove the existence of the ninth chord, it should

suffice to mention, aside from its appearance as a suspension, the dominant seventh chord with major or minor ninth, which no one seems to question. If one refuses to accept ninth chords on other degrees of the scale, at least it must be recognized that the secondary dominants can have major or minor ninths, making a secondary dominant ninth possible on each degree, even if they are not used also as scale-tone chords.

As far as they have minor ninths they are no more difficult to bring into the key than are the diminished seventh chords formed from them, and those with major ninths should make no more difficulty than the corresponding seventh chords. Obviously all the alterations usable with seventh chords can be applied also to these, for example:

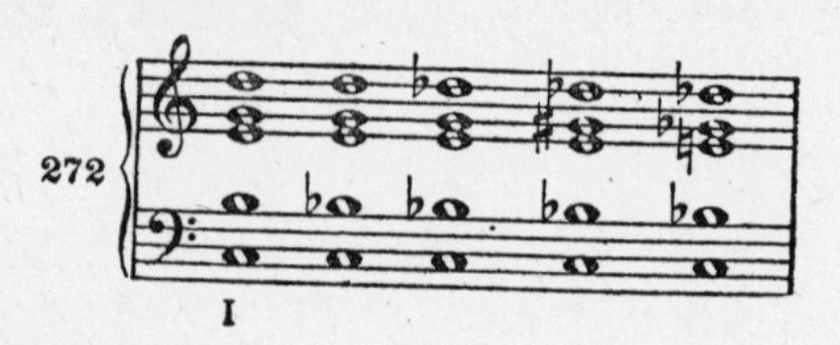

These chords are very useful when they are regarded as wandering chords or when they are joined to wandering chords as in the example from my *Sextet*.

In using ninth chords the student will do well to try for simplicity at first. Then he may investigate the variants, formed after the fashion of secondary dominants, following the suggestions given here. Later he may try the connections with wandering chords. Obviously he will do best here by following the rules as closely as possible.

SOME ADDITIONAL IDEAS THAT ENLARGE THE SYSTEM

1. Alterations of Triads, Seventh Chords and Ninth Chords

The important chromatic alterations to which triads are susceptible have already been made available to the student in the presentation of the secondary dominants, the minor sub-dominant relation, the Neapolitan sixth, the augmented $^6_5$ chord, etc. Here we shall undertake a survey of the whole matter, reviewing what has already been presented and supplying important omissions, though no pretension is made to completeness.

Every tone of a triad can be chromatically raised or lowered. One tone, two or all three can be altered simultaneously. I do not look with favor on the idea of an altered root, but prefer to consider it as a new or substitute root. My reasons for this view were given in the discussion of the Neapolitan sixth.

The lowered third in major triads and the raised third in minor triads give well known forms.

Alterations of the fifth in major and minor triads:

Major triads with fifth raised and third lowered:

Lowered third and fifth in a major triad, lowered fifth in minor:

Minor triad with lowered fifth and raised third:

Major or minor triad with lowered root:

Major triad with lowered root and third:

Major or minor triad with raised fifth and lowered root (by enharmonic change):

Major triad with raised fifth, lowered third and root; minor triad with raised fifth and third, lowered root (enharmonic):

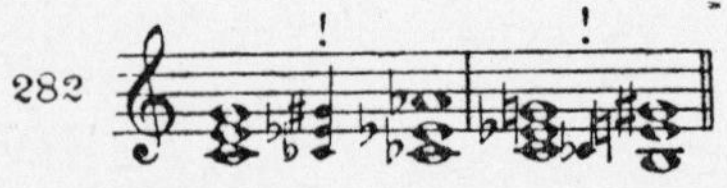

Major triad with lowered third and raised root, minor triad with raised root: 283*a*; major triad with lowered fifth and raised root, minor triad with lowered fifth, raised third and root: 283*b*; major triad with lowered third and fifth, raised root, minor triad with lowered fifth and raised root: 283*c*.

In some of these instances the altered root gives a chord built upon a different root. In other instances it is more practical, unless one wishes to enter the vain controversy on spelling, to use enharmonic notation and write, for example, *c-e♭-a♭* instead of *c-e♭-g♯*; although the rule for alterations is usually given: upward alterations are indicated with a ♯ or ※ (sometimes ♮), downward with ♭, ♭♭ or ♮; or, in general, the alteration uses the same degree of the staff with the appropriate sharp or flat.

I prefer, in place of a complicated notation, which often results from this pedantic exactness, to use a combination that recalls a familiar chord, as is possible with most of these chords. In other instances one will give attention to the voices and at least construct them simply. Thus I should replace 284*b* by 284*c* (as in 284*d* from the *Scherzo* of the *Sonata Op. 26* of Beethoven).

285 gives simple examples; 286 more complicated.

Neapolit Sixth

etc.

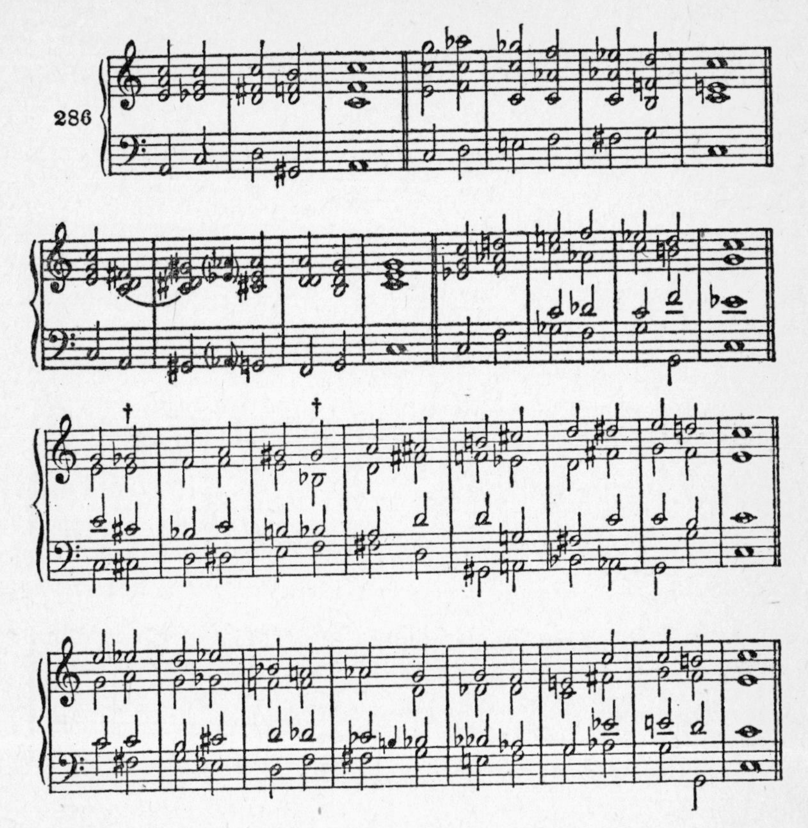

Sometimes a chord will sound harsh; 283*c*, for example, which appears in 286 at † (also on other degrees). It resembles an incomplete V_7; its missing third gives it an awkward effect. It is still not entirely useless. That a chord which is certainly harsh appears in a work of the "classical" period will perhaps reconcile the sensitive, if they realize that their sensitivity to harsh chords is the sensitivity of Figaro. Figaro, we recall, has not really sprained his toe; he only pretends to feel the pain.

In the alterations of seventh chords I shall only indicate the possibilities, giving a few of the connections.

The student should for a while keep carefully in mind that the main excuse for the use of alterations is the need for an artificial leading tone. The upward alteration should preferably proceed upward another half-step; the downward alteration, creating a falling leading tone, another half-step down. It is possible, however, for an altered tone to remain stationary, or sometimes to proceed in the direction opposite to its leading-tone tendency. Such progressions would seem to be necessary in appearances like that in 287 at ∮, of which the usefulness may be doubtful. Only alterations of the dominant seventh chord are shown here. To work out likewise the other seventh and ninth chords would be somewhat superfluous, as often the same forms result; also a discussion of all these chords would exceed the scope of this book. The student can investigate them for himself. Of course they progress to different triads of the key; otherwise there is no difference. I have already indicated how they should be brought in, and whether the student should use them.

288

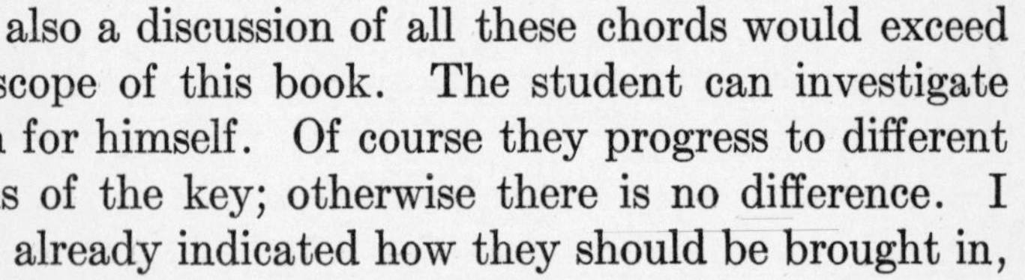

As can be seen, alterations can sometimes be used with very good effect, though their possibility may not be apparent at the first glance. Naturally their effectiveness can be attributed in part to melodic voice leading, and one might therefore be inclined to regard them only as chromatic passing tones;—not justifiably, however, for it is much more expedient in harmonic thinking to relate tones to a fundamental (root) than merely to make melodic adjustments. The latter may give some indication of the derivation of a chord; only the former gives a clear view of its functions and its tendencies.

289 gives alterations of the ninth chord; 290 shows possibilities of their use. Here I still adhere to the principle that the altered tone should progress in the direction indicated by the alteration. As a seventh chord can resolve deceptively, the ninth chord can of course do the same, also the altered ninth chord. Since even conservative theorists permit the seventh sometimes to rise, as is shown in 291 and allowed in nearly

289
290
etc.
etc.
NB

every textbook, it must surely be admitted that the ninth also may rise, at least chromatically. Thus the usefulness of the ninth chord is greatly increased.

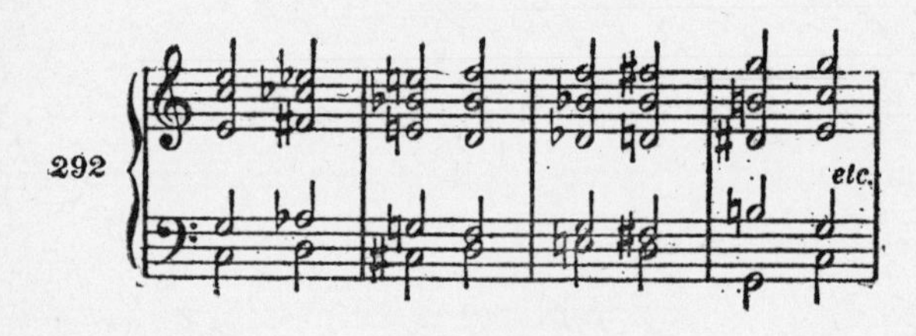

In 292 are shown two rising ninths. The student can find others for himself.

2. Abbreviation by Omissions in Familiar Progressions

This principle is not entirely new, but a brief statement here may clear up some things. We have often noted the effect of the cliché, of the familiar formula, some chord succession which has appeared so many times that it has become the established thing for a definite purpose. Once we hear the beginning of the well known pattern, automatically we expect the rest: the formula compels acceptance of a definite conclusion. With the formula begun, parts of it can even be omitted, perhaps only beginning and end placed side by side; the pattern is then abbreviated, represented only by its opening and close. Such an abbreviation is perhaps the progression IV—V, familiar in the cadence. I have already suggested that this should be regarded as a substitute for IV—II—V. Likewise the progression of the Neapolitan sixth directly to a V is an abbreviation.

For supposedly the complete progression would be:

Perhaps the Plagal cadence too is of this nature. Its impression of incompleteness may well result from an omission. Namely: IV—V—I or II—V—I is telescoped into IV—I or II—I. On the same principle the progression in 295*a*, appearing in cadences or half cadences, is condensed from 295*b*.

These abbreviations will ordinarily be used only in formulas that have a definite function, hence especially in cadences:

296

3. Connection of a Triad With All Other Triads; —of All Seventh Chords

In the following, connections of a major and a minor triad with all possible major, minor and diminished triads are systematically presented. Most instances are already familiar; in 298 several less well known are used in phrases, but omitting the diminished triad.

297 a)

b)

298

299
300

299 shows the connection of a triad with all the dominant seventh chords, 300 the dominant sevenths together.

In 301 and 302 some progressions are worked out that are hardly intelligible by themselves. It is evident that they could have an entirely good effect under certain circumstances. Obviously the same could be shown with ninth chords. I shall leave it to the student to work out such combinations. Anything may be good in the right place. The melodic treatment of soprano and bass can contribute especially to an effective result. The rhythm too must not be left out of consideration. Oftentimes a progression is very satisfactory when it is connected by passing tones. However, the use of passing tones, embellishments and suspensions, since it brings in quarter notes, causes an increase in the movement, which will have some effect on what follows. My advice to the student in this regard is this: when he has developed the ability to conceive the passing tones, embellishments and suspensions right with the

etc.
302

harmony, and he has fallen into a quarter-note movement, it will be best to continue it to the end. It is not impossible to let the quarter notes disappear, if they are avoided first on the first half of the measure and then on the second, or first in the melody and then in the middle voices. But this device is by no means easy.

4. Some Other Matters: Possibilities of the Rising Seventh; Basses for the Diminished Seventh Chord; a Mozart Chord; an Eight-Part Chord

With the assumption that the seventh can rise, it becomes possible to use the I_7 in minor built entirely of scale tones.

This chord can be transposed to other degrees of the key and can be especially effective there when joined to wandering chords (303*e*, *f*, *g*).

Another thing, which is not for squeamish ears but occurs often in modern music, especially with Richard Strauss, is the use of several different bass notes (as roots) with a diminished seventh chord,—because a diminished seventh chord can be regarded as a ninth chord in four different ways. If one supposes after each of the four (304*a*) a sufficient pause or a circumstance that enables the reinterpreting of the chord, then there is no obstacle in the way of joining these four chords in a series. There are in fact classical examples of this practice. If on the other hand we think of it as done quickly, or without a device to favor the change (this quick thinking [*rascher denken*] is one of the principal tendencies in development—it is always so, for too slow thinking, which can too easily become no thinking, has the opposite effect!) then we see the possibility

303

(304*b*) of an added voice along with a diminished seventh chord, consisting entirely of the four tones of another diminished seventh chord. A similar result is obtained when (304*c*) a scale is written against the diminished seventh chord, with these same tones appearing on the accents (first of each beat). This scale can also be constructed as in 304*d*, where (with quick thinking) the picture is changed at every moment. Here the weak eighth notes in the bass build the third diminished seventh chord, *e-g-b♭-d♭*. An analogy to the five-voiced dissonances appearing at these points is found in the organ point in 304*e*; they are then merely transpositions of this *g-f♯-a-c-e♭* to three other bass notes. From a comparison of 304*d* and *e* it is clear that the third diminished seventh chord (*e-g-b♭-d♭*) can be written against *f♯-a-c-e♭*, as in 304*g*; at every moment we have the equivalent of 304*e*. Since 304*f* is self-evident, since we have shown that the other eight tones can appear with this diminished seventh chord, since therefore each of the twelve tones of the chromatic scale can be sounded with the same diminished seventh chord, it is evident that any melody could be harmonized by one diminished seventh chord. We shall not actually do so, for it would be uninteresting and a little far-fetched. We should prefer characteristic changes of harmony. But it could be done! Naturally such procedure is not for a squeamish ear,—only for the trained ear that has learned to grasp ideas quickly!

I have noticed a chord in Mozart, which is passed through quickly. Obviously it could come slowly and be better understood. Then even squeamish ears can grasp it and examine it. This chord (305*a*) would make a pretty sequence (305*b*):

If inversions are used (305*e*) it can be even prettier. There can be no objection; it is Mozart!

I should like now to show a chord that does not indeed appear in Mozart, but could almost be possible with Bach. The leap from the *e* in 306*a* needs no explanation. At 306*b* it is equally acceptable over the organ point, as also are the figures in 306*c* and *d*, which are not unusual. If these are combined we have a chord consisting of eight different tones (306*e*†). This could

appear as in 306*f*. I do not know whether it can actually be found; but, in view of the six-toned chord which I have pointed out in Bach's eight-voice motets, which could please squeamish ears hardly more than this eight-toned chord, I really believe that if twelve-part choral works of Bach should be discovered, this chord might well appear, although there are no ninth chords.

5. Some More Devices of Modulation

A major key can be changed to the like-named minor, or a minor to the like-named major, by simple means.

There are of course many possible ways; here mainly the Neapolitan sixth chord and the augmented $\frac{6}{5}$ ($\frac{4}{3}$, 2) chord are used.

This principle can also be used in a modulation to a major key by modulating first to the like-named minor,

then changing to major. Vice versa, a modulation to a minor key may be worked out first to the like-named major, which is then changed to minor.

It will be recalled that the means recommended for keys three and four times removed on the Circle of Fifths rested on the same principle.

Another device: proceed to a wandering chord, a Neapolitan sixth, an augmented $\frac{6}{5}$ chord, an augmented

a)
C— D♭
309
b)
C— D♭
c)
C—D♭
d)
C— D♭
e)
C—f♯

f)
a—ab
g)
a—Db
h)
C—A

triad, etc., using it to complete the first part of the modulation.

Another way of looking at the same thing: every major triad can be treated as a Neapolitan sixth chord, every dominant seventh chord as an augmented $^6_5$ chord. Of course this should not become the only means of modulation.

In 310 is something that should be practiced by the student. A succession of two chords (++) is continued in various ways. The important thing here is not so much to accomplish a certain modulation as to try out the various possibilities for such a chord.

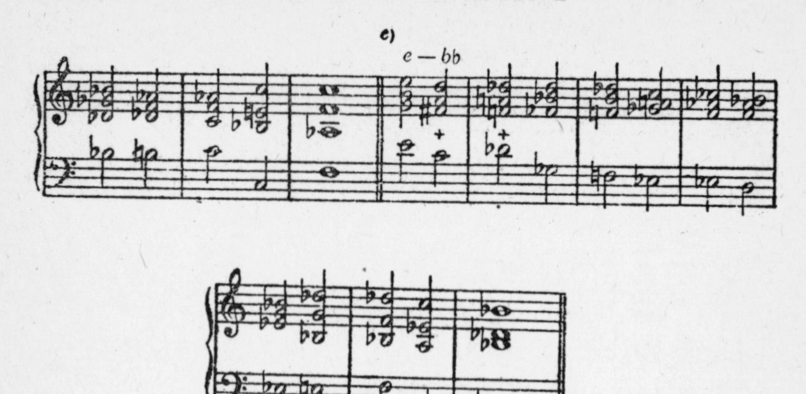

In 311 the possible leadings of another chord combination (++) are investigated.

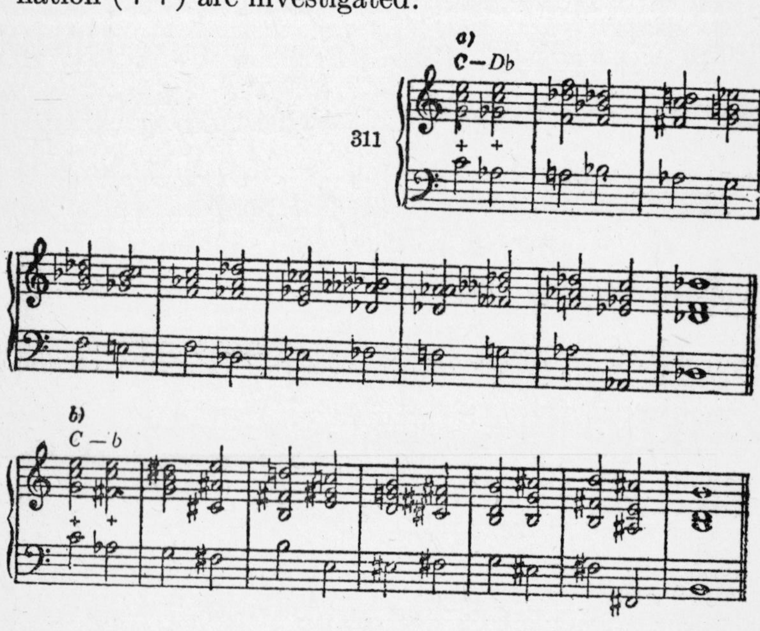

312 shows how it is possible to work toward a new key by a roundabout course. Here it is essential that some indication of the new key should be given first.

312
a)
C—d
b)
C — B
c)
C—Ab
d)
C—ab

I do not myself find these examples very good. They are unsatisfactory mainly because there is no motive present. With a freer movement through passing tones, embellishments and suspensions they could be much better, especially if, as in 313, some details develop gradually into a motive. I must repeat again here, however, that the student should not attempt to use these small notes until he can invent them along with the others.

6. A Few More Small Points

In the fourth section of this chapter was shown the possibility of harmonizing every melody with *one* diminished seventh chord. Here the reverse is suggested, that a melody can be harmonized by *any* diminished seventh chord (or by the corresponding ninth chord).

This construction is nothing new; it appears in the classical writers.

The suspension (or appoggiatura) at 314*a* and also the "returning" passing tone (or embellishment) over a diminished seventh chord are familiar. This *e*♭ used likewise over a ninth chord is nothing new (314*b*). Now if this same diminished seventh chord is considered a ninth chord with other roots (314*c*), the same melody can be used with it, but with changed significance (and notation). Since it evidently can appear with three different roots (*c*, *f*♯ and *e*♭), it must also be possible with the fourth (314*d*). Hence in 314*e* the same melody appears with all four ninth chords. The same principle is illustrated by a different figure in 314*f*, by which 314*g* becomes possible. This leads to 314*h*, and in *i* each ninth chord is resolved to a chord a fourth higher. The two figures can be combined as in 314*k* or *l*; then the same possibilities can be shown for this melody (314*m*). Obviously the figure in 314*n* can be treated in the same way, and certainly the same could be tried with other figures and other wandering chords. I shall show one of these possibilities in the next chapter with the augmented triad. It may not seem very interesting to have these four combinations placed in close succession, as here. But since it is possible, it becomes available for a better purpose, for harmonic variation, to enable a different continuation for a phrase.

315*a* illustrates another progression, by no means rare, which is best thought of as an imitation of the diminished seventh chord.

This progression (315*a*) recalls 315*b*. In 315*c*, it is familiar to us as one of the resolutions of the augmented $^{6}_{5}$ ($^{4}_{3}$) chord. It appears also with lowered fifth (*d*♭)

314

(315*d*) or (315*e*) as a sort of ninth chord. Even 315*f* is not unusual. This progression is well suited to strengthen a modulation. The first chord has here dominant character, so to speak, in spite of the falling fundamental progression.

Something more should be said about the $^6_4$ chord, especially in the cadence. This is of course treated fairly freely today. Generally, however, it is so used as to preserve its character; *i.e.*, it is either brought in or resolved as in the older music. Usually its character is preserved by its being placed on an accent, where it awakens the characteristic feeling of suspense. In the resolution even Brahms treats it rather freely. I do not so much mean an example like that in the third measure of the *Sapphic Ode*, where the $^6_4$ chord appears so as to suggest that the bass melody will continue through (as it does in a similar spot a little earlier), nor the place in the next to the last measure of the same song, where a $^6_4$ chord arises from an anticipation in the bass. Note rather in *Botschaft*, measures 14—19, where it is left freely by a leap (316).

Brahms here conceives the $^6_4$ chord simply as another position of the triad (no different from a sixth chord), which can then move directly to another position, the root position. More modern music is naturally still freer with it. Thus we see how the principle is confirmed

in the development of the art, that dissonances are treated with much less ceremony when the ear is trusted with them.

THE WHOLE TONE SCALE AND ITS FIVE AND SIX TONE CHORDS

During recent years there has been appearing more and more often in the works of modern composers a scale of six tones equally spaced: the whole tone (or whole step) scale.

In the works of modern composers (including my own) can be found two forerunners of the conscious use of the whole tone scale.

One: over an augmented triad the melody moves from chord tone to chord tone, taking on the way a passing tone that splits the major third into two whole steps. Naturally this progression is possible from each tone of the chord (318*a*, *b*, *c*), resulting in the whole tone scale (318*d*).

Two: the same result is given by passing tones over a dominant seventh chord with its fifth augmented (319*a*, *b*) or omitted (319*c*).

The two derivations are very similar, since the altered seventh chord is nothing but an augmented triad with added seventh, and the omitted fifth can be identified with the augmented fifth.

Likewise 320*a* is a further expansion of the seventh chord with augmented fifth, into a ninth chord. This chord includes five of the six tones of the whole tone scale. Surely one would as readily risk using these tones one at a time, in a melody, as all at once; *e.g.*, in 320*b*, where only *c*♯ is lacking to complete the whole tone scale.

321 shows a chord that comprises all six tones of the whole tone scale.

The resolution is:

Its derivation:

From the dominant ninth chord two tones are derived by the simultaneous raising and lowering of the fifth; result: a six tone chord.

These whole tone chords, regarded as wandering chords, have at least the multiple uses of the augmented triad. Hence they are of the greatest value in modulating, or in deviating from a tonality.

Each tone of this chord can be the root of a dominant; thus there are six possible resolutions to major triads.

Any other resolution of this chord will likewise be possible in six different transpositions, taking each tone in turn as the root. Hence six possible resolutions to a dominant seventh chord (327*a*), to a secondary seventh chord (327*b*), to a diminished seventh chord (327*c*), to two augmented triads (327*d* and *e*), to a seventh chord with lowered fifth (327*f*), to a minor ninth chord with lowered fifth (327*g*), to a major ninth chord (327*h*), to a minor ninth chord (327*i*), and finally to the other (there can be only two) whole tone chord (327*k*).

Here we have over sixty resolutions of the same chord, with no melodic progression greater than a half-step, hence with strict treatment of dissonances. Certainly many more could be discovered. If we permit a freer treatment of the dissonance, as we have often done, then the possibilities are very considerably increased.

FOURTH CHORDS

Built from superimposed fourths, chords of three, four, five and six tones are possible. All have manifold uses.

The four-tone fourth chord can be derived by alterations in the more familiar system of chords in thirds (333*b* and *c*).

Likewise the five-tone chord. This, as well as the four-tone chord, can take the place of a dominant, from which it can also be derived. For the four-tone chord we lower the root (if we admit this possibility), seventh and fifth of the dominant; for the five-tone chord we raise and lower the root (*a*♭ to *a* or *b*♭♭, and to *g*), raise and lower the fifth (*e*♭ to *e*, *e*♭ to *e*♭♭), leaving the third stationary. Here (334) inversions are used, but if one does not care to avoid fifths, naturally root position is possible.

335 shows several progressions with commonly used chords. The six-tone fourth chord has a minor ninth (from the bass note), hence is the first of the fourth chords to include a "sharp" dissonance. One will therefore be inclined at first to give this ninth the customary dissonance treatment, with resolution. I give here only progressions that permit resolution of the ninth.

Note that only resolutions to the commonest chords are given, though the less common can hardly call forth any objection, as in 337*a*.

337*b* shows how, through the lowering of three tones (*b* to *b*♭, *a* to *a*♭, *g* to *f*♯), the six-tone whole tone chord results (a progression that appears in my *Kammersymphonie*), and how this passes over into another six-tone fourth chord by the lowering of the remaining three tones (*c* to *b*, *d* to *c*♯, *e* to *e*♭).

INDEX

(Figures indicate pages; bold-face figures chapter headings or examples from the composers listed)